the FILM EDITING ROOM HANDBOOK

Norman Hollyn

ARCO PUBLISHING, INC.
NEW YORK

Published by Arco Publishing, Inc.
215 Park Avenue South, New York, N.Y. 10003

Library of Congress Cataloging in Publication Data

Hollyn, Norman.
   The film editing room handbook.

   Includes index.
   1. Moving-pictures—Editing.   I. Title.
TR899.H64   1983   778.5′35   83-8833
ISBN 0-668-05444-1 (Reference Text)
ISBN 0-668-05450-6 (Paper Edition)

Printed in the United States of America

10 9 8 7 6 5 4 3 2 1

the FILM EDITING ROOM HANDBOOK

Acknowledgments

I have yet to have an editing room job in which I did not learn something about editing, filmmaking, or people. Many of the people I've worked with don't even know how much I've been able to learn from them. Maybe now they will. I want to thank them all for those experiences. I also would like to thank the rooting section for this book—Bob, for kind words and sage advice, Terry and Ray at Datel for Apple help in a jiffy, my Mom and Dad for their support, and, of course, Janet. For everything.

CONTENTS

INTRODUCTION

At the end of my first week working on my first feature film I rushed out to the producer's bank to cash my very first paycheck. Though I saw long lines there I was not dismayed. I had in my hands a check from United Artists/Marvin Worth Productions that proclaimed in bold letters: *Lenny*. I was working on a film with Dustin Hoffman! Surely the bank officers would usher me to the front of the line and give me my money without so much as a glance at my identification.

Of course, it didn't work out that way. Not only did I have to wait on line with everyone else, but when it finally was my turn, the teller refused to give me any money because I didn't have an account with the bank.

Thus I learned my first and perhaps most valuable lesson about working in the film business—film editing is a job and make no mistake about that. After all of the mumbo jumbo that we read about *the movies* and their *glamour*, it is a bit of a shock to learn that everybody working in moviemaking is judged by the same criteria as the rest of the world: how well they get the job done. Film work, for the majority of those in it, promises no more "perks" than any other job. Your standing comes from how well you do the job, not just from the fact that you're doing it.

The second lesson that I learned about film editing is that there are a lot of ways to get the job done. There are almost as many systems for organizing a cutting room as there are people doing it. Many ways work, some do not, but the worst thing you can do is attempt to impose the system that worked on film A onto the very different film B. One of the tests of a good editing crew member is flexibility.

That leads to lesson number three—it takes a certain type of person to be comfortable in the field of editing. Flexible working habits are just the first necessity. You have to be able to work long days, long weeks, and long months in a small, dark, crowded room with the same small group of people. You have to be able to concentrate on the smallest detail and never give up until it is right. Editing can be an obsession, good editing almost certainly *is*. The editing of any film usually requires large amounts of energy, not all of it well or gratifyingly spent. To work under these conditions takes real dedication.

Anyone interested in a potential career in film editing would be well advised to internalize these rules before proceeding. For, while I try to talk about film editing rooms and the nuts-and-bolts techniques used in running them, I could never write about how to be a film editor. You either are or you're not—or you learn how to be, by living in an editing room day after long day, month after long month.

I can tell you that if you are interested in editing because it is a way to meet people or to become a director or producer, forget about working there. Some editors eventually make such a transition but that comes after years of editing and the only way to get through those years is to love it.

I can tell you that if you're a person who gets bored by details and constant repetition, forget editing. Eventually, editors get past this sort of thing, but until that point these details are their life, and it helps to be able to deal with that.

And I can also tell you that if you're a person who needs a separate, private life, you might as well forget most forms of editing. Fourteen-hour days and six- or seven-day weeks leave very little time for life as others know it. Unless your friends and loved ones are as flexible as you are, film editing's hours will leave you (and them) unhappy.

But, all of that having been said, I can tell you this—once you do it, it is all worth it.

Let that be lesson number four.

This book is written primarily for those who have an active interest in how a professional cutting room operates. To help those who are thinking of making it their career, I will often be quite detailed, though this may give more information than the normal film student would like. But there is an additional purpose to this. Editing room procedures have been developed over many years to expedite cutting. There are therefore many techniques which could be of help to all filmmakers, regardless of their budget or the type of film they are doing. However, since few film teachers or professors are also professional film editors these techniques are rarely taught. This book will, I hope, give film students, independent filmmakers, and others enough knowledge about editing room procedures that they can decide for themselves just how they can best organize *their* editing facilities to conserve the time and money that they rarely have enough of.

Film buffs will probably be both fascinated and overwhelmed by the sheer mass of technical data here. To them, my apologies. But I believe that to truly understand the art of film, the modus operandi of the film editor must be understood as well. In the years to come, as increasing sophistication opens the film audience up to an awareness of film editing, those film buffs who know *how* it is done will be in a much better position to say *why* it was done.

A friend of mine describes the assistant's job as "primarily cataloguing work."

An assistant editor is defined, under the IATSE Local 771 (East Coast) contract, as "a person who is directly assigned to assist the Editor(s) and a person who, among other duties, may be engaged in: synchronizing dailies, taking notes at screenings, obtaining cutting room facilities, breaking down daily takes, pulling out and assembling selected takes, making trims, ordering opticals, and performing other preparatory work in editing rooms."

The IATSE Local 776 (West Coast) contract defines the assistant as " . . . a person who is assigned to assist an Editor. His duties shall be such as are assigned to him and performed under the immediate direction, supervision and responsibility of the editor to whom he is assigned to assist."

Frankly, though I dislike all of these definitions, I much prefer the last one. The assistant's main task, as I see it, is to make sure that the cutting room runs smoothly for the editor. Period.

The implications of that statement are what this book is all about. Assistant editing always seems to boil down to this one question: "How can I make this run efficiently?"

Keeping the editing room functioning depends upon many things. One of the most important is controlling the film. An average film prints about twenty miles of film. A good assistant should be able to locate, almost immediately, pieces as short as one inch long. To this end, editing staffs have, over the years, developed a number of methods for logging, storing, and retrieving footage. As anyone who has ever looked for work and been denied it can tell you, this is what is called "the system." As a rule I (and almost every other person I know in editing) would rather hire someone who knows this system than someone who doesn't, all other things being equal. As we shall soon see, however, there is no real mystery to this system; it is all rather logical and straightforward.

The reason why people would rather hire someone who knows the system, though, is that the real difficulty in assistant editing comes in internalizing these procedures well enough so that every oddity one runs across during the course of a film can be accommodated and recalled with no disruption. This is where the experienced (and good) editing staff really earns its salary.

Network, for example, was nearly a textbook case in proper editing room procedure. Everything seemed so easy to me. It was a dialogue film, for starters. The director, Sidney Lumet, shot in a straightforward style using only a single camera (except in some of the television studio/control room material). There were no complicated effects or opticals. Lumet shot very little footage; usually no more than 3000 feet (about twenty-two minutes) were printed per day. The script supervisor, Kay Chapin, was a model of efficiency; her notes were explicit, fast, and accurate. I cannot remember a day when the picture and sound crews forgot to get slates for syncing purposes, or when their reports were inaccurate or misleading. There was only one editor on the film, Alan Heim, and he was wonderfully efficient. He worked on an upright Moviola, cutting primarily in the order that the scenes had been shot. Dailies were shown every evening after the day's shoot so we had plenty of time to prepare for them and still go about the business of cutting the film.

Less than one week after the completion of shooting there was a first cut of the film for Lumet to look at. And no wonder. The wheels of the entire process had worked exceedingly smoothly, helping us in the editing room do our jobs very fast and just as smoothly.

But *Network* was a rarity. Other films, with equally fine crews, can be very problematic.

Hair, for instance, was an organizational task of immense proportions. First, it was a musical and that complicated the task.

Then, the director, Milos Forman, was shooting with multiple cameras (most often with two, but on some days there were as many as seven) and shooting a lot of footage. Days where we had to sync 10,000 feet of film were very common; there were several days when we had 25,000 feet. Because of the subject matter of the film as well as Forman's personal style, much of the footage was neither as predictable nor as easily categorized as that from *Network*. Despite a superb script supervisor (Nancy Hopton), keeping up with the film was a herculean task. Not surprisingly, there were days when the script supervisor's notes, the camera and sound reports, and the processed footage and sound transfers bore little resemblance to each other. There were one, then two, and then three editors on the film, all working on KEM flatbeds. Flatbeds are more difficult to organize in general, but, the fact that three editors were cutting at once added to the assistants' tasks. Dailies were often shown in the midafternoon on the set, and when the film was shooting in California the footage would not arrive in the cutting room until afternoon. In both of these cases this gave the editing staff no more than a few hours to sync the rushes.

In short, *Hair* tested the organization of its editing crew to the utmost. The fact that we kept everything moving, accessible, and pleasant is a testament, I think, to what good, experienced crews can do with a good, workable system.

But organizing and accessing the footage is only one part of an assistant's mandate to "keep things moving." He or she must be the editing crew's link to the outside world, interacting with the suppliers, laboratories, job seekers, producers, and the general chaos that arrives at the editing room door every day.

Much of an assistant's day is spent on the phone making things happen. Equipment always seems to be breaking down; labs never seem to give you what you've asked for; supplies always seem to be used up too fast; job seekers always seem to show up with their resumes at the worst possible moment; and the editor *always* seems to need the piece of film that you happen to be working on for another purpose. The assistant editor must be able to cope with it all, sort it out, and make it all work on top of that. As we say in the business: "That's what they pay us so little money for."

The task of organizing an editing room is generally assigned to an assistant editor. For that reason, we will examine editing from the assistant's point of view in this book. There are three types of

editors in feature filmmaking: picture, sound, and music. Each of
the three assistants have some tasks similar to their peers and some
very different. Because the first assistant picture editor is usually on
the film before any other assistant it is he or she who often has the
information and the experience that the other assistants need. For
this reason, there is an unwritten chain of command in the editing
room. Both the sound and music departments maintain their own
semi-autonomous crews, with apprentices taking direction from
assistants who take direction from editors. The picture department
has a similar chain of command, but it is the responsibility of the
picture department to provide the sound and music people with all
the help and information that they can and, in exchange, the sound
and music departments are responsible to and report to the picture
department. Thus, the supervising picture editor is regarded as the
ultimate editorial arbiter (even though the editor is responsible to
higher powers like the director or producer).

Regardless of what kind of film you work on, you will find that
the *tasks* of these three departments have to get done one way or
another. In many documentaries and low-budget films, one person
does the work of all three departments. But the three tasks always
exist in roughly the same order and requiring the same struggle as
in feature films.

You will find this book organized, more or less, in chronologi-
cal order—the order that the assistant will normally have to deal
with the problems posed. As you read about how to make a cutting
room work, therefore, you will also get a tour through the filmmaking process itself, as seen through the editor's eyes.

What you will not find in this book is a discussion of the aes-
thetics of film editing except as they influence the assistant's job.
There are already several books and articles by people far more
qualified than I to talk about that subject (for a list of some of these
works see the bibliography). But what I hope becomes apparent
from this book is that there is also an "aesthetics of assistant editing." There are good and bad ways to organize, there are smart and
stupid ways to try to keep things moving. And when everything is
working properly, the organization has a beauty all its own.

the FILM EDITING ROOM HANDBOOK

1

EDITING WITHIN THE FILMMAKING PROCESS

Making a movie is often compared to running a war. It is a huge, complicated process, involving hundreds of people who must all be in the correct place at the right time. They are all involved in their own chains of command with one or two leaders at the very top who determine, for right or for wrong, the course of their work. It is an exhausting process that is not often very fulfilling until a film is complete and viewable.

Editing is just one part of the movie-making battlefield. It is, for me, one of the most important parts since it is where all of the disparate elements come together. Whoever controls the editing process (and this can be the director, the producer, the distributor, or the editor) controls how the film is presented to the public and can, with the changes that can be made through editing, save or ruin a film. If the shooting process is one of creating, the editing process is one of recreating.

The overall filmmaking process is divided into three handy categories—preproduction, production, and postproduction. Much has been written about the general process and I won't attempt to delve very deeply into it, but here is a brief description of this tortuous road to the neighborhood theatres.

Preproduction

The very earliest stage of preproduction is the idea. Either a writer, producer, director, or agent gets an idea for a film which is then sold to a movie company. As soon as the money is exchanged the writer begins writing and the other facets of the production begin to come together. A director must be chosen, if there is none already involved. A cast and crew are hired. Chief among these is the production manager, who will supervise the day-to-day operations for the producer. It is this production manager (sometimes called the line producer) who determines the budget and shooting schedule, arranges for the equipment and locations, makes most of the deals with the crew members (cast salaries are more often handled by the producer) and, in general, makes sure that everything will be in place for the first day of shooting.

Production

When that day arrives a battery of people descend on the set. On *Four Friends* there were days when over 120 cast and crew were working. There are departments for every job from the lighting to the greenery, and from transportation to *effects* (they'll make it rain or snow for the director—on cue).

While all of this chaos is occurring on the set, the editor and staff are quietly working away in another location, perhaps even another city. They are organizing it so that the people on the set can see the results of the previous day's work (called the *rushes* or *dailies*). At the same time they are beginning to cut the film.

Requests flood in from the set every day. "We need to reshoot a scene, how was the lead character wearing his tie?" or "The sound on one take last night wasn't very good, can you do something to help us out or do we have to reshoot?" or "There was a scratch on the negative in such and such a scene, can the scene be cut without that shot?" Each question is important and the answer can't come too soon. And, all the while, the film is being edited together.

Postproduction

When the film is finished shooting, the crew goes off to find other work and the director returns to the editing room and begins to work with the editor toward the first cut. There are several screenings and slowly a film emerges from the mass of raw material shot on the set.

Publicity people from the distributor begin to make plans for the publicity campaign—posters, trailers (those "coming attractions" you see in the movie theatres), television spots, promotions, etc., etc.

Sound editors are hired to begin work on the sound effects and dialogue where the soundtrack needs to be cleaned up. If some of the lines need to be redone for quality, members of the cast are brought into a studio to rerecord their lines. A composer is hired and a music editor assists in creating a score for the film.

Finally the film's sound is mixed together into one soundtrack for the film's release. The original negative is cut to match the editor's cuts and the color balance is corrected on the film. The picture and the soundtrack are *married together* and the first full screening of the movie can take place.

After that, the film opens and (everyone hopes) is very successful. All of the editing crew members go off to find other work on other films.

2

PRELIMINARIES

The first time I ever entered a feature film cutting room I was looking for work. I had heard of a film called *The Taking of Pelham One Two Three* that needed an apprentice film editor. I had gone over the few film books that I could find trying to gather enough information so I wouldn't seem like a complete dunce when I went up for an interview. I called the editor, Jerry Greenberg, made an appointment, got reasonably well dressed (but not *too* dressed; mustn't look too green, I thought) and arrived about five minutes early on the appointed day.

I took only two steps into the cutting room before I realized just how useless all of my reading preparation had been. From ceiling to floor on several walls of the room were stacked hundreds of white boxes, each labeled with one of three or four colors of tape. Some boxes had red writing on them, some had black. On each of the editing tables was stacked an array of equipment and supplies that none of the books had mentioned. A stack of looseleaf notebooks lay open on a table and though I couldn't read anything in them I suspected that even if I could I wouldn't be able to understand a thing.

No one had prepared me for the sheer awesome complexity of the thing.

I still think of that day when I see job seekers visit the cutting rooms where I work. What now seems simple and logical to me must look awesomely complex to anyone seeing it for the first time.

How does a professional cutting room look? Depending on the film's budget the "cutting room" may actually be several rooms. Or it may be the back of someone's office or home. But whatever the situation, every cutting room has many things in common—they all have a place to store the film, they all have a place to work on the film, and they all must have the equipment to do both adequately. Figure 2.1 shows a typical editing room.

FIGURE 2.1   A typical editing room, albeit cleaner than most. This
one is minus the cutter Moviola. The editor has attached a large velvet cloth below the picture gate, on the right side of the Moviola, to
protect the film from rubbing against the Moviola and scratching.
(Photograph by Janet Conn)

An average cutting room on a medium budget feature begins
with a place for the editor to do his or her work. The editor will
need an editing machine or two, an editing table complete with all
of his or her favorite supplies, the film logbooks, a series of trim
barrels, and plenty of room.

Let's examine each of these in turn.

An Editing Machine or Two

There are two types of editing machines common in today's
cutting rooms: uprights, usually called *Moviolas*®; and *flatbeds*,
called, variously *KEMs*®, *Steenbecks*®, *Moviola*® *flatbeds*, or by any
number of other manufacturers' names.

The Moviola has been *the* editing machine for many years in
the film business, and at least in 35mm, it is still a very popular

FIGURE 2.2 A normal Moviola
with reels for taking up the film and
soundtrack. (Photograph by Janet
Conn)

choice. It retains this loyalty for several reasons: (1) most editors
working today learned on these machines and old habits die hard;
(2) it is much cheaper to buy and rent Moviolas than flatbeds, making them the preferred choice for filmed television and low-budget
films; (3) they generally take up less space in the usually tight con-
fines of the editing room; and (4) they make certain kinds of editing
easier. (Sound and music editing is, in my experience, easier on

uprights—they are easier to thread with short pieces and they stop on a dime.) In addition, as we shall see later, setting up a movie's logging system is easier for an upright than for a flatbed and, therefore, less expensive and time-consuming.

Basically, a Moviola is an instrument which pulls the separate rolls of picture and soundtrack from reels on the bottom of the machine to the top, either independently or in synchronization (see Figures 2.2 and 2.3). One of the first things an apprentice editor usually learns is how to thread a Moviola for the editor, and it's no wonder—next to his or her hands, the Moviola is the editor's most important physical tool. In fact, with the best editors, their hands actually become part of their Moviolas.

There are several types of Moviolas. Picture editors use two of them. The first is the kind that you saw in Figure 2.2. The second is often called a *cutter Moviola* or, simply *cutter* (see Figure 2.3). It is much the same as the first type except that it is designed to be softer on the film and faster to thread. The gentleness is a serious concern if you're going to be cutting a movie for six months or more—making, unmaking, and remaking splices all of the while. The cutter has no take-up arms and no threading wheels above and below the picture gate. This means that it is simplicity itself to thread the machine—simply drop the picture in at the picture gate, the sound at the sound head and "let 'er rip" (figuratively, of course). This speed is of great help to the editor during the cutting process—the fewer physical encumbrances placed between the editor and the process of editing, the happier the editor will be.

Most editors like to cut with two Moviolas. This enables them to make their selections of good cutting points on one machine and then add them to the roll of already cut material on the other. We'll see more about this later but, for now, it is only important to remember that most editors work best with two machines—one to keep the cut film going on and one to select the next cut from.

The other type of machine now in use is the flatbed. Simply, a flatbed is an instrument which pulls the separate rolls of picture and soundtrack from left to right, either independently or in synchronization (see Figure 2.4). The flatbed has a few advantages over the upright. First, it is extremely gentle on film. As a result, it is my only choice for 16mm film—the upright Moviola can be so brutal on film that it is a rare editor who can cut a complete film without damaging it at least once. Second, it has several fast-forward speeds.

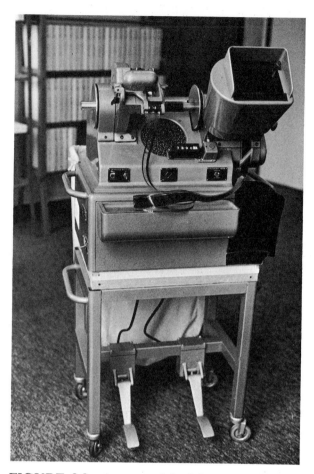

FIGURE 2.3   A cutter Moviola, which has no gates above or below the picture head and is softer on the film. The film and track are fed through their heads by hand and fall into the bag hanging behind the machine. Note that on both machines, the picture head has been masked off with black tape. In this way the editor will be able to see only that portion of the picture which will fall within the 1.85:1 frame (which is the ratio that most films are shown in theatres today) even though the film may have been shot full-frame (1.33:1). (Photograph by Janet Conn)

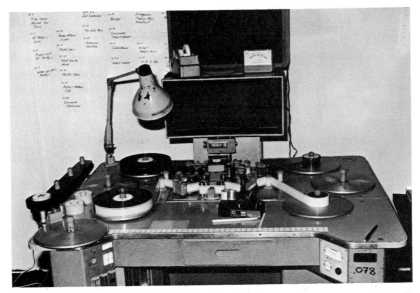

FIGURE 2.4 A flatbed editing table, in this case a Steenbeck. (Photograph by the author)

This makes it extremely easy to make fine-cut corrections in an already cut film, to find a few selected sequences in a large roll of film, or to rapidly compare two similar takes. A third advantage is its large screen size. Directors love this feature as it enables them to see the film without hunching over the editor's shoulder. Some editors, therefore, find this to be a bit of an encumbrance. Even these editors, however, will admit that a larger screen does help one to see things in a frame. Finally, compared to the upright the flatbed is also very quiet which makes it nicer for screening. An editing room with more than one upright running can leave you wondering when the man with the earplugs will be coming around.

Most flatbeds can run up to four separate rolls of film at one time (three picture/one sound, two picture/two sound, or one picture/three sound—though the last is not too common). This enables the editor to, on one machine, run the equivalent of two uprights—leaving the cutting on one pair of *gangs* (as each path is called) and the selecting of cut points on the other pair.

Each of these types of editing machines has its own pluses and minuses and, therefore, its own set of supporters and detractors.

The editor will make his or her own decision on what type of machine to cut on. The assistant editor is expected to be able to set up a logging system for any of them.

I have my own preferences, of course. I like to cut sound and music on upright Moviolas. I like to cut 16mm and complicated 35mm films (musicals, action pictures) on a flatbed. Dialogue pictures are no easier on one machine than on the other. I like to screen cut pictures and selected takes on a flatbed.

There are times when these uses overlap. What, you may ask, do you do then? Do the best you can.

An Editing Table with Supplies

In the United States a normal editing table (or bench) looks much like the one shown in Figure 2.5. (For a fairly thorough discussion of how an English editing table looks, see Ernest Walter's *The Technique of the Cutting Room*.) The essentials on it are as follows:

Synchronizer: In much the same way that the Moviola or flatbed can pull the film and soundtrack along together in sync with each other, editors need to have a way of doing that on an editing table. The synchronizer (see Figure 2.6) does this so well that it is regarded as the ultimate sync setup. It is a passive mechanical device that usually has four identical wheels which are permanently locked together so that they spin with each other. Film locked into one of the four gangs will travel at exactly the same speed as film locked into any of the other gangs. Moviola and flatbed synchronization has been known to slip, but there is no way that film locked into the synchronizer can slip. Everyone in the editing room will have their own synchronizer. They are that useful.

Sound Reader: Some way of hearing the soundtrack must be provided. This is accomplished by placing a little sound head on one of the gangs (usually the second from the front) and connecting that up to a low-quality amplifier with a built-in speaker. This amplifier/speaker combination is known as the *sound*

FIGURE 2.5   An editing bench. The film and soundtrack are fed from the reels on the left rewind (picture first and soundtrack behind it), through the synchronizer, and are taken up on the right rewind. The wheel next to the right rewind is a *Reddy-Eddy,* a time-to-footage converter. Behind the synchronizer is the sound amplifier, also called the *sound box* or *squawk box.* (Photograph by Janet Conn)

reader, *squawk box,* or "that damned box." Sound *never* sounds as good as it should through a system like this, which is why some sound editors rent better amplifiers and separate speakers. On *Hair* we rented a good speaker and installed a better amplifier in our KEM flatbed. It helped give us a better sense of the picture against music.

Rewinds: These are two stands at either end of the editing bench. The reels containing the picture and sound film are slipped onto their protruding shafts, clamped together, and can then be moved in forward or reverse by using the handles. These handles can be pulled out part way from the stand, disengaging the handle from the shaft. This is helpful if you're winding very fast. When you've gotten up to a good speed simply pull the handle out and let the film coast along, virtually rewinding itself.

Splicer: There are a few types of splicers. The two most popular are the Rivas® (see Figure 2.7) and the Guillotine®. Both do the same things: provide a cutting edge for cutting the film

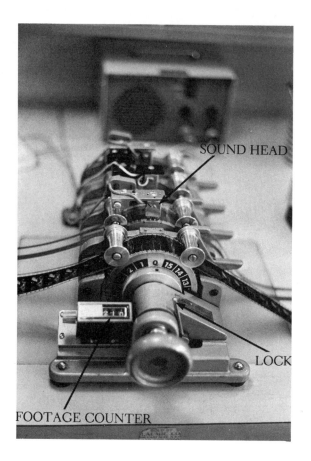

FIGURE 2.6   A synchronizer. It is made up of (usually) four wheels all locked together. Each wheel, or gang, has sprockets on it so that it can transport film or soundtrack. In this case, the first gang is running picture and the second gang is running sound. The wheel on the first gang is marked off in frames (zero to fifteen). Notice from the footage counter on the synchronizer that the frame of picture on the zero mark is at 210 feet and zero frames exactly (210'00). The lock on the right enables the editor to freeze the wheels at a particular frame. Normally, the wheel turns freely. (Photograph by Janet Conn)

FIGURE 2.7   A Rivas splicer. The film is placed across the base of the splicer so that it fits onto the pins. The tapper (A) is brought down lightly onto the film to smooth it out. The cutting blade (B) is then brought down to cut it at the metal wedges (C). Soundtrack splices are made by placing each piece of track on the pins so that the two butt up at the metal wedges. The white tape is then used on the bottom side only to splice the two together. The splice will then extend over four sprockets (two on each side of the cut). Picture is spliced differently. One piece of film is placed so that *two* sprockets overlap past the pins on the right. The other piece of film is then butted up against it (no sprockets will overlap). The clear tape is then used to splice the pieces together. The resultant splice extends over no more than two sprockets, *one* on each side of the splice. These two-sprocket splices will not be seen on a projector. (Photograph by Janet Conn)

evenly on a frame line, and a setup block on which two pieces of cut film can be aligned and then taped together. This is the extent of the "cutting" part of film editing. Cut piece number one, cut piece number two, lay them side by side, and tape them together. It is ridiculously simple, which is why many editors (including myself) get touchy about being called "cutters." Cutting and splicing is easy, we say. It's the editing that is difficult.

Both of these splicers use tape to fasten the cut film together. There is virtually no use for cement splicers in a film editing room today unless you intend to cut your own camera original. If you don't, stick with the tape splicers.

There is one other type of splicer—the diagonal splicer. It is used for soundtrack only and it cuts on an angle rather than straight up and down. This splicer is used primarily to finesse difficult sound or music edits.

Supplies: First, the list. Then the explanations.
Splicing tape—clear and white
Leader—white and black
Fill leader (also called *slug film*)
"Scene missing" leader
Academy leader
Pencils, pens, paper, rubber bands, paper clips, etc.
Spring clamp
Loupe
Rulers
Reddy-Eddy® and/or calculator
Trim tabs
Beep tone roll and virgin stock
Spare take-up reels and cores
Gloves
Webril® wipes
Cleaner
White boxes
Differential
Q-tips®

Splicing tape—Obviously, this is the tape that you use to splice the film together. Clear tape is used for pictures, white tape for sound.

Leader—Solid white or black film. Its uses are myriad and we'll discuss each of them as we come on them in the text. For now, let's say that on the average feature you can expect to go through white leader as if it were water and black leader like it was gold. Order accordingly.

Fill leader—Fill is waste film. It is usually old movies or rejected lab prints which would have been discarded. It is added to the soundtrack when a length of silence is needed. Rather than hunting for a piece of neutral sound to add, the editor will drop in a piece of fill of the proper length.

"Scene missing" leader—As cut scenes are put together on rolls for projection, scenes which belong in between two cut scenes

but which have not yet been cut are indicated with a short length of leader which says "scene missing" on it. You can purchase this kind of leader already made from a film supply house. When you do, purchase very little.

Academy leader—The numbers that you sometimes see at the beginnings of films (you know, 8-7-6-5, etc.) are part of a standard developed by the Society of Motion Picture and Television Engineers (SMPTE). They count down in seconds from eight to two and then go to black before the picture begins (an alternate standard counts down from twelve feet to three feet, which is the same thing). Also imprinted on these standard leaders are all kinds of helpful information. There is a field for the projectionist to focus on, there are markings showing the borderline of the screen area (since, normally, only part of the frame is meant to be projected the rest has to be covered up by a plate in the projector). One academy leader should be placed at the head of everything that is to be projected, so order a lot of it, either from your lab or a supply house.

On *Four Friends*, the cinematographer, the late Ghislain Cloquet, shot his own head leader, which he felt represented the way his cameras were shooting. The editing crew had to cut a short length of this into every leader. I found no real value in this after the first several days of shooting but it does suggest an alternate (and cheaper) way of getting the scene missing and focus leaders—have your camerman shoot them. A word of warning though—industry standards are to have exactly twelve feet from a "picture start" mark to the end of the leader (four feet and thirty-two frames in 16mm). You must keep this length constant in every leader you make.

Stationery—Editors use grease pencils (also called china markers) to write on film because the marks are easily wiped off. In addition, a healthy supply of regular pencils, pens, markers, various sizes of notepaper, rubber bands, and paper clips will keep the editing room humming along happily. It is the assistant's job to make sure that the editor never runs out of anything that he or she needs. Often this job is delegated to an apprentice, if there is one on the job.

Spring clamp—Something has to hold the multiple reels on the rewind shafts together, or they won't roll up at the same rate. A clamp will do it (make sure you get one with the table setup when you rent it).

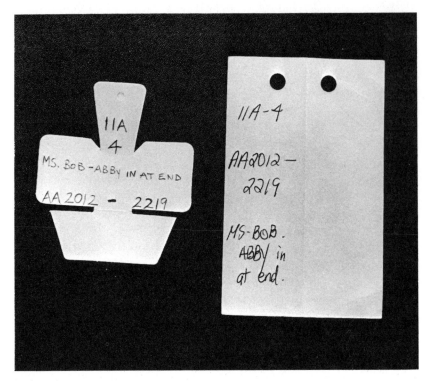

FIGURE 2.8 Two types of cinetabs. Both are made of stiff cardboard. The version on the left is used primarily in New York. The version on the right is used in California (it is folded lengthwise down the center and inserted in between layers of rolled-up film). Both types of tabs give the same information. In England, usually no trim tabs are used. A piece of tape is placed on the top of the rolled-up film instead. (Photograph by Janet Conn)

Loupe—This is just a little magnifying glass that the editor can set on top of the film if he needs to examine a single frame on the table. In the center of most benches there is a lamp set in the table and covered with a sheet of frosted glass or plastic. The editor turns on the lamp to provide back illumination of the frame.

Rulers—There are a few times when it will be necessary to draw straight lines onto the film (usually to indicate fades, dissolves, or other types of opticals). A two-foot ruler will take care of most of these needs. Music and sound editors usually need three-foot rulers for their markings. I find it helpful to have rulers in half, one, two, and three-foot lengths.

Reddy-Eddy—This is a little wheel that converts footages to timings. Calculators can do the same thing. In the appendix of this book there is a conversion chart. A copy of it might suffice too.

Trim tabs (also called *cinetabs*)—These are heavy cardboard markers onto which everything from code numbers to personal notes can be written. There are two main types of trim tabs in the United States (see Figure 2.8).

Beep tone roll—This is a roll of soundtrack onto which a continuous tone (usually 1000 cycles) has been recorded. This has a lot of uses which we will discuss later. Along with this beep tone roll, a small roll of soundtrack which has never been recorded onto (called *virgin stock*, for all too obvious reasons) is useful. The assistant can check out the fidelity of all of the equipment with it.

Take-up reels and cores—On a Moviola, film is wound on these reels and a healthy supply of them is valuable. On flatbeds film is wound onto cores, small plastic spools, which are slotted onto the flatbed or into a split reel (which is nothing more than a take-up reel which splits in two).

Other editing supplies—White editing gloves, film cleaner (acetone or Ecco®—but use Ecco for picture film only, it will erase soundtrack), two-piece white boxes for storage, a few film cans for shipping, Q-tips® for cleaning machines, and whatever other effluvia the editor likes to have surrounding him or her. Also, a phone list, placed prominently by the editing room telephone, will save everyone a lot of time looking for the numbers of suppliers and contacts.

None of these supplies magically appear when you sign onto your job. It is the job of the assistant to rent what can be rented and to purchase the rest. Typically, you can rent a cutting room complete with an editing machine, a table, synchronizer, sound reader, rewinds, splicer, and take-up reels for one flat price (on a daily, weekly, or monthly basis). Supplies will have to be purchased.

The Film Logbooks

We will discuss the nature of the logbooks in several chapters but you should know that there will be a few types of logs. Some will be on clipboards hung on the walls and some will be in looseleaf

FIGURE 2.9   A trim bin. Film is hung beneath its trim tab so that it can be easily located. Note that very large trims are flanged off and hung on a roll. In this example, rubber bands have been stretched across the pins over the film to prevent them from falling off when the barrel is rolled from place to place. (Photograph by Janet Conn)

notebooks near the editor. A small table will be helpful for those. Editing tables get crowded almost immediately. They're no place for logbooks.

A Series of Trim Barrels

These are also usually rented as part of the editing room package. Each is a rectangular barrel, almost waist-high, lined with soft cotton material, and topped with two parallel rows of metal (see Figure 2.9). Out of these two rows stick a series of tiny pins which neatly fit through the sprocket holes in the film. As the editor is cutting, he or she will hang anything not used on one or another of these pins. This keeps the film hanging in an orderly manner near the Moviola. When the editor is done, it also keeps the pieces hanging in an orderly manner near the apprentice who spends hours splicing and wrapping them all back together.

Plenty of Room

Actually, this is the one thing that editors get all too little of. Editing rooms are usually small and ancient with barely enough electricity to run the equipment without blowing a fuse. This is the norm in most New York City editing rooms and in most independent houses in Los Angeles. Editing rooms at the major studios in Hollywood range from the luxurious to the closet-sized.

The assistant editor must be part interior designer and come up with a comfortable and efficient layout for the room, whatever size and wherever it is. Remember, you'll be living in it for the duration of the film.

For example, let's say that you have one editor, two Moviolas, one assistant, and one apprentice to fit into one room. My first questions always involve the editor's comforts. Does he/she like to work facing the windows or away from them? Near the door or far away from it? Near a phone or isolated from it? Some editors like to be insulated from the outside world; others like to be part of it.

Figure 2.10 shows one arrangement that I've used in a New York City editing room. It is a typically cramped example. This layout is a good compromise between many bad elements. It insulates the editor from traffic a bit, provides easy access for the assistant to the phone and the door (an assistant spends much of his or her time dealing with the outside world), and it provides working space for the editor as well as some nearby rack space.

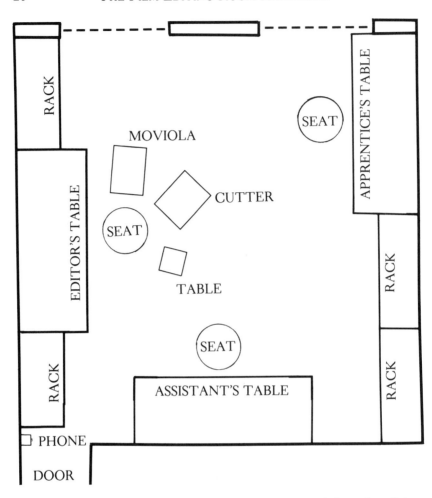

FIGURE 2.10 Floor plan number one. This Moviola-style editing room houses three people and four racks for film. Additional racks can be lined up against the windows if they are needed. Note that in this position the editor works to his or her right and that the Moviola picture screens face away from the windows, avoiding glare.

An alternate arrangement (for an editor who likes more isolation) would be to place him or her where the apprentice's table is. Note also that the arrangement in Figure 2.10 works if the editor is right-handed and prefers to have the Moviolas on the right side.

In the case where an editor wishes to work on a flatbed I might arrange the room as shown in Figure 2.11. Many flatbed editors pre-

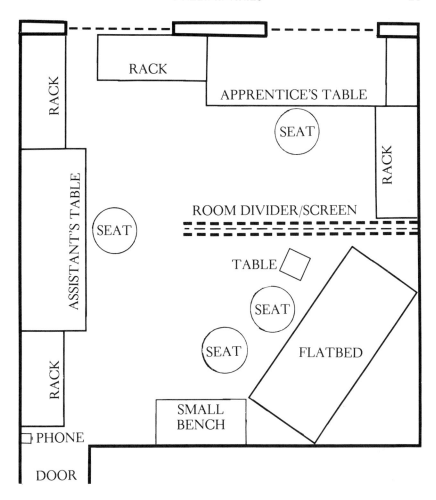

FIGURE 2.11   Floor plan number two. Notice how much more room is needed in a flatbed system. There is no room for additional racks.

fer to have their own editing bench, especially in a room of this size, using the space on the flatbed to cut. A small table to the editor's left would contain the logs and perhaps a small synchronizer (with no sound attachments) for use in obtaining precise footage counts. If the editor needs an editing bench a small one might be set up nearby out of the way. Often, a smaller flatbed is rented in addition to the larger one. This goes nearby.

Often, on a feature, you are able to rent two rooms, or one

room with a smaller room off it. In this case I prefer to put the apprentice and the film library into the smaller room, and leave the editor and assistant in the other. This is always preferable since apprentice work is, by its nature, noisy and can often be distracting. Once again, it is the assistant's job to think of the editor at all times. The more comfortable the editor, the faster and better the film gets edited. And, in the hierarchy of editing room personnel, if the assistant or the apprentice must be a little bit less comfortable in order to make the editor more so—so be it.

There are, of course, many other possible situations in editing rooms. Most nonfeatures don't have apprentices at all. Some low-budget films can't even afford an assistant. Some high-budget films have more film than can fit in the same room with the editors. On *Hair* we had one room stacked ceiling to floor with film. Some editing rooms are set up with videotape systems. But the principle remains the same—make sure that the editor is comfortable and can get the work done. That is, after all, the job everyone is there to do.

3

BEFORE THE FILM BEGINS

Even before the Moviolas and the flatbeds move into the editing room there are things an assistant editor must do. The first, of course, is to get hired on the job, but let's assume you've already managed that (for an exploration of that topic see Chapter 18).

Let's say that you've just been hired onto Adam Free's new picture, entitled *Silent Night, Silent Cowboy*. Your editor is a woman named Wendy Libre (editing has traditionally had more women in it than almost any other film trade).

The first thing to do after Wendy hires you is to determine your salary, if this hasn't already been determined for you by Wendy or the film's production manager. I've found that the odious job of talking money is always better done at the beginning of the film so that there are no problems later. Be aware that people get paid in more ways than money. Working on a good film with good people, learning a lot about the craft, and making more contacts are all legitimate forms of payment on films. And while your landlord probably won't want to get paid with that kind of currency, they all should be taken into account when you are deciding whether to take the job or not.

Silent Night sounds like a good film for you. As soon as you've taken the job, get a copy of a script. The script will tell you a lot about how you should organize the film. A musical will be organized differently than a straight dialogue film and on an action film, you will get different kinds of footage than on either of the other. You will see if a lot of special effects work is planned (*opticals, matte shots, stock footage, on-set projection, et al.*). You will see if there are a lot of short scenes or if the film is made up primarily of longer shots. For the sake of complicating this example, let us assume the following about the movie you are going to do.

Silent Night, Silent Cowboy is a film about the shooting of a western. It focuses on the scriptwriter's life, which is (naturally) falling apart just as the film is being made. There are going to be three weeks of shooting in a desertlike location (for the western film-within-the-film), two weeks on various locations in the city, and five weeks in a studio. Because of the nature of the film there will be scenes of people watching projected film, some opticals, and some on-set music. Though there might be one or two scenes in the western with fast action, most of the film appears to be dialogue-oriented, with a lot of long scenes intercut with the western.

This may be all that you can tell from a few readings of the script, but this has already given you a lot of information. As you learn more and more of what different kinds of films demand of you in the editing room you will be able to read scripts much more easily for these kinds of clues.

After you've read the script you will discuss the job with Wendy. She will tell you how she wants things handled. Some editors have more demands than others, but all of them have *some*. Most of them are reasonable requests that they have learned help them do their job better. In this case, Wendy wants to work on a Moviola. She tells you that she is not going to be on location during the three weeks in the desert. Instead, she will be cutting. She will also be able to tell you the results of any conversations she has had with the director—how much coverage he intends to shoot, any special requirements *he* has, what kind of cutting he wants done without him, when he wants to see the cut if at all.

The production manager will also be able to give you a lot of valuable information. You'll want to know how much footage to expect since you will have to organize 80,000 feet differently than 500,000. He will probably also have decided what lab will be processing the dailies, what sound house will be transferring the sound dailies, and where you will be cutting. The production manager or production office coordinator (called the P.O.C) can also give you some idea of where and how to obtain supplies, how you can obtain a supply of petty cash, and who is on the crew. Get your name and Wendy's on the crew list immediately (as well as your apprentice's name if you have one) and get a copy of the latest one. Often, you will be working with people who you already know. This can help you to see the strengths and weaknesses you will be faced with during the film.

The people you will need to know most directly are the director (of course), the sound recordist and whoever is taking the sound notes, the second assistant camera (this person takes the camera notes), and, most importantly, the script supervisor. The script supervisor's paperwork will be your most direct link with the set. If you have a good rapport with him or her, everything will run that much smoother.

Finally, something that seems so obvious to me that I'm always shocked by how many people never bother to do it. I make a point of meeting the people with whom I'll be dealing. I drop by the laboratory to introduce myself to the customer contact person and the shipping clerks. I say hello to the *dailies projectionist*. I go by to see the person doing *sound transfers* and the *sound house shippers*. In fact, I introduce myself to as many people as I can—at the editing rental house, in the production office, on the set. At each stop I'll try and iron out procedures. What time will I be getting my dailies? Should I pick them up or will you deliver? When do you need the negative and quarter-inch tapes? Where can I reach you after hours if there is any emergency (though editing staffs often work late and on weekends, many of your contacts won't)? I tell the projectionist all of the details about the film (aspect ratio, what format the dailies will come to him—on reels or cores, Moviola or flatbed wind, et al.). I work out a system for the delivery of all paperwork to the editing room. I find out how to submit time cards and get paychecks.

The assistant's job is to keep things moving smoothly during the editing process. A little bit of advance work here will ease your path later in countless ways.

If you are lucky you will have a production manager who will hire you early enough to do all of these things (two or three days is plenty). But one rarely is that lucky. On most films you will probably find yourself put on the payroll on the first day of shooting. The dailies will be arriving early the next morning and you will have only this one day to organize everything. With the general lethargy of suppliers you will find that one day isn't enough time to get everything done properly. In that case I usually spend a day or so during the preceding week making those contacts and ordering supplies. This is not, of course, a completely satisfactory solution. There are always a thousand personal things that you must do the week before you start a film (that dentist appointment really won't wait another ten months) but production managers seem to expect that you will give them this free time and, in order to avoid hassles later in the film, you should oblige them.

Meeting people before the film really *is* that important.

Another major task at this point is hiring the crew. On some films it is obvious at the outset that the complexity of the film will exceed the crew's capacity to get it done effectively, and the hiring of an extra assistant (or an apprentice) may be permitted. In any case, if the crew of *Silent Night* is to exceed you and Wendy, the two of you will have to decide who to hire.

From reading the script you and Wendy have decided (quite rightly) that no second assistant will be necessary on this film. The crew will consist of the two of you and an apprentice. There are many ways of finding qualified editing crews. After having worked in the business for a while, you will probably know of people with whom you're comfortable working. Wendy might have someone that she wants to hire. You may have worked with an apprentice before who knows how you work and could handle the job with a minimum of fuss. The unions also keep lists of qualified people and you can call them for this "availability list" (though I have often found these lists to be quite out of date). In many cutting rooms, job seekers come by in a seemingly never-ending stream leaving their resumes behind. I have sometimes hired from among these people after talking to them.

One word of warning on this last method. For union jobs in unions on either coast there is a rule that you must first give all out-of-work and qualified union members a chance at the job before hiring outside of the union. In practice, this means interviewing the people on the eligibility list first. The Los Angeles union is very strict about this rule and sometimes enforces it with crippling severity. So—be careful before you hire.

However you've chosen to find additional crew, the one guiding factor in making that decision is to realize that this person must help to move things smoothly during the editing process. That is why many people prefer to hire from among the people with whom they have already worked.

Let's say that Wendy and you have decided to hire Philip Spring, a young man who worked with the two of you on your last film. You've all settled on your salaries and read the script, you have already set up the cutting room with Wendy's Moviolas and other supplies. Maybe you've even met the director to say hello.

The first day's shooting has been completed. It is now Tuesday morning. You real work is about to begin.

4

SHOOTING

Dailies Preparation

If everything is moving smoothly, on Tuesday morning you will receive three different packages from three different locations. From the film laboratory you will receive the picture dailies and their accompanying paperwork. The sound transfer house will deliver the track dailies and their accompanying paperwork. And, from the production office, you will receive a copy of the script supervisor's rough notes (after a few days you will also begin to receive the typed-up final notes as well). If you are lucky enough to be working at a studio in Hollywood where everything is done on the lot your apprentice can pick up everything in five minutes. On films with tight deadlines I often have the dailies picked up very early in the morning so the syncing can be finished early. Most days I like to start at 9:00 a.m., on tougher days a 7:00 a.m. start may be more helpful (I've found that starting times in Hollywood are usually earlier than elsewhere—7:00 or 8:00 a.m. is not uncommon).

The papers you should get with the picture dailies are the laboratory report and the camera report. You should also get at least a verbal report from the customer contact person if there is anything wrong *whatsoever* with the printed dailies. By the time you walk into the dailies screening you should know everything that there is to know about the footage that everyone else is going to look at for the first time. If something looks wrong everyone will want to know immediately whether it is a problem with the print or on the camera original and whether or not it's correctable. You, as the assistant, will probably be the only one who can know the answer and you'd better know it.

One note about lab contact people. I have only twice met anyone in this position who did not think that part of their job description was to protect their lab—even by lying, if necessary. This is

TECHNICOLOR, INC.	EAST COAST DIVISION	(212) 582-7310-13	ROLL #	SHEET #
321 WEST 44th STREET	CAMERA REPORT		1	1
NEW YORK, N. Y. 10036				

PRODUCTION: *Silent Night* DIRECTOR: *Adam Free* CAM #: 2 MAG #: A
JOB #: CAMERAMAN: *M Cerne* RECORDIST: MIKE TYPE:
DATE: *10.7.83* ASSISTANT:

SCENE	TK	SD	FTGE	REMARKS	SCENE	TK	SD	FTGE	REMARKS
10	1		70		10E	1		775	TS
	2		105			(2)		800	TS
	3		178						
	4		250						
	(5)		322					800	
	(6)		390					20	
10A	1		410	MOS	Exposed			-180	
	(2)		435	"	Waste				
10B	1		485		Short				
	(2)		535						
10C	(1)		585						
10D	1		625						
	(2)		675						
	(3)		755						

INSTRUCTIONS: PRINT - CIRCLED TAKES ONLY TYPE NEG: 5247

PRINT NORMAL *1-Lite*

FIGURE 4.1 A camera report. As this is the first roll shot on the film, it is labeled "Roll #1". Note that both takes on setup 10A are MOS and that both takes on set-up 10E have been tail slated (noted as "TS"). Only the circled takes will be printed. The processed negative from the rest of the takes (called "B-negative") is stored separately. (Courtesy Technicolor Inc.)

why a good rapport with them is absolutely essential. You'll find out fast if you can trust them or not.

The camera report that you receive from the laboratory has been passed from the set to the lab and from the lab to you (see Figure 4.1). It lists a lot of information that is helpful to the lab and a few useful tidbits for you. For one, it shows you everything that was shot on Monday. *Takes* which your director, Adam Free, wanted printed for editing are circled. Each camera roll is usually 1000 feet in 35mm and 400 feet in 16mm (approximately 11 minutes). As each take is shot, the second assistant cameraman/woman marks the approximate ending footage of each take on the sheet. This runs until the camera roll is used up.

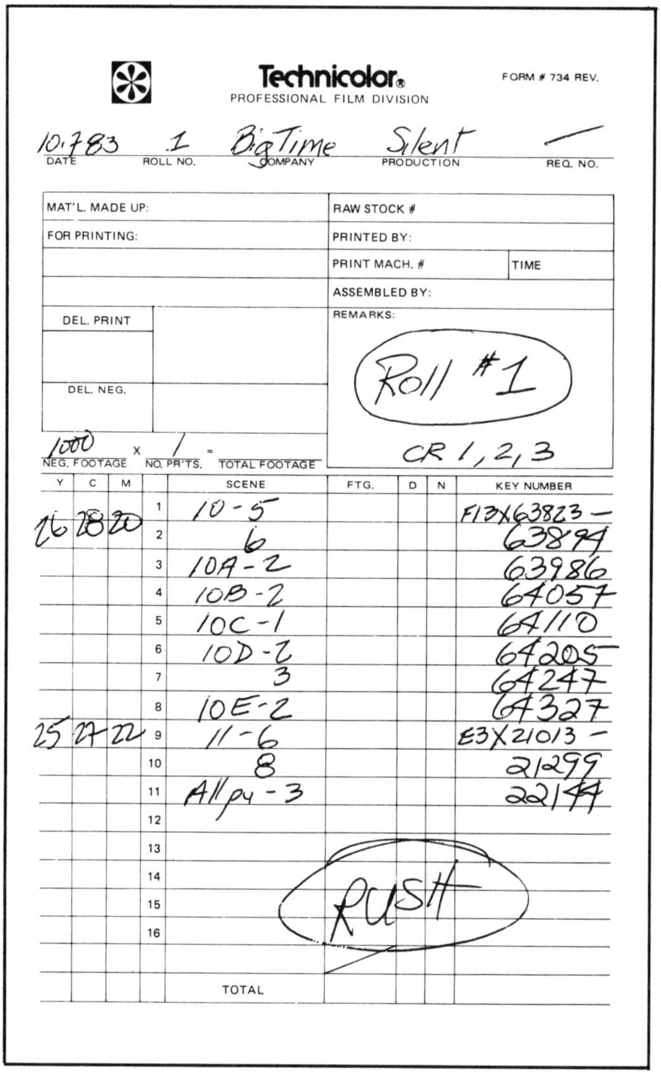

Technicolor®
PROFESSIONAL FILM DIVISION
FORM # 734 REV.

DATE: 10-7-83 ROLL NO.: 1 COMPANY: Big Time PRODUCTION: Silent REQ. NO.: —

MAT'L. MADE UP:
RAW STOCK #
FOR PRINTING:
PRINTED BY:
PRINT MACH. # TIME
ASSEMBLED BY:
DEL. PRINT
DEL. NEG.
REMARKS: Roll #1
CR 1, 2, 3

NEG. FOOTAGE 1000 x NO. PR'TS. 1 = TOTAL FOOTAGE

Y	C	M		SCENE	FTG.	D	N	KEY NUMBER
26	28	20	1	10-5				F13X63823 —
			2	6				63894
			3	10A-2				63986
			4	10B-2				64057
			5	10C-1				64110
			6	10D-2				64205
			7	3				64247
			8	10E-2				64327
25	27	22	9	11-6				E3X21013 —
			10	8				21299
			11	All pu-3				22144
			12					
			13					
			14					
			15					
			16					
				TOTAL				

RUSH

FIGURE 4.2 The lab report. Only the circled takes from the camera reports have been printed. This one lab roll contains material from three camera rolls. The numbers listed on the left are the amounts of yellow, cyan, and magenta used in color balancing the film. The numbers listed on the right are the initial key numbers for each take. (Courtesy Technicolor Inc.)

SOUND REPORT

COMPANY _Big Time Films Inc._   DATE _10/7/83_
DIRECTOR _Adam Free_   ROLL # _1_   SHEET # _1 OF 1_
TITLE _Silent Night_   PROD. # _____
Recorder _T.A. Edison_ Mic. _____   Speed _7½ ips_____

ƒOUND ONE
1619 BROADWAY, NEW YORK, NY 10019 (212) 765-4757

SCENE	SOUND	REMARKS	SCENE	SOUND	REMARKS
		1K Tone	11	2	
				③	Print for sound only
10	1	Bad hum		4	
	2	" "		5	
	3	OK		⑥	
	4			7	
	⑤	Best for sound		⑧	
	⑥		All pu	1	
10B	1			2	
	②			③	
10C	①				
10D	1		INSTRUCTIONS FOR TRANSFER		
	②		Nagra Stereo Sync		
	③		Combine tracks		
10E	1				
	2				
WT 100	1	Room Tone			
11	1				

FIGURE 4.3   A sound report. Since setup 10A was MOS there is no sound listed for those takes. Note the wild track taken and the printed take marked "Print for sound only." No picture will be printed for this take. Note its presence in the lined script and the log, then file this extra print along with the wild track. The instructions in the lower right-hand corner are for the transfer house. In this case they note that the sound has been recorded in stereo and that the monaural dailies track should comprise a combination of both of the two stereo tracks rather than just one of the two. (Courtesy Sound One Corp.)

On the top of the camera report are two items of information that are also important—the shooting date (in this case September 12, 1983) and the camera roll number (this is the cumulative count of rolls shot over the entire movie shoot—in this case number one). Each camera roll gets one or two sheets, depending upon how many takes were on the roll. In no case does any camera report include data for more than one camera roll.

With the camera report and the picture dailies, it is common for most labs to send a lab report (see Figure 4.2). After processing, the lab pulls out the selected takes, strings them together, and prints just these selections (the remaining nonprinted takes—called *B-negative*—are stored for possible later use). Since a lot of negative has been removed from the camera rolls, selected takes from several camera rolls usually end up on a single lab roll. The lab report is a list of all takes on that lab roll. Also listed will be the timing lights (the amounts of red, blue, and cyan used in the printing process) for the lab roll, the date, and a few other pieces of information. Of all these lists, the total footage should be quite helpful to you.

At some point your soundtrack dailies should also arrive. And, like almost everything else involved in your job, they come with some paperwork. The sound report is analogous to the camera report—it lists all takes recorded and indicates which are the selected ones. It also lists the sound roll number (the cumulative roll number for the original quarter-inch tape reel), the date, and any special transfer instructions (see Figure 4.3). In addition, a report similar to the lab report will come from the transfer house. This transfer report will list everything that was actually transferred along with any special things that were done to the sound dailies.

A final, but crucial, piece of paperwork you will receive is the script supervisor's notes (Figure 4.4). These will list all the takes made during the day and which takes the director asked to be printed (often the script supervisor will add *why* the takes were good or not good). This paper is the only real link you have with the director (see Figure 4.5).

The first thing that you'll want to do is to compare all the pieces of paper to make sure that everything that was supposed to be printed was actually printed. You may be surprised to find out how often things go wrong, either because the second assistant camera or assistant sound didn't ask for a take, or because the lab or sound house made an error. If there is any discrepancy, you should call and get it corrected immediately. If the dailies screening is not scheduled until late in the day it is often possible to get a nonprinted take printed in time (sound transfers are usually easier to get than picture reprints).

This ability to phone in for a quick print is why I prefer to have the original negative and quarter-inch sound rolls stored at the lab and sound house, respectively. On some documentaries or low-budget films the sound tapes and sometimes even the negative are stored in the editing room. I don't like this idea because labs and

PICTURE _Silent Night, Silent Cowboy_   DIRECTOR _Adam Free_
                                              DATE _10.7.83_

Sc.	Tk	SR	CR	Comments	Description
10	1	1	1	0:40 "Horrid"	40mm - ABBY enters room screen r., x's to desk and throws mss. onto table. He reaches for cabinet, gets shocked, then pulls out liquor. He drinks, hears typewriter, then exits cam. r.
	2			0:20 INC	
	3			0:41	
	4			0:38 "Rushed"	
	⑤			0:45 "Good"	
	⑥			0:45 "Best"	
10A	1	MOS		0:10	40mm - ABBY's P.O.V. of the room.
	②			0:12	
10B	1	1		0:35	60mm - ABBY reaches for cabinet, gets shocked, hears noise, and exits cam. r.
	②			0:37	
10C	①			0:29	90mm - Closer of 10B
10D	1			0:21 "NG"	75mm - ABBY walks in from S.R. and throws mss. on table. He exits S.R.
	②			0:20 "Good"	
	③			0:30 "Best" (slated TK4)	
10E	1 B			0:15	75mm - ABBY enters D.S.L., goes into bedroom hall, and exits.
	② B			0:10 "Good"	

FIGURE 4.4   Script notes. See Fig. 4.5 caption.

sound houses are better equipped to store and handle this material than an editing staff. All you need is one friend stopping by to say hello carrying a big radio (or any other item with a large magnet in it) and stepping too close to the tapes and—presto!—instant blank tape. There is a scene in Brian DePalma's _Blow-Out_ in which sound editor John Travolta returns to his room to find all of his sound

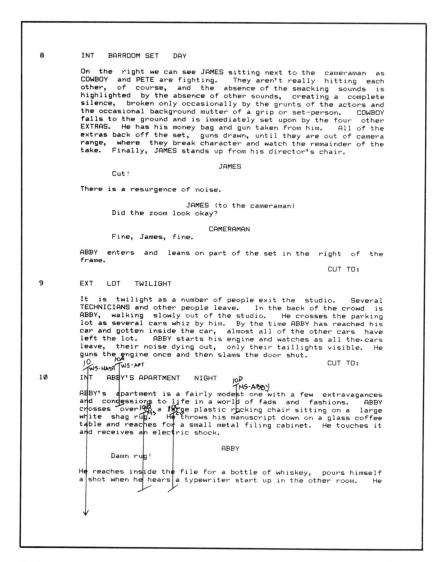

8   INT   BARROOM SET   DAY

On the right we can see JAMES sitting next to the cameraman as COWBOY and PETE are fighting. They aren't really hitting each other, of course, and the absence of the smacking sounds is highlighted by the absence of other sounds, creating a complete silence, broken only occasionally by the grunts of the actors and the occasional background mutter of a grip or set-person. COWBOY falls to the ground and is immediately set upon by the four other EXTRAS. He has his money bag and gun taken from him. All of the extras back off the set, guns drawn, until they are out of camera range, where they break character and watch the remainder of the take. Finally, JAMES stands up from his director's chair.

                  JAMES
    Cut!

There is a resurgence of noise.

                  JAMES (to the cameraman)
    Did the zoom look okay?

                  CAMERAMAN
    Fine, James, fine.

ABBY enters and leans on part of the set in the right of the frame.

                                    CUT TO:

9   EXT   LOT   TWILIGHT

It is twilight as a number of people exit the studio. Several TECHNICIANS and other people leave. In the back of the crowd is ABBY, walking slowly out of the studio. He crosses the parking lot as several cars whiz by him. By the time ABBY has reached his car and gotten inside the car, almost all of the other cars have left the lot. ABBY starts his engine and watches as all the cars leave, their noise dying out, only their taillights visible. He guns the engine once and then slams the door shut.

                                    CUT TO:

10   INT   ABBY'S APARTMENT   NIGHT

ABBY's apartment is a fairly modest one with a few extravagances and concessions to life in a world of fads and fashions. ABBY crosses over, a large plastic rocking chair sitting on a large white shag rug. He throws his manuscript down on a glass coffee table and reaches for a small metal filing cabinet. He touches it and receives an electric shock.

                  ABBY
    Damn rug!

He reaches inside the file for a bottle of whiskey, pours himself a shot when he hears a typewriter start up in the other room. He

FIGURE 4.5 The lined script. The script notes (see Fig. 4.4) and the lined script are your best links with the set. Every take made is listed along with comments on the script notes. By looking at any given line on the lined script you can easily see the shots used to cover the scene. For instance, for the last line on the second page of the script you can see that there were two types of wide shots, two closeups on ABBY and three closeups on BOB. The squiggly lines denote action or dialogue that is not on camera in the given setup.

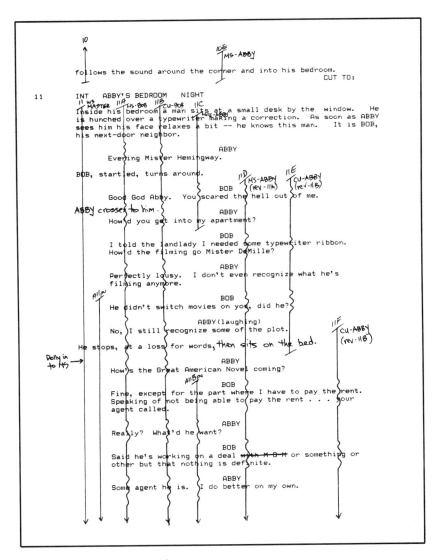

FIGURE 4.5 (continued)

tapes demagnetized. He plays roll after roll and hears no more than tape hiss on any of them. It is a sound editor's ultimate horror.

So I prefer to let the sound house store the tapes.

After you've checked all the paperwork you can plan the dailies rolls. Based on the camera and lab reports you can know how long each printed take is. Based on the other paperwork you can now make a plan for how to lay out the dailies rolls. Generally it is a good idea to keep the rolls in the 800- to 900-foot range (not too big but also big enough to give the projectionist time to thread up the next reel). If possible, I like to leave the takes on the dailies rolls in the same order as the lab rolls. That way there is no cutting and pasting of picture to do. This is very helpful if you are pressed for time. What this means, though, is that the crew will see the film projected in the order it was shot. This is no problem unless the director prefers to see it another way.

There are times when the lab rolls have to be cut apart and respliced. When a director is shooting with more than one camera he or she will usually want to see both cameras for each take, one right after another. Since the takes will come in different camera rolls (coming from different cameras) they will almost never end up in the proper sequence on the lab rolls. You will then have to cut the takes apart and resplice them into the proper order.

Once you have determined the content and order of each dailies roll make up one little list for each reel. Tape them somewhere prominent.

Up until now you've done a lot of paper pushing and haven't even touched the film. Now you can do that (about time, huh?). Assuming that all of the paperwork arrived at 9:00 a.m. (this almost *never* happens but let's make believe), by 9:15 a.m. you should have had your morning coffee, chatted with the crew of the film down the hall from you, checked out all of the paperwork and are now ready to proceed.

So, let's *sync* the dailies already.

Philip, your apprentice, should have already made up a complete set of leaders for each reel you're going to do today (I usually have the apprentice make up a lot of leaders before the job begins— on a Moviola job, where leaders can be reused, about twenty is enough). Use white leader for both picture and track leaders. Then put a long piece of white tape on the leader and write on it with black felt-tip pen (all picture labeling should be in black) as shown in Figure 4.6. The soundtrack leader should be written in red as in Figure 4.7. All track labeling should be red; this will help you to easily differentiate between reels of picture and track.

After ten 35mm feet, splice the picture leader onto the academy leader about one foot before the picture start mark (some labs will print an academy leader at the head of every lab roll if it is

FIGURE 4.6   Picture head leader (to be written in black). A small wedge is cut on the top of the leader and reinforced with splicing tape. This prevents the end of the leader from becoming frayed with use.

FIGURE 4.7   Soundtrack head leader (to be written in red).

FIGURE 4.8   Picture start mark.

FIGURE 4.9   Soundtrack start mark. Note that the mark does not extend down into the bottom of the track since that is where the sound head will be.

requested; in this case you can use the academy they give you). Put a piece of tape over the picture start mark and write on it (with black marker, naturally) as shown in Figure 4.8. Punch a hole in the middle of the start mark frame. From this frame there are exactly twelve feet to the end of the academy leader. If you put your start mark in at the zero frame on your synchronizer and set its counter to zero you should cut your leader off at the frame line between the fifteenth frame after the eleven-foot mark and exact zero frame of the twelve-foot mark. This is easier than it sounds now.

[NOTE: To make our lives easier, we will standardize our method of notating these frames. If I want a length of twelve feet I'll write 12'0 feet (12 feet, zero frames). By the same token, a footage of 370'07 means the seventh frame after the 370 mark. On a synchronizer you would always place your first frame (which we will call the zero frame) on the white zero mark in your synchronizer. 370' 07 would therefore fall on the frame marked "seven." When I want to mark the frame I am cutting on I'll write 11'15/00, which means on the frame line between 11'15 and 12'00. A cut at 370'07/08 means cut on the frame line between 370'07 and 370'08. So, an academy leader begins at 0'00 and cuts at 11'15/00.]

The length of the soundtrack academy should be the same but it will be made entirely out of white leader. After ten feet on the track leader, put a piece of white tape on the leader and mark it as shown in Figure 4.9. Mark it in red, of course (DO NOT write in the bottom half of the leader because this passes over the magnetic head and may leave some residue on the head that will lessen the sound quality). Once again, put a hole punch in the start mark frame. Now, put that frame in the 0'00 mark and make a cut at 11'15/00. Your picture and track leaders will now be the same length *from the start marks* (where it counts). I like to prepare the picture and track leaders at the same time in the synchronizer. That way I am just that much surer that the two really are the same length.

A final word or two before we get to the actual syncing. Film has two sides to it—a shiny side called the *base* and a slightly duller side called the *emulsion*. When film is projected it reads correctly if the emulsion is "up" (meaning up as it spins off the reel). You can usually tell which side of a piece of film is which by holding it near a light and moving it around. The emulsion side will show some raised edges within the frame. This is actually the picture image. If you can't see them well enough a surefire test is to touch the film with your lips. If you've just "kissed" the emulsion side the moisture on your lips will leave marks on the film. Any moisture left on the base side will wipe off very easily. The disadvantage of this method is, of course, that it leaves marks on the film. If you have to, try to kiss a section of the film that won't be needed (like the handwritten lab ID).

When soundtrack *fill* (or *slug*) is inserted into a roll of sound for any reason at all this fill must be cut in so that the base side is on the same side as the soundtrack. The emulsion side peels off too easily and would come off on the sound heads, ruining the sound and, possibly, the sound head.

Tail leaders are much less complicated to set up. They are ten feet long and end with the inscription shown in Figure 4.10 (the example shown is for a *track* tail leader only).

At the tips of both the head and tail leaders I like to cover four to six sprockets with splicing tape cut into a wedge as shown in Figure 4.10. This wedge helps you thread the film onto a reel and prevents the ends from being slowly shredded away by the constant wear and tear they get.

Dailies Syncing

You've already decided what is going into each dailies roll. You even have the little pieces of paper listing them. For today's dailies you have decided to make the lab rolls the dailies rolls. You will notice that this means that one of the dailies rolls will be a little large (lab roll 1 is 980 feet long), but this is not inordinately large (1025 feet or more is too large). I prefer to keep the rolls smaller, but in this case it just isn't worth the extra work to begin splitting everything up into smaller rolls. This would involve splitting A11p.u.-3 (the pick-up of set-up 11) off of lab roll 1 and putting it onto the head of lab roll 2; and then splitting 11D-5 off the end of lab roll 2 and putting that onto the head of lab roll 3.

This illustrates one of the conflicts you will be getting into nearly every day on a film. No matter how many sensible rules you may have set up they won't help the editing room run smoothly if you don't know when to bend them. You must have a sense of priorities. When there is time to do everything you want to do, you do it. When things are moving slower than you would like, it is wise to sacrifice some things in order to make sure that there is a complete set of dailies for the director to watch.

About now, the producer or the production manager will probably be calling you to find out "if everything looks all right." Everyone is naturally nervous. Can the camera operator follow focus properly? Is the lighting what we really wanted? Did the lab do the job they were supposed to? You tell him, "Hey, I'm not finished syncing yet. I'm still moving the takes around on the lab roll so I have reels under 900 feet," and he's not going to feel very happy or secure.

So you now have several rolls of film and several rolls of soundtrack. Things move much faster if the film is already marked. Let's do that.

Take the first roll of film. The chances are that it is tails out. If it is not, don't worry; this system works just as well from the head of the roll as from the tail, but let us assume for now that it is tails out. Attach a tail leader to the end of the roll, cutting off anything that is truly garbage. Generally you will not want to remove anything from the picture roll in case someone needs to see it. But there are some things that are plainly not needed. Cut off portions of the picture before or after the takes which are completely clear or black. Cut off long pieces at the ends of takes where the assistant cameraperson has put his or her hand over the lens. Do not cut out, unless asked, *color cards*, *gray scales*, or pauses at the end of takes where the actors are still visible. On *Fame*, one take was going badly for one of the actresses. She stopped in the middle of the take and waved for the director to cut. Later on, the editor, Gerry Hambling, was able to utilize that wave to make another point altogether. Had I thrown away this "obviously bad" end of the take, he never would have known that it existed on the negative and we would have had a problem with the scene.

So take the tail leader for the first dailies roll, attach it (on the frame line please) to the end of lab roll 1, and begin to rewind it until the beginning of the last take on the roll (take 11-8). This gets quite easy to do with practice. In between takes there are usually one or two completely clear frames called *flash frames*. Even if you are rewinding quite fast you can see these very easily.

TAILS PIX (No. 7.(3) DALIES Roll 1 // "SILENT NIGHT, SILENT COWBOY "

FIGURE 4.10   Picture tail leader. The soundtrack tail leader will say "TRK" instead of "PIX."

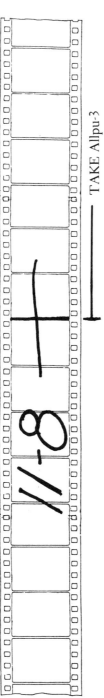

—— TAKE Allpu-3

FIGURE 4.11   The head picture ID is written in grease pencil on the film.

FIGURE 4.12   The exact frame where the slate is closed (no light can be seen coming through the clapper and the slate itself) is marked with an X and the take is marked with its ID.

At the point where take A11pu-3 is cut together with 11-8 put a cross on the frame line and, just to the left of this cross (on the very beginning of take A11pu-3) write the take number very large in yellow or white grease pencil (see Figure 4.11). Then, using your loupe if you have to, find the first frame where the slate is completely closed. Check the setup and take number on the slate to make sure that this is the take that you want. If it is then mark that frame much as you did the start mark (see Figure 4.12), large and in grease pencil. On some takes you will see a frame where there is a blurred slate, which is completely closed but also has a blurry trail showing the top of the slate closing on the bottom of the slate (see Figure 4.13). If this is the case with the take you are working on mark that frame with a big circle in addition to marking the next frame with the X.

The theory behind this is very simple but it requires a little sidetrack, while I explain how film projection works.

Film is a series of still pictures shown twenty-four every second. The way in which this works in a projector is quite simple. One frame is shown for one forty-eighth of a second. A plate drops in front of the film, blacking out the image for another forty-eighth of a second. During this time the next frame is pulled down. The plate moves out of the way and this next frame is shown for one forty-eighth of a second before the plate drops in front of the film again. If that plate were not dropping down in front of the film we would actually see the image of the film being pulled down into view. But since the projector is synchronized so that the film is only pulled down while the image is blacked out we never see that happen.

A similar thing happens when film is shot. But instead of the light going out to the screen from the projector, the light is coming from the set *into* the camera. The film is exposed for one forty-eighth of a second, during the time the film is steady in the camera. The plate then drops down in front of the lens and the film is moved down one frame. What this means is that every forty-eighth of a second the film is not recording anything (it has always fascinated me that during one-half of the time we watch a film, we are watching a blank screen).

So . . . back to marking up the picture frames (you thought I'd forgotten about that, didn't you?). In the normal case you can look at the frames and see one in which the slate is open and see it closed

FIGURE 4.13 In some cases there is one frame where the clapper is visible as both moving towards the slate and closed. In these cases the frame which is fully closed is marked with the "X" and the blurred frame is marked with an "O".

FIGURE 4.14 The sprocket where the first sound of the slate can be heard is marked as the beginning of the slate frame.

in the next. We can assume that the slate closed during the time the plate was in front of the camera. In other words, it happened in between two exposed frames—on the frame line. But in the case where there is a blurred slate, we know that the actual moment when the slate made contact was during the frame we are looking at. To be precise in syncing dailies, I like to note the difference. Thus the big circles on the blurred frame.

After marking A11pu-3 move along to the next take back in the reel—11-8. Mark this in the same way. Then do 11-6. Normally you would continue along the roll after this, doing 10E-2 and so on until you finished the roll. But 10E-2 is marked "T.S" on the reports. This means that, for one reason or another, the slate comes at the tail of the take. It is therefore called a tail slate. This means that you should not spin up to the top of the take to find and mark the slate, but that you should find and mark it (in exactly the same way as before) at the tail. On all of your markings (at the slate and at the top of the take where the identification is repeated, as well as on your paperwork) list this take as 10E-2ts.

After you've marked the slate then go to the head of the take and make your cross dividing 10E-2ts from 10D-3. Mark the head identification. Then continue on back to the top of the roll.

When you get to the very top of the roll and have finished with take 10-5 attach (at a frame line please) your head leader to the head of the take. When this is done the very first frame of the film should begin at 12'00, if the head leader is inserted into the synchronizer in the standard way—at 0'00. You have now completed marking your first roll of picture dailies. When you complete the other two rolls you will have three rolls of picture dailies, all marked up, and all heads out. If the picture came to you heads out and you marked it that way you would have ended up tails out. In this case all three rolls should be rewound so that they are heads out and ready for syncing.

But before you are completely ready for syncing you must similarly mark up the soundtrack dailies. These also will probably come to you tails out but very rarely will they be divided in the same manner as the picture dailies were. To help you out of this you should begin marking them from the last take, and building them into the rolls that you've already determined as you go along (you can now see the advantage of figuring out the reel breakdown ahead of time).

There is a slightly different procedure for marking track dailies. For now, don't put any leaders on the rolls. Just spin them onto reels in the order you want them. Run them through the synchronizer on the gang with the sound head so you can listen to them. At the beginning of every take sound recordists usually beep the track once. At the end of the take they usually beep several times. Just as you look for the flash frames when you are looking for picture slates, you are going to be listening for the beeps as you mark track slates. As you rewind and hear the beeps, stop and roll forward, listening to the track. You should hear the assistant camera call out the take number (it will sound something like "Scene 11F. Take 7. Marker!"). Continue to roll forward until you hear the sticks hit. Listen carefully since there are sometimes noises on the set which can be confused with the sticks.

When you have found the area with the sound, rock the track slowly back and forth under the sound head until you find the exact point where the sound begins (this is called the first modulation). Slate boards are designed to have very sharp attacks on the sound so there should be little problem with this. Mark this with grease pencil as the first sprocket of your slate frame (see Figure 4.14) and then mark the entire frame much as you did the head leader marking. Be careful not to extend your slate down into the area where the sound is as the grease pencil will rub off on the sound head if you do.

After you've marked and identified the slate, move back to the next one, continuing in this fashion until you've got to 11E-4. In between the point where there is a double beep signifying the end of the preceding take (11D-5) and the beep signifying the beginning of 11E-4, make a cut. This is, as you've already determined, the top of dailies roll 3. Put this up on the shelf next to the already marked picture reel for dailies roll 3. Tape the piece of paper that lists the takes on the reel to the front of the reels. You can now move along to the other takes.

After you've gotten to 11A-4, you'll break the reels again (this does not mean you will take an ax to them; it means you will make a cut between 11A-4 and A11pu-3), and then continue back to the beginning of the roll.

A few words of warning. There are times when the sound recordist will take some wild sound (sound for which there is no picture). These wild tracks, along with any sync sound takes that have no matching picture (either because of a director's request or because something was printed that should not have been), should be saved on a separate roll. There is often a need for them in editing or sound editing. There are also times when a take is shot *MOS*, without sound. Such a take is 10A-2. We will see how to deal with this in a few pages.

We now have three rolls of marked picture and three rolls of matching marked track. If there have been no terrible problems with paperwork or slates it is now probably about 10:00 a.m. We are now ready to sync them up.

Put the matching picture and track rolls up on your bench. Thread them up on the synchronizer so that the picture is in the first gang and the track is on the second, where the sound head is. With this arrangement you will find that the track will not take up at the exact same rate as the picture. That is what the differential is for. You put that in between the two reels on the take-up side and it corrects this problem. If you don't have a differential and are using 16mm cores to space the reels out (or using actual spacers) you might want to reverse the order of the picture and track by putting the track in gang 2 where there is a sound head and putting the picture in gang 3 where there is not (you want to avoid putting any kind of scratches on the film, and a sound head slipping down onto the film will put an embarrassingly long gouge on the film).

Pop the reels in so that the start marks are at 0'00 on the counter, although, since you have no head leader yet on the track only the picture leader can be put in at 0'00: the track can be put in anywhere. Then run until you reach the first picture slate—for take 10-5. The chances are infinitesimal that the sound slate will line up exactly. In fact, it's quite likely that your sound slate is many feet away. Removing only the track from the synchronizer, pull the sound off of its reel (by hand) until you find the marked slate. Now put this in on exactly the same frame as the picture slate is on. The picture and sound are now locked into sync with each other. Now roll backwards until you see the cut point, which in this case is where the top of take 10-5 is cut to the head leader. Cut the track at this point and attach the track head leader to it. When you run back to the picture start mark the track start mark should line up perfectly with it, at the 0.00 mark. If this has happened, congratulations, you've just sunk up your first take ("sunk up" appears to be the past tense for sync up; it looks silly but that's what everybody says).

At the head of the take on the track you can now write 10-5 (the scene and take number) in the position corresponding to the mark on the picture.

The theory behind syncing dailies is quite simple really. Because the recording of sound and picture is done on two different machines you will end up with materials of different length. In order to sync the two you leave the picture as it comes to you and adjust the length of track to match it by adding or, more often, removing lengths of track as necessary.

Now, move down to the end of 10-5. Where you have made the cross dividing the two picture takes, make the same mark on the corresponding point on the track. The cross will be a sync point for you.

Now, repeat the process by going down to the picture slate, locking in the synchronizer at that point, removing the track until you get to the track slate, putting that back in the synchronizer in sync with the picture and running back to the cut point. In this case, the cut point is the cross that you've made on the picture. Make a cross on your track at this exact point and write "10-6" at the head of the take just as you have on the picture. You now have scene 10-6 in sync but because you've changed the position of the track from 10-5; scene 10-5 is no longer in sync. But you have marked, with the cross, the exact point where 10-5 ends. You have also just marked the beginning of take 10-6. You want to make these two points come at the same place—opposite the cross on the picture. So, without removing anything from the synchronizer, cut the track at both crosses and resplice the track together leaving the excess track out. Since 10-6 is already in sync in the synchronizer you must make sure to make these cuts on the *right* side of the synchronizer. When you've done that both of your takes will be in sync.

What you have done, essentially, is find the end of 10-5 and the beginning of 10-6 on the track (you have done this by lining up the track slate to the picture slate and matching the beginnings and ends of the track to those points on the picture), removed the excess track between them, and then butted the two takes together so that the end of 10-5 comes at the same point as the beginning of 10-6— the cross.

If there had not been enough track at the end of 10-5 before 10-6 began (rather than too much, as is usually the case), you would have found the beginning of 10-6 and added as much fill onto the end of 10-5 as was necessary to butt it up against 10-6.

You can now move onto the next take. Spin down to the end of 10-6, and mark the cross on the track. However, you can see that the next take, 10A-2, is MOS, without sound (this is why I actually write MOS after the take number on the all of the identifications; i.e., 10A-2mos). The next take on the sound roll will be 10B-2, not 10A-2. This is how to handle this situation. Make your cut at your already marked cut point on the track but splice fill leader onto the track. Making sure that the cut point on the track lines up with the cut point on the picture (and, after putting an ID on the fill in the track) spin down to the end of the take and mark the cut point as you normally would. Then cut it at that point, remove it from the synchronizer and continue as normal, finding the slate for 10B-2.

To simplify, you do everything as usual except that you don't have to find the slate and line it up.

Continue until the end of the roll. When you've finished, cut the track tail leader on at the last cut point and you are finished with your first roll of dailies. Continue on to the next two rolls and, by 11:00 a.m. you should be done with the day's dailies.

A word about those pieces of track that you cut out. These will eventually end up in the trash barrel but you should not throw them out until you've checked that the dailies are all in sync. Hang them in order in a *trim bin* (one reel per pin). This way if you've made an error in syncing that requires something be put back into the roll you can locate it without a problem.

One final note. Remember those takes with blurred slates? Remember how I asked you to put a big circle on the blurred frame? Now I'll tell you why, and it involves a slight adaptation to your syncing method. For these takes we can assume that the actual first modulation occurs, on average, two sprockets before a normal slate. That is, instead of it happening on the frame line before the frame you've marked with an X, it is happening somewhere in the middle of the preceding frame. So, as I am syncing a take like this (and I can know which takes they are because I've marked that big circle in the preceding frame), instead of making the first modulation fall on the first sprocket of the X frame I make it come two sprockets before that frame line, in the middle of the frame with the O on it.

When I put the track in the synchronizer I put it in two sprockets earlier than I would and then I erase the old slate mark and correct it (see Figure 4.15). This enables you to get to within two sprockets of what the correct sync must be, and as that is one forty-eighth of a second, that is close enough for everyone. Of course, in 16mm you won't have the option of sliding it a fraction of a frame as there is only one sprocket per frame. This is an inaccuracy that one must live with. For consistency's sake I usually put the slate on the first fully closed frame. But you should use your own judgment about which frame to mark on the track for the first modulation.

Now comes the time to check your work. It is essential for the assistant to look at the dailies before anyone else, unless there is absolutely no time to do so. Not only can you check sync that way but you can prepare all of the paperwork that will help the editor take notes at dailies. It also gives you the first real look at any problems inherent in the footage. If there is anything serious that hasn't come to your attention by now, a viewing (and, let us not forget, a listening) will bring them to your attention now.

Thread the Moviola (see Figure 4.16). There is a special way to accurately thread the film at the picture and sound gates and it is tied in with how you've marked the slates. You've sunk the film up so that the sound of the slate hitting occurs in between two frames; you should line them up in the Moviola that way.

To do that, place the start marks for the reels in their gates. Then disengage the two heads so that you can move the picture separately from the track. First frame up the picture so that it is positioned correctly in the gate (use the academy leader for this), then go back to the start mark and, rocking it with the connecting bar, position it so that with one more little turn of the bar it will begin to bring the picture into the frame. In other words, position it so that it is midway through its pulling-down motion. Then position the sound so that the first sprocket of the start mark frame line is under the sound head. Now you can lock the two of them together and know that they are in as close a sync as the machines can give you.

At this point you should also set the footage counter on the Moviola to 0000'00. It is a good idea to get in the habit of *zeroing out* the counter before running any roll on the Moviola.

Now you can run the picture/sound dailies together. Listen using headphones; the clatter of the Moviola is so loud that it is

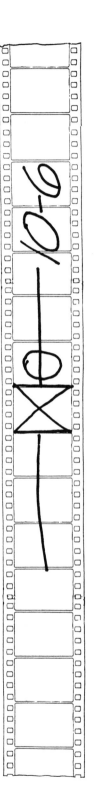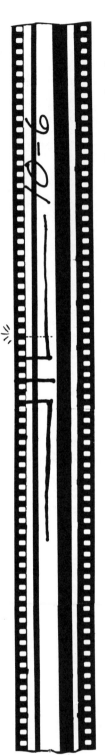

FIGURE 4.15   Syncing takes with blurred frames requires making the marked slate on the track fall two sprockets later so that the actual sound of the slate falls in the middle of blurred frame (where, presumably, the slate actually struck). The dashed line on the track indicates where the first sprocket of the marked slate *used* to be before it was moved to accommodate the blurred slate.

FIGURE 4.16 The picture is threaded up from the feed reel (A), around a set of rollers (B), through a series of gates (C), under the picture head (D), through another gate and a roller, and into the take-up reel (E). Care must be taken to leave adequate-sized loops between the gates and the picture head. (Photograph by Janet Conn)

impossible to get a good idea of what the dailies sound like otherwise. As you watch the dailies you should have the script supervisor's notes to refer to as well as your lists of what is on each dailies roll.

You are now going to make the *Editor's Dailies Notes* sheets for Wendy (see Figure 4.17). Some editors like these notes on loose-leaf paper, some like them in a spiral notebook. Whatever their preference, the basic concept remains the same. At the top of the page is the dailies roll number and the date of the shooting. Following each take on the reel is a brief description of the shot. Leave some room for any notes that Wendy or Adam will want to make during the dailies screening. Your description should be fairly standardized and short. List the size of the shot (WS-wide shot, CU-close up, etc.) and a description that will help identify the shot for the editor (Master of Room, Dolly to CU of ABBY, etc.). You can decide what to write as you watch the shot on the Moviola (using the script supervisor's notes as guides if necessary). And, as you watch the dailies, check that everything is in perfect sync.

When you've finished with checking the dailies the picture and track should be cleaned with an editing glove or a velvet as your apprentice, Philip, rewinds (make sure no scratches are put on during this handling), packed into some transporting device (the most common are fiber cases which hold six reels comfortably and have a handle on top for easy carrying) along with the notes and a little penlight for Wendy to see and write with in the darkened screening room.

When you're done with all of this, you're done with the dailies syncing.

Dailies Screening

Later on that day, your film, Wendy, and much of the shooting crew will march into a screening room ready to watch the first day's dailies. Actually, you and your film had better arrive ten or fifteen minutes before the scheduled time for dailies to make sure that everything is going to flow as smoothly as it can. Philip should have rewound and cleaned each reel of dailies so that the picture and track are both wound correctly for projection (remember what we discussed about KEM versus Moviola wind?) and are free from dirt.

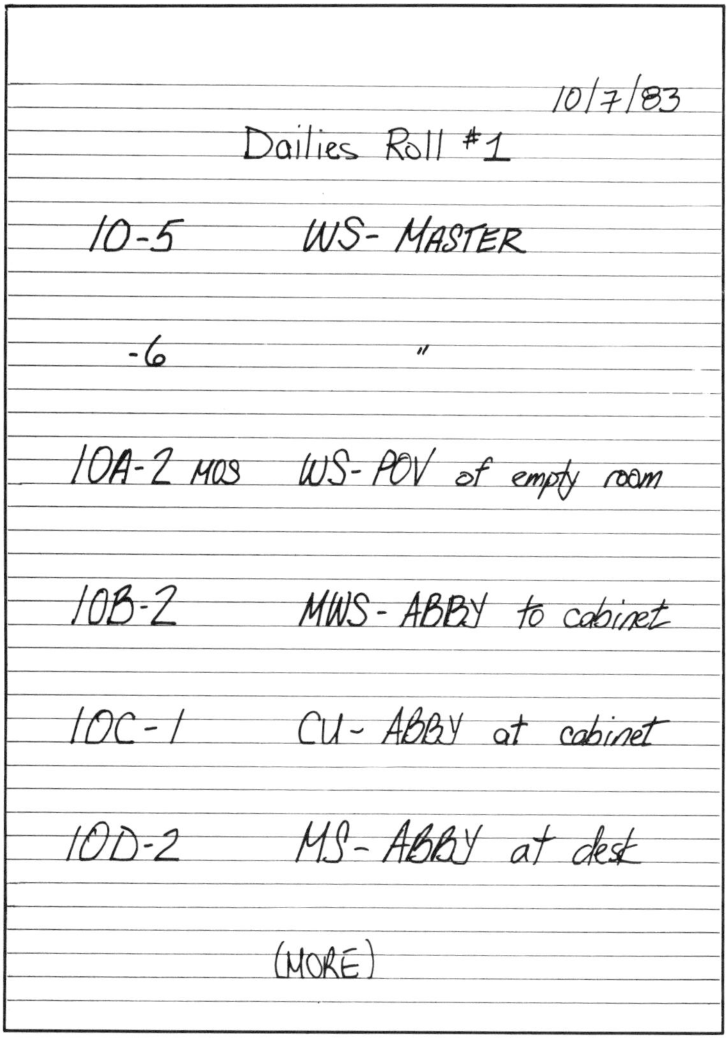

10/7/83

Dailies Roll #1

10-5   WS- MASTER

  -6   "

10A-2 MOS   WS- POV of empty room

10B-2   MWS- ABBY to cabinet

10C-1   CU- ABBY at cabinet

10D-2   MS- ABBY at desk

(MORE)

FIGURE 4.17 The Editor's dailies notes. Enough room is left so that the editor can write his or her comments after each take.

Give Wendy all of your notes and check everything out with the projectionist (I usually tell him—it is still usually a him—what reel numbers he is showing that day, what format the picture is in, and what wind) and then you will take your seat in the room.

Seating preferences vary from film to film. I've worked on movies where the director has opened the dailies to anyone who wanted to come, and I've worked on others where attendance was very restricted. Some directors prefer that everyone sit in the same places every day and some don't really give a hoot. The most important thing for you, as the assistant, is to be near the sound level controls and the intercom to the projectionist so that you can relay the seemingly endless stream of instructions up to him.

Some directors like the assistant or the editor to call out the number of prints of each setup as they are screened (e.g., "Scene 10 master, two takes"), some don't. It's best to ask ahead of time.

Once everyone has arrived and the doors have been closed, someone (guess who?) will signal to the projectionist to begin. Then you will notice several things beginning to happen. For one thing, every person in the room is going to be looking at the film for his or her own reasons. The camera crew is going to want to be sure that they shot the film correctly. The sound crew is going to be listening for sound problems. Costume and makeup will hate certain takes because the lead had his hair messed or his handkerchief wasn't folded properly, and the producer is going to want to be sure that the production is looking good and is also getting usable footage without wasting time and money. In fact, about the only people who will be looking at the film as a whole are the two people whose jobs depend on it—the director and the editor.

This is going to put you in a very interesting spot. For one thing, you are going to have to be noticing all of the things that the other people are noticing. It *is* important that the star's handkerchief matches from shot to shot. It will be important to remember just which shots have lousy sound or focus problems (these things are often difficult to see on a Moviola or flatbed back in the editing room). It will also be important to notice which shots have the best performances in them, and which are the most consistent with each other.

All of these things are important to the editing of a film and Wendy should be taking careful note of all of them. Yet, very often, it is the assistant who must take note of things like technical problems so that he/she can mark it down on all of the paperwork as necessary. There's a good chance that at some point during the editing, Wendy will turn to you and say, "Which shot was it that had that bump in the middle of the camera dolly?" Since you'll never know if you don't write it down it helps to take your own notes. And since you'll never write it down if you don't notice it first, pay attention at the dailies.

At the same time that you will be taking some of your notes, Wendy will probably be taking hers. She will most likely be seated next to Adam, who will be giving her some feedback on what things he likes best and least in the dailies. Some directors prefer that their editor do no first cutting until they are there with them, but the more normal practice is for the editor to be cutting day by day as the crew shoots. Adam's notes on what takes he liked and didn't like (and why) will be very helpful to Wendy as she cuts the footage.

As a result of these notes Wendy may ask you for certain things. For instance, she may ask you to print up an unrequested take, or to reprint a take with a slightly different color balance. Or she may ask that you listen to the original quarter-inch tape on a particular take to see if some annoying sounds can be gotten rid of. Write all of these requests down (it helps to buy a nice supply of those flashlight pens; it is difficult to write in the dark of the screening room otherwise) and act on them immediately after the screening or the first thing the following day if it is too late in the evening.

After the screening is over, collect all of the paperwork and film and arrange to get it back to the editing room, either by messenger or by your own hand. That footage is too important to get misplaced by screening room personnel who don't really care about your troubles. Unless you feel 100 percent sure that your film will return to you safely, always move it yourself.

One final word about dailies screenings. Many production managers, in their desire to be thrifty, think that banning assistants and apprentices from dailies is a good way to save money. My experience tells me exactly the opposite. The more that you and Philip know the film, the more help you will be to Wendy in the editing. This will, in the long run, save a lot of time and money. There is no better way to examine the film than to see it on a large screen. In addition there is also the very human side of things. Philip will be working with you for many more months (possibly a year or more) and there is no faster way to alienate someone than to ban them from a project that they are working on. Besides, he can help you get all of the film back to the cutting room after the screening.

So, we will assume that you and Philip have gathered up Wendy's notes after the dailies. You have dutifully written down all of your instructions, including those comments that the set personnel have given to you. Wendy is going to go out to dinner with Adam to discuss the footage with him (and, presumably, a dozen other department heads, all of whom need to know some crucial information in order to plan for future shooting). The two of you, therefore, bring the film back to the editing room, rewind it (most projectionists will not rewind your film for you, unless they're given something extra—like money), clean it, and set it out on the film racks, ready for tomorrow's work.

What do you do now? Since we have been to an evening dailies screening, it is probably about 8:00 or 9:00 p.m. before you've finished with all of your work. Now, it's time to go home to your other life.

5

PREPARING FOR EDITING

Coding and Logging

One of the greatest tasks of an assistant editor is making sure that the editor will always have any piece of film whenever it is needed. It is this vast librarianlike task that make good assistants so valuable. If Wendy cannot find the three-frame addition to a shot that she knows that she needs to make an edit work, then she's not going to be able to edit the film, is she? There are assistant editors who always seem to work in a chaotic state of near-hysteria, in which the three frames are always misplaced, always madly searched for, and always belatedly found. A good system will enable anyone—be it the editor, assistant, or apprentice—to find anything within seconds. If Wendy wants to see a take, it should take no longer to get it than it takes to walk over to a box, lift it out, and bring it back to her. Anything less breeds confusion. If I seem rather insistent on this point it is only because it is one which I see as the cornerstone of good assistant work. Unless *everyone*, including the director, editor, apprentice, and producer, works better amid chaos, I see no reason to have chaos in the editing room. Relaxed but tightly run editorial situations make for better filmmaking.

So it is important that every assistant get serious about the setting up of the system for a film. There are virtually as many systems as there are assistants organizing them. Yet nearly all are based on certain principles that make life easier for the editor(s).

The cornerstone of any film editing system is the code number. With over 100,000 feet of film printed on most features, finding individual frames could get very complicated if there were no way of identifying each frame. How, pray tell, does one differentiate between one take of a close-up of our hero ABBY from another take of the same camera angle? There is no way simply by looking at the picture. And how does one identify a piece from the soundtrack? There is nothing on it to see.

One thing you definitely DO NOT do with unidentifiable pieces is throw them out. That tiny little piece of film that you need today is almost always the one you threw away two weeks ago. Nothing should ever be thrown away. That's rule number one for a system.

So, how will you identify the film and track? Luckily, this is a problem solved long ago. Before any film gets cut you will send it to a place where it will be *edge coded* (sometimes called *edge numbered*).

What this means is that your film (both picture and track) will be run through a machine which will print inked numbers on one edge of the film (see Figure 5.1). One number will be printed for every foot, which means that there will be one number every sixteen frames in 35mm and one every forty frames in 16mm (unless you ask for special 16mm coding that is also coded once every sixteen frames). The coding machine that prints the numbers automatically increases the printed number by one every time it prints a new number. In that way every foot of the film will have a different code number assigned to it. In practice, this will be just as good as if you had coded every frame of the film. In fact, it will be better, since film with code numbers on every frame would make the work of editing much messier.

The numbers that get printed on the film are almost completely up to you, within the limits of the printing blocks that the coding services own. The most common setup is to have two letters followed by four numbers (such as AB3456). Another increasingly common arrangement is to have seven digits, of which only the last four need be numbers (e.g., 3BC4567 or 1234567 or ABC4567, etc.). In England one can use an eight-digit coding system (called the *Moy* system after the coding machine). Once again, the last four digits are numbers (like 123A5678). The need for this kind of system is not very acute in the United States (except at Warner Brothers in Hollywood, where they run a very similar system) so I won't discuss it until Chapter 7, in the section on foreign systems.

Though using code numbers for identification is a very important item for the assistant editor, the editor has an even more important use for it. If matching rolls of picture and track (such as the pix and track rolls for dailies roll) are coded in the same way, then each code number will also serve to sync up the picture and track in much the same way that the slate does. In this manner, the editor can instantaneously line up his picture and his track in the Moviola and run them in sync.

Don't worry if this is a little confusing in theory. It is actually much easier in practice, as we shall now see.

After the dailies have been returned from the dailies screening you can send them to the coding service. For our system we will use the common New York system (that is, after all, where we are working on this mythical film) and code them sequentially by dailies roll numbers. In this way, dailies roll 1 will be assigned the code number AA1000 at its start mark. At the start mark tape a piece of paper tape which says exactly that ("Start Code AA1000") on both the picture and the track reels. Dailies roll 2 will be coded AA2000, roll 3 will be AA3000, up to roll 10 which will be AA0000. Then I would cycle to the codes BB1000, BB2000, etc. Generally, it is a good idea not to use both EE and FF, or VV and WW prefixes (since they look alike) or OO codes (since it can get confused with the number zero).

There are many variations on this particular coding system. In one, some attempt is made to use code numbers on each take that will coincide with the setup and take numbers. The Moy coding machine is particularly good for this as it has eight digits (so you can code something like 010E2000 for Scene 10E, Take 2).

Another variation is to cycle the code numbers in this manner: AA1000, AA2000, . . . , AA9000, AA0000, AB1000, AB2000, . . . , AB0000, AC1000, and so on. This system is of most value when you expect a large amount of footage and you are worried about running out of numbers (26 letters of the alphabet with 10 rolls used for each letter gives room for only 260 dailies rolls). In actual practice most coding services don't have all of the letters of the alphabet. Most don't have the letter *I* or the letter O, for instance, and many Hollywood coding services only have from AA through KK. Plus, many of the letters that you *do* have should be reserved for other uses which we shall discuss later.

Practically speaking, if the director intends to print more than 120,000 feet of film I would choose the second method. If there is some doubt I prefer the first method, always leaving open the option of cycling back to the letters AB, AC, etc., if I run out of

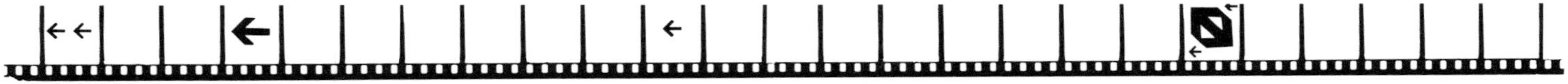

FIGURE 5.1 Coded film. The frame with the design in it is coded AA1047. The frame with the single large arrow is AA1048. Thus, the frame with only the two small arrows is called AA1048+3. Note that the frame with the single small arrow in it can be called either AA1047+9 or AA1048−7. The arrows all point in the direction of movement of the film.

Pg 1

LR	EDGE NUMBERS	CODE NUMBERS	SC	TK	CR	SR	DESCRIPTION	COMMENTS
1	F13X63923-63893	AA1010-1082	10	5	1	1	WS - Master	Dailies Roll #1 (10-7-83)
	63894-63966	1083-1155	10	6			''	
	63986-64000	1156-1170	10A	2	HOD		P.O.V. - Empty Room	
	64057-64109	1171-1223	10B	2		1	MWS-ABBY to cabinet	
	64110-64164	1224-1278	10C	1			CU-ABBY at cabinet	
	64206-64246	1279-1320	10D	2			MS-ABBY at desk	
	64247-64304	1321-1378		3			''	Misslated on TK4
	64321-64347	1379-1399	10E	2?			MS-ABBY sits down	
	E3X21013-2128	1400-1605	11	6	3		WS - Master	
	2129-21513	1606-1820	11	8			'' -Pick up	Pick-up f/ "Great American"
	22149-22176	1821-1983	Alt	3	2		'' -Pick up	Dailies Roll #2 (10-7-93)
2	F23X14132-14339	AA2012-2219	11A	4	4	2	MS-BOB ABBY in at end	
	14590-14750	2220-2451	11B	3			CU-BOB	
	F13X62107-62137	2452-2482	11B	1	5		'' -Pick up	Pick-up f/ "oh alright"
	62167-62260	2483-2576	11C	2			MS-ABBY	
	62401-62576	2577-2742	11D	3			CU-ABBY	
	62746-63123	2743-2920		5			''	

FIGURE 5.2 A code book page showing lab roll number (LR), edge numbers, code numbers, scene number (SC), take number (TK), camera roll number (CR), sound roll number (SR), and shot description. This log will be your main bible during the editing stage of the film. It will give you almost all the information you need to find any piece of film. Any oddities (misslates, special editing notes) should go in the "Comments"

prefix letter combinations before the end of dailies.

When the footage is returned from coding it will be tails out and will have a lot of funny yellow or black numbers running down one edge of the film. Two things need to be done now—checking that the coding was done properly and logging the numbers into a logbook for easy reference. Both of these things can be accomplished quite easily if we make one small adjustment to the procedure that we've already discussed. Before you send your dailies reels out for coding put them up on your table, run them through your synchronizer, and log them in. This is how you can do that.

Run the film through the synchronizer and put the start marks in at 0000.00 . This is where the AA1000 code number will fall *after* the reel is coded. Take out a blank code book sheet. Gather all of your paperwork around you and then begin rolling down on the synchronizer until you get to the first take on the roll (in this case 10-5). Begin to fill out the sheets as shown in Figure 5.2. Enter the dailies roll number and the date the footage was shot at the top of the page. Then enter the information pertinent to this particular take—the lab roll number, scene and take number, camera and sound roll numbers, and the short description which you gave the take in the editor's dailies notes.

Now, look at the footage counter at the first frame of the take. It should read "0012." This means that, when this roll comes back from the coding service, the code number AA1012 will be on that frame. Enter that under the column "Code Numbers." Now look at the edge of the film which has a color band on it. Every foot there is a number imprinted within that usually blue or black band. For 35mm film the number will usually look something like F32X12345. In 16mm the numbers are much smaller and less visible. They look something like $\frac{12}{55}0938$. This is called the *latent edge number* or the *key number*. This is a number which Kodak (or whoever the lab is that your film bought the raw stock from) imprinted in the original stock. These numbers become visible after processing and printing. These are the only numbers on the original negative and these are the numbers that your laboratory will understand. Enter this number in your logbook under the "Edge Numbers" column. Don't worry if the first number is many frames down from the first frame of the take. Use the first number within the take.

Now, spin the film down (through the synchronizer of course) until the end of the take. Note the last code and edge numbers within the take and write them down. Now, on the next line, list the pertinent information for the next take (10-6, in this case). Continue until you have gotten to the end of the dailies roll. You should now have gotten the code numbers for every take on that roll, along with the other information necessary to find any of them later.

At this point your tail leaders should be beginning to come into the synchronizer. At the first code number in the tail leader put a small piece of white tape on both the picture and track, mark the exact frame where that code number would fall, and write on that tape what the code number would be (in the case of dailies roll 1 it would be AA1983).

Now you can send this reel (and the other dailies rolls when you have logged *them* in) to be coded and when they are returned to you, tails out, all you need to do is to check that the first code number that falls on the tail leader falls on the exact frame that you marked on that small piece of white tape and that it is, indeed, the same number. If all is well then the reels have been coded correctly and you have entered them in the logbook correctly.

Breaking Down the Footage

At this point you've got an awful lot of paperwork and some coded footage sitting tails out on your film rack. Wendy is probably dying to begin editing and to do this she will need that footage. After all, at this point in the film, there is nothing else for her to cut. Once you are further along into the film the chances are good that she will be cutting slower than the film crew is shooting so that there will be a bit less pressure to provide her with footage.

So, can you just give her the footage and paperwork and let her cut? Of course not. There are still two more major pieces of paperwork to account for.

The first thing are those trim tabs I mentioned back in the list of supplies. These tabs will always be stored with the film—one tab for each take (see Figure 5.3). Listed on them will be the shot (10-5, in this example), the code numbers (AA1012-1082), and the short description you gave the take (WS—MASTER). Now you can see why I encouraged you to be concise in these descriptions—there just isn't much room on these damned things. These trim tabs can

FIGURE 5.3 Note that the descriptions used on these tabs are the ones used in both the dailies log and the code book. (Photograph by Janet Conn)

be made up as soon as the logbook has been done since all of the necessary information is in it.

The final bit of necessary paperwork to be done is filling in the code numbers in the lined script. On the notes pages you should fill in, next to each printed take, its proper code numbers (see Figure 5.4). The script pages should then be put in a three-ring binder so that they can be added to every day as the new script pages come in.

Writing the codes into the script can save Wendy a lot of time

PICTURE _Silent Night, Silent Cowboy_   DIRECTOR _Adam Free_
DATE _10·7·83_

Sc.	Tk	SR	CR	Comments	Description
10	1	1	1	0:40 "Horrid"	40mm - ABBY enters room screen r.,
	2			0:20 INC	x's to desk and throws miss.
	3			0:41	onto table. He reaches for
	4			0:38 "Rushed"	cabinet, gets shocked, then
AA1012-1082	⑤			0:45 "Good"	pulls out liquor. He drinks,
AA1083-1155	⑥			0:45 "Best"	hears typewriter, then exits cam r.
10A	1	MOS		0:10	40mm - ABBY's P.O.V. of the room.
AA1156-1170	②			0:12	
10B	1		1	0:35	60mm - ABBY reaches for cabinet,
AA1171-1223	②			0:37	gets shocked, hears noise, and exits cam. r.
10C AA1224-1278	①			0:29	90mm - Closer of 10B
10D	1			0:21 "NG"	75mm - ABBY walks in from S.R.
AA1279-1320	②			0:20 "Good"	and throws mess on table.
AA1321-1378	③			0:30 "Best" (slated TK4)	He exits S.R.
10E	1 T3			0:15	75mm - ABBY enters o.s.l. goes
AA1379-1399	② T3			0:10 "Good"	into bedroom hall. and exits.

FIGURE 5.4 Marked-up script notes. The editor can find takes using the lined script and these notes without ever referring to the log book.

when she's looking for takes. All she has to do is look at the script, find the setup she needs, and she knows the code number.

Once these things have been done the individual takes can be flanged off and made ready for the editor. To flange off a take and get it ready, place the picture and track rolls on the right rewind, tails out (this is how they came back from the coding service anyway). Put them in the synchronizer, in sync. Take off the tail leaders and hang them up in a trim bin (you can reuse them by simply

FIGURE 5.5 These three takes have been flanged off and fastened with a rubber band. With their cinetabs in them, they can now be given to the editor for cutting. Some people prefer to put their tabs in the center hole rather than as shown, but the other method enables you to stack takes on top of on another and still read their tabs. (Photograph by Janet Conn)

taping a different dailies roll number and date over the old information). Now, wind the take onto your flange until you get to the head of that take. Wind it *through* the synchronizer so that it is on the left side of the table and cut the two takes apart at the grease pencil mark you used to divide the takes when you were syncing them up. This will leave the single take by itself on the flange, heads out.

Remove the single take from the flange by giving the flange a little quick turn in the opposite direction from the way in which you were winding it up. Wrap a rubber band around the take so that it won't flap loose, tuck the trim tab in between the first and second layers of film, and set it up on your table. It's now ready for the editor. Of course, one take isn't going to do her much good so continue this process until you've got all of the footage for one scene broken down (see Figure 5.5).

Now, and only now, can Wendy actually cut the scene.

Odds and Ends

You will notice that you've got some track left over from the syncing of the dailies that you never used. This *wild track* or *wild sound* was sound taken on the set with no picture rolling. This is often done to get the ambience of the room (helpful for the sound effects editors later on), specific effects peculiar to the location, or readings of lines that the director wanted to do on the set (off-camera lines, on the other end of a telephone for instance, voice-over speeches and the like are often done this way; they are often redone in a looping stage near the end of the editing process but having temporary lines here can help the editor pace out the scene properly).

This soundtrack material can be very helpful to Wendy as she cuts. (Then again, it may be of no use to her whatsoever, but give her the opportunity to make that decision.) For that reason, it should also be coded and logged. The easiest way to do this is to build up a reel of wild sound as the dailies progress. Unless Wendy has an immediate need for the sound let it build up until there are five or six hundred feet on the roll. Then send it in for coding and, when it returns, log it into your logbook on a separate page reserved for wild sound. Most assistants will code this wild track with the prefixes WS, WT, and WV (if there is that much of it) so make sure not to use these codes for any of your dailies. When you do the trim tabs do them all in red (to indicate soundtrack, of course).

The way in which you divide the work described here between you and Philip depends entirely upon your work load and your confidence in him. At the beginning of any film the assistant normally syncs the dailies. As the shooting progresses it is not uncommon to hand this task over to the apprentice. It is a good way for your apprentice to learn as well as a good way to free you up for other tasks, especially if Wendy is the type of editor who wants you to stand next to her as she edits.

However, you should always be the one to screen the footage before dailies and prepare the editor's logs. In this way you will get familiar with the film. Also remember that, ultimately, it is *your* job to make sure that every task in the editing (whether you or Philip does it) is done correctly.

Different editors will ask for their film in different ways. I generally put all of the takes for any given scene in order, into a series of white two-piece boxes. I mark on the outside of the box (on a long strip of white tape placed horizontally down the middle of one of the box's sides) what takes are inside. I never put takes from different scenes in the same box. I then file the box on a shelf reserved for material that the editor has not yet begun to cut.

Thus, when Wendy asks you for the footage to Scene 10 you can go to the boxes on the shelf marked Scene 10 (which includes all takes and wild sound) and either give them to her in the boxes or set them out for her, as she wishes. When she asks you for Scene 11 it will also be ready for her. As you get more and more footage in for preparation you should always check with her to see if she has a priority as to which scenes she would like to cut next. In that way if you have four scenes to prepare you can know the order you should code and log them. Most of the time you will be able to keep up with the dailies on a day-to-day basis, so that you will never be more than a day behind in getting footage ready for Wendy. Sometimes, however, you will fall behind. On *Hair*, one scene took two and a half weeks to shoot and ran through nearly 80,000 feet of film. It took us nearly a week to get it all prepared. The bottom line, though, is to ensure that Wendy has the film she wants to cut when she wants to cut it.

6

THE EDITOR EDITS

While the Editor Edits

At some point Wendy is going to want to begin editing the movie. On some films the producer or director may be in a mad rush to get the first few scenes cut to see whether a particular actor or actress can really act, if a director is getting the proper coverage, or if the editor can edit.

In any case, Wendy will begin editing. Her first step will probably be to screen all of the footage shot for the scene she is about to edit. If she has already cut the scene that comes immediately preceding or following it she may screen them as well. All the while she will probably be taking notes as to what her preferences are and what the problems are with each take. She will integrate these notes with those that she took at the dailies screening so that she has a thorough idea of what both she and Adam want to do with the scene. She will then make a little plan (either in her head or on paper) as to how she wants to cut the scene. Placing the first take in her Moviola she will run it until she gets to the point where she wants to cut to her second take. Leaving the first take in the Moviola she will screen other takes on her cutter Moviola to remind herself of her options. When she finally decides on the correct take to cut to, she will find the exact frame she wants to cut out of on the first take and the exact frame she wants to cut into on the second take. She will mark these two frames, rewind the film back out of the Moviola until she has the frame she marked over her splicer on the editing table. Then she will make the cut. Then she will remove the picture and track of the second take from the cutter Moviola, find the marked frame, and cut it there. Some editors will immediately cut the sound to match. Others run the picture cut first to make sure that they have chosen the correct cut points and, if they decide that they have, then cut the soundtrack to match the picture.

If you think about it, this will leave several things around the editor's table. There will be the first part of the first take (from its very beginning including the slate) cut onto the second part of the second take (all the way until its very end including the flash frames) all together on the Moviola. This piece, because it contains the cut (or cuts) that Wendy has already made, is known as the *cut*. You will have no film on the cutter. You will have two loose rolls—one of them will be the remainder of the first take and the other will be the first part of the second take. Pieces left over after a cut has been made are called *trims*. A trim that comes *after* a piece which is in the cut is called *tail trim*, and a trim that comes *before* a piece in the cut is called a *head trim*.

Let's assume that Wendy was cutting Scene 10. She has decided to start with the master shot and to use take 6 (i.e., Scene 10-6) for the opening of the scene. She wants to cut out of it after ABBY enters and stops to look around the room; then she will cut to a shot of ABBY looking (she will use 10D-3 for this).

After she has made this cut you will have the following:

Head trim on 10D-3
Tail trim on 10-6
Cut-together pieces of 10-6 onto 10D-3 (the cut)

You will also have the master shot, take 5, which she did not use. Takes which are not used at all are called *outs*. So, unless Wendy uses 10-5 later on in the scene you will have 10-5 as an out.

Some editors will leave the slate and excess material on the head of 10-6 with which they started the scene until they have Scene 9 to cut it onto. Others do not. Let's assume that Wendy does not want to keep the head piece on. She makes a decision as to where she will want the scene to begin and she removes the very head piece. You will now have two trims from 10-6—a head trim and a tail trim.

Well, what do you do with these trims? If Wendy is the kind of editor who works by herself you will do nothing, she will do it all. But some editors like to have their assistants standing by them doing all of the filing work. In that case you would have one of the trim bins right next to you. When Wendy goes to use a take you (or she) would take the trim tab from the take she is using and hang it (and the rubber band around it) onto the top row of pins. You and she will then be able to see the code numbers, scene/take numbers, and description quite clearly.

When Wendy hands you the two pieces of 10-6 you hang them on the pin on the bottom rack *immediately below the matching trim tab.* It is all right to spool off the film from a short roll so that it is all unwound in the barrel. If the trim, however, is too big you can take the rubber band, thread it through the center of the roll, loop it back onto itself to make a sort of rubber band hook, and hang the trim (as a roll) from the proper pin. In this way, all trims from any particular take are located immediately below their identifying trim tab. They will be easy to find this way (see Figure 6.1).

As Wendy gets further into Scene 10 you will have more takes to hang up and, doubtless more individual trims from any particular take. If you are standing right by Wendy and the barrel it would be very helpful to you to make sure that the trims are hung in numerical order (I like to hang them with the lowest numbers on the top but some assistants hang them in the opposite order; it really makes no difference). Later on, when you or Philip puts away the trims they will have to be put away in numerical order so this will save time later on as well as making finding individual trims just a little bit faster while you are working with Wendy.

So, Wendy is going to have a cut on her Moviola. It would be nice if she could look at it from the very beginning but since she has cut it to the very first frame she (or you) won't be able to thread it up on her Moviola. You deal with this problem by having Philip prepare a number of leaders that can be used for thread-up purposes. He can make them just like the dailies reel leaders except he should leave the identification section blank (the leader will, then, list just the name of the film followed by a blank space, then the designation "Cut pix" or "Cut trk," and finally the word "Heads"). Tail leaders can also be made for this purpose. The cut scene number with a description will be inserted into the blank section (Sc. 10—ABBY arrives home).

Some editors don't like to have all of that leader before their film. They prefer just four or five feet of blank white leader onto which they can write the scene number. They will use the first frame of picture and track to sync the footage up rather than a start mark.

About that description you will write onto the leader. You will

FIGURE 6.1   These trims are hung under their respective trim tabs. Note that very small trims are hung underneath the tab so they won't be lost among the longer trims and accidentally dropped into the barrel. (Photograph by Janet Conn)

find it extremely helpful to make a list at the very beginning of the shooting of the film listing all of the scene numbers in the film followed by a short four- or five-word description of the scene. As you get further into the editing of the film it will be easier to identify scenes by this description rather than by their scene numbers. If you make up the scene list everyone can get to know them faster. These descriptions can be merely a few words of memorable dialogue from the scene (Scene 11 might be called, "How'd the filming go Mister DeMille?" or just "Mr. DeMille"), a reminder of a particular shot in the scene, or a piece of scenery from the scene in question (on *Hair* we entitled three musical numbers shot together in a Central Park tunnel as "The Tunnel Suite").

The idea of these descriptions is to give everyone in the editing room a handy set of short cuts to describe and remember the scenes in a film.

To return to the scene of the editing . . . Wendy is now cutting away. As she looks at the cut again, she realizes that she would like three more frames of the mastershot 10-6 before she cuts to 10D-3.

Those three frames are hanging in the barrel. She will look at the code numbers on the cut film, see that last code number before the cut is AA1032, and ask you for "the tail trim of AA1032" or for "the tail trim AA1033." You can look across at the trim tabs and, at a glance, see in which take AA1033 falls, go to the take immediately underneath the tab and find the piece that she's asking for almost at once (since you've put the trims in numerical order on their proper pin). This additional piece that she is going to cut in (sometimes called an *extension*) will normally always be called for by code number since she has the code number of the piece staring up at her on her cut picture. Sometimes she may ask for the extension by its description—"the trim on that big wide master shot," for instance. You can determine which take she wants from the description on the cinetab or, if there are several "big wide master shots," you can ask her which one she means.

There is an alternative to asking Wendy for the code number and, as you get better at assistanting, you will get better at this method. If you are paying attention while she is editing, you will be following her progress as she cuts. By the time she asks you for a trim you should know the footage and the cut points almost as well as she does. All you have to do then is look at the point that she is examining on her Moviola and you can know what take she will need. It is these kinds of shorthand that make an observant assistant editor so valuable. There were times, when I was working on *Hair* or *Fame* or *Starting Over*, where I would try to guess ahead as to what my editors' needs were going to be and have the piece ready for them before they even asked for it. When they did, it was fun to have it ready for them.

Assistants get their kicks from strange things, don't they?

After the Editor Edits

When Wendy is finished with Scene 10 she will want two things to happen. First, she will want to go on to Scene 11. You should have everything ready so that she can begin cutting the next scene as soon as she is ready for it. I try to stay at least two or three scenes ahead of the editor, whenever possible. Once again, being ready means that all footage, wild sound, and paperwork is complete and ready for the editor's use.

The second thing that Wendy will want is to have the trims from Scene 10 taken away and to be given an empty barrel for Scene 11.

Once she is working on Scene 11, put the trims away, or have Philip do it. Trims must be put away in an orderly manner so that they may be retrieved rapidly, upon demand.

The best system that I have seen for this is to file the trims in one set of two-piece white boxes, arranged by code numbers, and to file the outs separately by their scene numbers. This is handy because if Wendy needs an extension she will generally call for the needed trim by its code number (since she will have the adjacent code number on the film in the cut). But if she wants an out to give her another option for a shot, she will normally ask for it by scene number or description (e.g., "Do we have alternate on Scene 10-6?").

You will, therefore, have three kinds of film to store away after a scene is cut—trims, outs, and wild track. Each is handled differently and stored separately.

Filing the trims is the most tedious task of the three. The trims should be organized in the trim bin in numerical order with particular attention to two problems. The first is that those pieces Wendy cut apart but which actually belong together. Splice them back together, checking to make sure that the sequential code numbers are sixteen frames apart (or forty frames, in 16mm). The second problem is those pieces that don't belong together but which have been spliced together by Wendy. These trims must be separated and hung on their own pins.

Once all of the trims have been set into order, remove them from the pin while still holding them together in the proper order. Wrap a rubber band around the top of all of the trims about an inch or so down from their ends (see Figure 6.2). Wrap a rubber band around them two or three times to get them to hold together, then flange the trims up starting from the end with the rubber band. When you get to the other end the trims will be tails out. Wrap a rubber band around the entire roll, slip the trim tab back in as you did originally and go on to the next trim (see Figure 6.3).

If Wendy has cut into the wild track, splice the roll back together in order even where pieces have been removed. Differentiate these splices from continuous ones with a red grease pencil X across the cut.

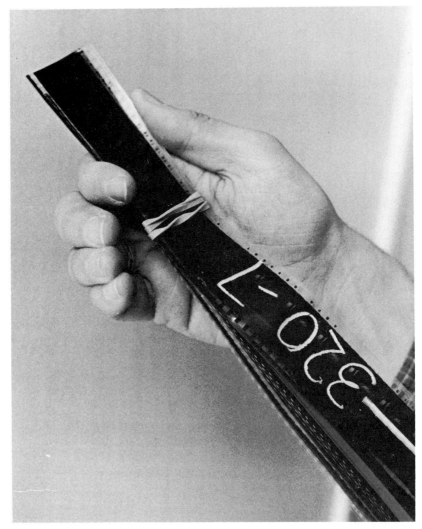

FIGURE 6.2   After the trims are put together in numerical order a rubber band is wrapped around them at the head (top). They are then flanged up from their head. (Photograph by Janet Conn)

When you are done you should have a set of trims wound tails out, a number of outs wound heads out, and the wild track. Now you should box them up for easy access.

To do this, take a white box, run a strip of white tape horizontally down one of its sides, and write on it as shown in Figure 6.4. Then put all of the trims pertaining to those code numbers in the

FIGURE 6.3   After the take has been flanged up, a rubber band is put around it and its tab is removed from the trim bin and put into the trim. Note that this tab has been put in the center hole rather than at the edge. This has been done to show you the rubber band in the center. Normally, you should wind trims as shown in Figure 5.5. (Photograph by Janet Conn)

box. In this way you will have one box for AA1000, one for AA2000, and so on. At times you may find that you will need two boxes for each set of code numbers (this often happens when there are long takes). In that case mark the second box with the starting number of the numerical first take within it (AA1606, for instance, if 11-6 were to start this box). Try to leave enough room (but not too much) for additional takes which may be added to the boxes later.

The outs will be handled differently. I like to write vertically on the box, rather than horizontally (see Figure 6.5). Each take inside the box should be listed on its outside. In that way, when Wendy asks if there is an out for a particular setup you can look at

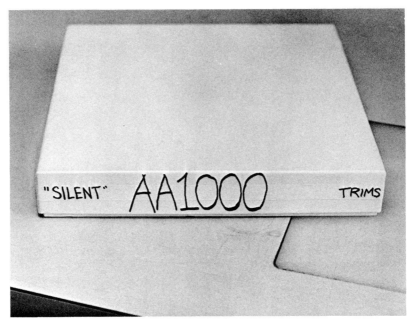

FIGURE 6.4   A trim box. (Photograph by Janet Conn)

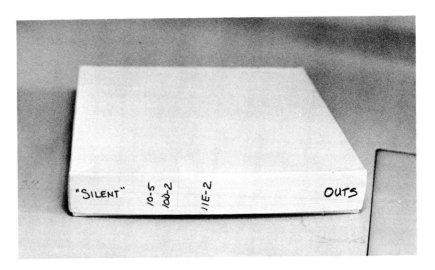

FIGURE 6.5   An outs box. Note that one take which has been an out has been removed from the box, and presumably, used in the film. Its number has been covered over with tape. (Photograph by Janet Conn)

the outside of the box and tell her the answer. When you remove the take cover over its number with a piece of white tape; in that way if she decides not to use the trim you can just peel the tape off, exposing the number again.

Wild track is filed, as I've said, wound up in individual takes and stored by code number (which, since you are coding in the order that the wild track is coming to you and since wild track numbers increase in the order in which they are shot—WT1001, WT1002, WT1003, etc.—is the same as by wild track number).

As scene after scene is completed and the trims and outs are done, you will find yourself building up quite a number of shelves of trims and outs. In order to keep them orderly I would store the boxes for trims on a separate rack from the outs and leave one or two shelves for the wild track (you rarely need more than this). You should mark the front of the shelf crossbar with a long length of tape. You can write on the tape what kind of footage is on that rack (trims, outs, etc.). Right now, when all you have are trims, outs, and wild track this may seem like a silly idea. But later on, when you have *opticals, dupes, scratch mixes, temp music transfers, temp sound effects,* and more, these categories may be helpful to those trying to locate material in the cutting room.

All at the Same Time?

You may have noticed that a lot of things happen simultaneously during shooting. Dailies have to be sunk and screened, logs must be maintained, there's footage to be readied for the editor, scenes to be cut, and trims and outs to be stored. All of this happens *right now* and this can be a problem. An assistant editor must be a good office manager in order to accomplish everything without forgetting someone.

Quite often there will be special requests from the producer, director, or some other people on the set. On *Fame,* one rented lens was out of focus and ruined a day's shoot for us. In order to claim the insurance money we had to ship the takes in question to Panavision out on the West Coast and screen them for our insurance company. This meant separating them out from the dailies (I got them coded first so that the coding process could go on uninterrupted) and shipping them from one place to another. It was my responsibility to make sure that I knew where the footage was at all times and that it got back to me safely.

On the same film we had to send selected takes out to Hollywood for screening by M-G-M executives every week or so. You can appreciate how that disrupted the normal flow of the film from screening to cutting. I had to keep logs of exactly what the executives had seen and what they hadn't. I had to keep a record of the status of the footage at every moment (some of the footage had been coded and some, unfortunately, couldn't be). I had to keep Gerry Hambling, the editor, informed of exactly what scenes were completely ready for him to cut and what scenes were partially in Los Angeles.

On *Hair* we were always sending clips of previous scenes out to the set so that they could check matches on hair, makeup, lighting, and set.

In short, there are always too many disruptions and never enough time. But, if the editing room system is set up efficiently, then everything can flow very smoothly anyway. Gerry never lacked scenes from *Fame* to cut, the *Hair* set people always got their clips, the M-G-M executives always got their takes to screen, and everyone seemed happy. Everything depends on creating a system that can function so smoothly that even when things mess up the works they can't stop the work.

7

SPECIAL CASES

The procedures I outlined apply primarily to straight dialogue movies being cut on an upright Moviola in the U.S. There are a lot more kinds of movies and ways to edit them than that. We'll consider a few of them now.

Musical Systems

I mentioned earlier that *Silent Night, Silent Cowboy* had a few musical scenes in it. One of them takes place on a saloon set where the lead in our movie-within-a-movie, COWBOY, enters the town saloon for the first time and gets involved in a fixed poker game. As he enters, he walks around the room amazed at the newness of everything. One of the sights he sees is three cowboys singing together accompanied by a guitar.

This scene could be shot several ways. One of them would be to hire actors who could sing and have them actually play and sing live on the set. This creates two problems. First, since they would rarely be singing at the exact same rhythm and pitch from take to take and from angle to angle it would be difficult for the editor to cut the takes together. In addition, sound recorded on the set couldn't be musically as clean as sound recorded in a music studio.

Many songs are recorded this way, however, to the chagrin of the director and editor when they see (and hear) it later on in the editing room. Often an absolutely clean wild track of the song to be sung is recorded and used as the main soundtrack against which the editor cuts his or her picture, hoping that the actor's lips will match the tune in all of the takes that are cut in (after some adjustments).

A better way, from the standpoint of lip sync, is to record to playback. One clean track is obtained, either through a recording in a music studio (this is the way musicals are done) or by recording a wild track on the set before the shooting of the scene. This sound-track is then played back over loudspeakers to the actors on the set who sing and play back to it, attempting to copy it as exactly as possible. In this way there is only one musical track, and this would therefore be at the same rhythm and pitch in all takes. Later on, in the music editing, variations in the lip sync can be corrected so that any sync mistakes the actor or actress made during the shooting can be modified or eliminated.

The way a playback sequence is handled on the set of a major feature is to have two Nagras (or other recording machines). One of them is used to play back the quarter-inch tape to the actors. The output of this machine is also fed to another Nagra, which records it as well as the syncing slate and any other sounds that the sound recordist is able to isolate from the din of the played-back song.

If this method is used the dailies proceed as normal. Each take will have a slate as recorded live on the set. The soundtrack will then segue into the direct feed of the song from the playback Nagra.

However, on lower-budget films, it often is not possible to rent two tape machines. As a result no recording is done and the tape machine is used for playback only. This creates much extra bother in the syncing. Since no sound was taken during the playback takes the dailies will either have to be looked at in silence or the sync tracks will have to be created by you in the editing room. To do this you would need a copy of the original playback quarter-inch tape (you will need this tape anyway, even if you were supplied with dailies soundtrack from two Nagras; so you should make sure that your music editor or sound recordist gets you a copy).

From this tape, make as many transfers of the song as there were takes made on the set that used the song (you will need to have the script supervisor's daily notes for this). On a Moviola, you must then match up by eye every take to its own transfer of the music. Be aware that the singers or guitar picker will rarely be exactly in sync for the entire length of the song. You should choose the sync position that puts most of the song in comfortable sync. Then mark a fake slate mark near the top of each take. This will help you to sync and Wendy to line up the takes on her Moviola later on. Then you can prepare the dailies rolls just as you normally would.

Now, regardless of whether one or two Nagras were used, you

will have sync dailies with sound for all takes. When these dailies rolls come back to you after the dailies screening your coding complications will begin, for coding musical takes is a much different process than coding normal dailies.

Once again, the problem stems from the fact that all sound has been generated from only one source—that original quarter-inch tape. When Wendy cuts the picture it will be much easier for her to cut all of her picture takes to only *one* soundtrack. In that way, she will end up with a cut picture that will run in frame-to-frame sync with the original recording.

For Wendy to cut take after take to one soundtrack she must have all of her picture takes coded in sync to that one track. To do this you must *spot code* each of the takes individually. You will need a synchronizer with sound heads in both the second and third gangs.

To start you must have one copy of the complete song on 35mm sound film. Before you code any of your dailies, this track must be coded. My suggestion for what to code it is to figure out how many musical playback numbers there will be in the film and then assign each one its own prefix code. For instance, in our film, let's say that there are three musical numbers. For convenience's sake we shall code the playback for our first song, "Jimmy the Baby" (see Figure 7.1, script pages for this scene), with the prefix code 1. We will use a seven-digit coding system for playback numbers, leaving the six-digit numbers for the straight dialogue scenes. This will make it immediately apparent to us whether a trim is from a musical playback take or from a dialogue. We will code this "Jimmy the Baby" master 35mm track with the code 1AA0000 (if we had only six digits to work with we might code it P10000; and reserve all codes with the prefix P for musical takes).

Actually, I usually don't code my musical masters beginning with 0000, I start several hundred numbers in. For now, let's code this playback master (as it is called) 1AA0300. You will see the reason for this in a minute.

After the playback master comes back from coding you will be ready to code each of the takes. Let's say that there were four setups involving our singers. They are as follows:

19—takes 4,6,8—Master shot of the entire scene
19E—takes 2,4,7—MWS of the two singers

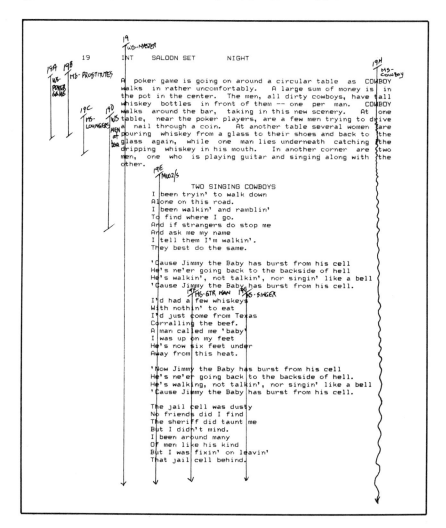

FIGURE 7.1   Script pages for a musical scene.

19F—takes 2,3—MCU of the singer/guitarist
19G—take 2—MCU of the singer

All of the other setups involve portions of the scene where the musicians are not visible and were, therefore, not shot to playback. Let us also assume that Adam, knowing that he would not begin the scene with the medium close-ups of the singers, only shot them singing from the second verse until the end, as shown in the line script.

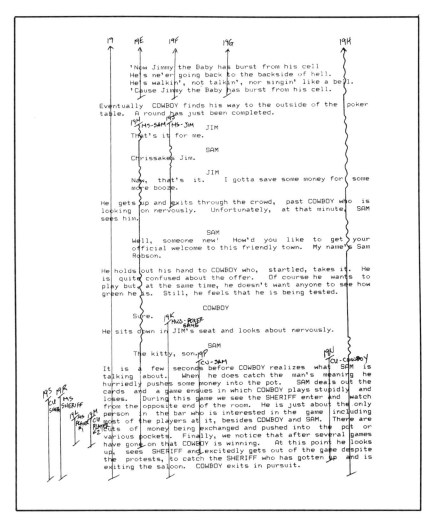

```
 19    19E     19F        19G                    19H
  ↑     ↑       ↑          ↑                       ↑

        'Now Jimmy the Baby has burst from his cell
        He's ne'er going back to the backside of hell.
        He's walkin', not talkin', nor singin' like a bell.
        'Cause Jimmy the Baby has burst from his cell.
    Eventually COWBOY finds his way to the outside of the  poker
    table.  A round has just been completed.
            19H  MS-SAM  19J MS-JIM    JIM
        That's it for me.

                                SAM
        Chrissakes Jim.

                                JIM
            Naw,  that's  it.    I gotta save some money for  some
        more booze.

    He  gets up and exits through the crowd,   past COWBOY who  is
    looking  on nervously.   Unfortunately,   at that minute,  SAM
    sees him.

                                SAM
            Well,   someone  new!   How'd you  like  to  get  your
        official welcome to this friendly town.   My name's Sam
        Robson.

    He  holds out his hand to COWBOY who,   startled, takes it.  He
    is  quite confused about the offer.     Of course he wants  to
    play but, at the same time, he doesn't want anyone to see how
    green he is.   Still, he feels that he is being tested.

                                COWBOY
            Sure.   19K  MWS-POKER
                           GAME
    He sits down in JIM's seat and looks about nervously.

                                SAM
            The kitty, son. 19P
    It  is  a  few  seconds before COWBOY realizes  what  SAM  is
    talking  about.    When he does catch the  man's  meaning  he
    hurriedly  pushes some money into the pot.   SAM deals out the
    cards  and  a game ensues in which COWBOY plays stupidly  and
    loses.   During this game we see the SHERIFF enter and  watch
    from  the opposite end of the room.   He is just about the only
    person  in  the bar who is interested in the game  including
    most of the players at it, besides COWBOY and SAM.   There are
    outs  of  money being exchanged and pushed into the pot  or
    various pockets.   Finally,  we notice that after several games
    have gone on that COWBOY is winning.   At this point he looks
    up,  sees SHERIFF and excitedly gets out of the game despite
    the  protests, to catch the SHERIFF who has gotten up and is
    exiting the saloon.  COWBOY exits in pursuit.
```

FIGURE 7.1 (continued)

Put the dailies roll with the playback takes up on your synchronizer. Any takes without playback in them should be separated so that all playback takes are on one reel and all nonplayback reels on another (note that they will still all be entered in the logbook as from the same dailies rolls; they are being separated here for coding purposes only.)

Then take the playback master and run it down on your synchronizer until you can hear the song from your soundbox. Now, choose a word of the song that has a definite *hit* to it. This means a sound that is as sharp and identifiable as, for instance, the slate is. Good choices for this are words which begin with the letters *b*, a hard *c*, *d*, *g*, *k*, *p*, or *t*. In this song, a few good bets would be the words *been*, *tryin*, or *down* in the first line. Listen to your playback master on your synchronizer and find a few of these easily identifiable hits. Find them by sliding the track back and forth under the sound head exactly as you did when you found the sound slates as you were syncing the dailies. As you find each word mark the exact sprocket down on the track and note the word that you've found as shown in Figure 7.2. Since you know that some of the takes don't begin until the second verse mark some points down there as well (the second syllable in the word *whiskey* might be a good choice as well as the word *Texas*).

Now take the playback master out of the synchronizer and put your playback dailies takes in. Run them down until you get to the first take (19-4). Run down even further until you get to the first word that you decided was your sync point (*been* in this case). Listen for it and mark it with a grease pencil. In the third gang place your playback master at the same point so that the two sync points line up sprocket for sprocket. If you roll down to the next word that you marked on the playback master you should find that it lines up exactly with the same word on the dailies take. Do this for a few more sync points so that you verify that the two tracks are running exactly in sync.

There is an additional way of verifying sync on these two music tracks, though it is very difficult to describe in words. If you run both tracks at the same time with both at the same volume you should hear the two sounds *phasing* with each other. This phasing sounds like a very slight echo; I've heard it described as a "tunnel" effect. If the tracks are one or two sprockets out of sync you would no longer hear this phasing but a very fast echo instead (the further out of sync they are the longer the echo delay will be). If this happens move the playback master one sprocket at a time and listen. When you no longer hear this echo but hear the sound take on an eerie, hollow quality then you know that the tracks are phasing and are in as close a sync as possible.

It is sometimes difficult to hear this phasing, especially with poor quality sound equipment. Phasing occurs more easily on instruments like strings or on single vocals than it does on drums or

FIGURE 7.2   Section of a playback master with three sync points marked on it.

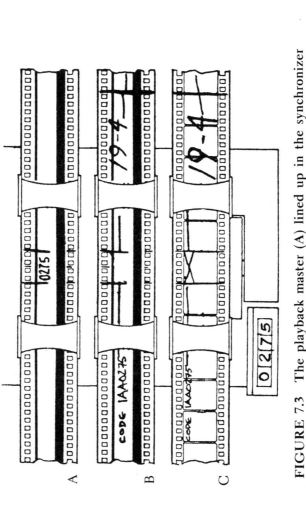

FIGURE 7.3   The playback master (A) lined up in the synchronizer with the dailies track (B) and picture (C). The code number 0275 on the playback master would actually be edge coded on the side of the film. It is shown in the center for legibility only.

brass instruments. As a result, don't count on hearing phasing as the only measure for whether you're in sync. Always use the individual sync point technique and use phasing as a final verification.

After you are sure that the tracks are in sync with each other, roll backwards to the top of the picture take. Then look at the first code number on the playback master that lies within the take. The last four numbers are the code numbers that you are going to tell the coding service to begin coding this take at.

For an example, look at Figure 7.3. The first code number on the playback master that lies parallel to the beginning of 19-4 is 1AA0275. The reason why this is before 1AA0300 is because there was some time when the camera was running before the men began singing the song, perhaps because of the camera slate or because they were talking first.

We can now see why it was better to start coding at 1AA03000 rather than at 1AA0000. In this way we can have enough room before the song begins to accommodate these sorts of occasions.

Always be careful that the starting number you assign a playback master is not so high that it gives an ending number which is over 1000. A playback master which begins 1AA0300 should run no longer than 1AA0999 (699 feet).

Now, 1AA0275 is the first code number on the master. You will want to code each dailies take differently, of course, while still preserving the last three digits for Wendy's sync. I recommend coding this take 1AB0275. In this system you would code succeeding reels 1AB0 ... , 1AC0 ... , 1AD0 ... , etc. After you run out of letters (1AY0 ... , 1AZ0 ...) you would change to the next thousands number (1AB1 ... , 1AC1 ... , etc.). Though other assistants use other methods I prefer this one. It is very flexible. If Adam ever decides to go back and print up any B-negative or to reshoot the scene it gives you many more numbers to play with without changing your basic system.

Let us, therefore, code take 19-4 1AB0275. Put small pieces of white tape across the exact frame of the picture and track that this number will fall on. Write on it "Code 1AB0275"—black for picture and, of course, red for track.

Now comes the tricky part. Every coding service has different approaches to how they like these spot-coded reels. Some want them each on their own individual reels (most of them charge by the reel for their coding services). Others use electronic sensing equipment so you either have to attach a piece of foil to the end of the preceding take or cut out a little notch on one edge of the film. Other services prefer the takes strung together on one set of reels but with leader connecting each take so that it is easy for their operators to see where they should stop their machine and set up for a new take.

On *Fame* we had our own coding machine and an apprentice was hired to run it. This apprentice carefully watched the footage for flash frames or for the white tape splice on the track.

After you set up each take for coding you can enter their beginning numbers in your logbook. It is also possible to put end code tapes on each take so that you can check that each take has been coded properly. I find, however, that this requires so much extra time and effort that it is easier to check them *after* the reels have come back from coding by running them through the synchronizer.

The only other slight adaptation you will have to make for these musical takes is how you file your trims. I usually list the code numbers of several takes on the outside of the box (for instance, "1AB0275-1AE0216" or "1AB-1AE").

Nonslated Takes

Sometimes, through problems on the set or some other exigency, you will get a take where you have no visible slate to mark for syncing purposes. On *Hair* several shots during the song "Good Morning Starshine" were shot from a helicopter too far away from the action to have slates.

In this case there was nothing to do but to *eye-sync* each take on the Moviola in much the way that I described for musicals where sound was taken with only one Nagra.

Sometimes, the camera operator will miss the slate either by being out of focus during it or by being pointed just slightly too far up or down to catch the slate. At other times the lab will cut off the top of the shot, losing the slate with it.

In these cases you will have some tricky eye-syncing to do. Once again, the trick is always to find something that would have a definite hit sound to it. In many cases you can use car door slams, an actor pounding on a table, or any number of other sharp sound effects to sync things up with (you can usually find the exact frame where these effects happen). Always be sure to check the footage in the Moviola to make sure that you really *do* have the proper sync.

At other times you must use dialogue. Here, you can use the same technique as in lining up takes with the playback music master. Look for the letters *b, c, d, k, p,* or *t.* These usually have fairly definite sounds as well as being reasonably identifiable by lip movements. If you need to, say the words of dialogue while you feel your lips move to see what shape the lips of the actor on your Moviola should be making. And, as always, check sync on the Moviola before moving along to the next take.

KEM and Other Flatbed Systems

Until now we have discussed only upright Moviola systems. In these systems takes are individually broken down before being given to the editor. Each take is treated as a separate entity.

But one of the advantages of a flatbed is its ability to high-speed from one take to another. This advantage would be lost if all of the takes were broken down individually as we do for a Moviola. Therefore, a flatbed system is set up with completely different parameters than a Moviola system.

To examine the basic tenet of a flatbed system let us reexamine the mode of cutting on a Moviola. On *Silent Night* Wendy uses two Moviolas—one to examine potential cutting points and another on which to make the cuts. On a flatbed she would do much the same sort of thing. Let us say that she was using an eight-plate KEM. On four of these plates (one reel of picture and one of track) she would have her picture and track for the cut and on the other four she would have the picture and track for her examined takes.

One of the problems of a flatbed is that it is more difficult to thread and rethread each roll of film. One of the tasks of an efficient flatbed system, therefore, should be to minimize such setup time.

One way of doing this is to put as many takes on the same roll as are comfortable. These cutting rolls are called KEM rolls. A KEM roll has no equivalent in a Moviola system since all takes are broken down individually before they are cut. But on a flatbed system takes are not broken down for the editor but are *rearranged* into more orderly cutting rolls.

There must be some intelligence put into the organization of these KEM rolls, however, otherwise Wendy will spend more time finding takes within a roll or changing them than she would save by using the flatbed.

To give an example: Let's say that to save time you decided to take the dailies rolls that we've already discussed and make them the KEM rolls for Wendy to cut from. You would then have all of the setups for Scene 10 on one roll. If Wendy decided to cut take 10A-2 onto take 10-6 she would have a problem. First she would roll down on the KEM roll until she found the frame on 10-6 that she would like to cut out on. Then she would have to roll *further down* on the same roll (losing her place on 10-6) to find the frame of 10A-2 that she would want to cut into.

This is far more difficult to do for an editor than having both frames visible simultaneously and it doesn't take advantage of the flatbed's other picture head.

An obvious solution, therefore, would be to make sure that shots 10-6 and 10A-2 were on different KEM rolls.

This, in fact, is the basis of the flatbed system. Any shot that the editor might want to cut *to* should be on a different KEM roll than the shot that the editor would be cutting away *from*.

There are times when this won't be possible to know in advance. In the music playback scene I described earlier in this chapter you would probably never know ahead of time in just what order all of the cutaway shots at the beginning of the scene (19A through 19D) would be used. In general, however, there are some rules which will work for your planning. First, keep all shots of the same person (no matter what their size—wide, medium, or close) on the same roll. In the scene in Abby's bedroom (Scene 11, Figure 4.5) I would keep all of the shots of Bob separate from Abby's shots. Next, keep the master shots on the same roll with the insert shots. These are very close up shots of some action (an example would be an extreme close-up of Bob's fingers making a correction at the typewriter) which would be inserted into a medium shot—let us say—of him. Master shots will very rarely be intercut with insert shots, as the cut from very wide to very tight shot is usually much too disconcerting. Insert shots are usually cut to medium-close or close-up shots. By the same token, wide shots are usually cut to medium-wide shots or medium shots. This rule obviously depends upon the footage that you get so that it is imperative that you use your brains and your experience in making these kinds of choices. Lastly, in a montagelike sequence (which may be as complex as a car chase or as easy as all of those atmosphere shots at the beginning of the music playback scene described earlier) almost anything can be cut to anything else. In this case it is helpful to have all of the montage elements on the same KEM roll, as close to each other as possible. I would put all takes of scenes 19 A through 19D one right after another on a KEM roll (though not the same KEM roll as the master shot). In this way, Wendy could roll down past each one rather rapidly and decide which one she wanted to cut into the master shot *on the other roll.* She would then make the cut, and then find another cutaway if she wanted one immediately afterwards. This is not a perfect solution but it is an acceptable one.

Obviously, if this method of cutting is to make any sense at all all takes of any given camera setup should be on the same KEM roll. It would do the editor no good to have to put up two different KEM rolls to see two takes of the same setup. So, unless the lengths of the individual takes are too long to permit it, put *all* takes of the same setup together.

KEM rolls should be neither too short nor too long. If the rolls are too long (over 800 feet) then it will take more time to fast-forward or rewind between setups than it would to put up a new roll. If they are too short (this minimum size will vary depending on the lengths of the takes involved but let us say, for an example only, less than 400 feet) then the assistant will spend more time threading up the KEM rolls than the editor will spend looking at them.

As you work more and more with editors, you will find out how they like to cut. As you pay attention to this you will learn better ways to organize KEM rolls for them. It is not an easy task to think ahead as to how the editor will *probably* cut, but it is an important one, and it is one which you will get experienced at with time.

What changes will this new system cause you to make in your paperwork and work-style? As you might expect, there will be many. The most obvious one is that rather than breaking the dailies rolls down into individual takes you will be breaking them apart only to rebuild them again into the KEM rolls. This also means that, if you coded the film when it was still in dailies roll form, all of the numbers would get jumbled up once the takes were rebuilt into the usually very different order of the KEM rolls.

For this reason, it would be wise to wait until after the KEM rolls are built before you code and log them. This will, inevitably, slow down the process by which the editor gets his or her film to cut but it is an unavoidable side effect of using a flatbed.

In some cases it might also be helpful to have an *extra* logbook which would be organized by scene numbers rather than by code number. In most Moviola systems, the arrangement by code number is the same thing as arrangement by setups within the scene (19 is followed by 19A which is followed by 19B). But since this will rarely be the case in a flatbed system some assistants like to have a log organized by scene and setup. Frankly, in most cases, this is an indulgence as very similar information can be obtained from the numbers you insert into the lined script notes (which can include KEM roll number as well as the code number). However, if the lined script is badly organized or inaccurate then such an extra log might be a good idea.

As the film is being shot, this KEM system also creates more work in the editing room, resulting in a slightly different work flow for everyone involved there. In an average editing room the assistant editor would supervise the syncing of dailies, determine the KEM roll breakdown, and supervise the building of the KEM rolls. The apprentice would then have to sync dailies, build KEM rolls, and put away trims. Unless there is going to be very little footage every day it would be wise to think about putting on a second assistant to sync the dailies, freeing the first assistant up to work with the editor and organize the editing room, and allowing the apprentice to do the work of trims and building KEM rolls (which is a very laborious task).

Building KEM rolls involves pulling the takes for each KEM roll from all of the dailies rolls that are involved. The best way to do this is to organize the paperwork first. You would determine exactly what takes would go on what KEM roll while, at the same time, noting from which dailies roll each take came.

You or Philip would then take all of those dailies rolls and spin down on each one on a synchronizer until you found the necessary take which you would then built into your KEM roll on another synchronizer. In actuality, this process is far more time-consuming than it would appear from this description, very often involving four synchronizers (and/or KEM plates) and much running around with splicers and pieces of paper. And, all the while that you are building the KEM rolls, you should also be logging in the footage and setting it up for coding.

On many films, KEM roll building resembles an early Three Stooges film and requires one person's complete attention. It is an unfortunate fact of life, however, that most production managers do not realize the necessity of an extra assistant (or even an extra apprentice) and insist that everything be handled by a three-person crew. This works on easy dialogue films but is usually a disaster on larger projects. Editors should insist on a fourth person but they rarely do (or, if they do, can rarely get one). What this means is that you and your apprentice will be doing a lot of overtime hours and that your editor will be getting less of your time and, ultimately, less work done.

You can see that KEM systems, in general, create much more work for the assistant than Moviola systems do. But, for the editor, there are often distinct advantages to the flatbed. You will learn about these as you work with the flatbed. Until then I can only reassure you that all of the extra work you will have to do is definitely worth it.

Location Shooting

Three weeks of the shooting of *Silent Night* involve location shooting in a desertlike area. As mentioned, Wendy will not be going on location but will be staying back in New York, continuing to cut as the footage comes in. But Adam and the rest of the crew will still need to see the film every day. This will inevitably complicate your life but it is necessary.

In order for the crew to see the film on location they will need three things—a projection system, a projectionist, and the sunk film. The first two should be arranged for by the production manager who will have already scouted the location. Sometimes a local movie theatre can be outfitted with a double-system projection so that the crew can see the dailies there. At other times, a portable projector must be brought in to the location. In either case it will be important that you find out the projectionist's requirements before the first day of location dailies. Some projectors will not accept film on cores and the film must be shipped on reels. For others, the reverse is true. Some projectors can handle reels a little over

1000 feet, others cannot. If there are any special requirements that you must meet you need to know about them before you send the first day's footage or the dailies will not be able to be shown.

You, or the production office coordinator (a person who supervises the production office traffic), should determine the best way to ship the film to the location. Prompt delivery must be assured and it is for this reason that the film's production assistants are often utilized rather than messenger services which are doing runs for many other clients at the same time. Film can be shipped by air, train, or bus. If delivery is to be made out of the country a customs broker should be hired to prepare all of the shipping papers that the various governments will require at the airports. In any case, the fastest, most reliable method should be chosen. (A side note—some editors are afraid of the security machines at airports, fearing that they will damage the soundtrack; I have done several experiments with these machines and have never had a track damaged.)

The major change in your dailies schedule will obviously be one of time. If the dailies screening on location is at 7:00 p.m. and the film takes three hours to reach the location you will obviously have to be finished syncing and checking the dailies in time for the film to make it to the airport by 4:00 p.m. If possible, try to leave yourself two hours of spare time for inevitable delays.

A copy of the editor's notes should be sent out to the set so that someone can take down Adam's notes for the selected takes just as you or Wendy would if the dailies were in New York.

Of course, arrangements should also be made to get the film back to New York as fast as possible so that you can proceed with the coding, logging, and cutting. Often it is possible to ship the sunk dailies back with the unprocessed film and quarter-inch tape. When film is shipped to location it is not uncommon to expect a one-day delay in being able to code and log everything.

There are times when the editor will be asked to come onto location. In this case, it will be up to the assistant to create a completely functioning editing room there. Editing rooms have been set up in such diverse locations as Bora Bora, Morocco, and Norway. Obviously, you can't just get on the phone if you need a roll of splicing tape, so you will have to bring enough supplies to last you the length of time you will be on location. I should warn you, though, that being in an editing room in Bora Bora is not as much fun as it sounds.

Film-Within-Film

In several scenes in *Silent Night* people watch projected film, dailies for instance. In order to set this up, you will have to provide the film for the shooting.

An example was the *Rocky Horror Show* sequence in *Fame*. In it, several of our characters were in a large audience watching the famous midnight show film. I had to prepare the film for that showing.

Several segments of the film were used. Each was cut from a new print of the movie supplied to us by Twentieth Century-Fox. Each segment was placed on its own reel (along with a backup copy on another reel in case the first one was damaged), each with its own academy leader so both the projectionist and the cameraman could quickly focus. In this case, since the film already had a sound-track on it, the actual sound of the movie was used for playback to the extras who were playing the audience (in other cases, an inter-locking 35mm magnetic soundtrack might have been needed).

In addition to the film I supplied the soundman, Chris Newman, with playback tapes of the soundtrack of the sections we were using. I did this so that when the camera was shooting at the audience (and the screen was not visible) the projector would not have to be run to give the audience the soundtrack to the movie. This saved a lot of time and confusion on the set.

Foreign Systems

If you have been reading this book in sequential order you will have noticed that there are many times when the organization will be up to the assistant. As a result almost every assistant has a slightly different way of organizing an editing room. It should come as no surprise to you then that editing systems in other countries vary from those I've described. If you are ever called upon to assist an editor from a foreign country (as I did with Gerry Hambling on *Fame*) you will have to learn the differences. Always keep in mind, however, that film is film and that editing is editing. Though there are differences between the countries they are mostly surface ones. Film is still spliced together by a person concerned with the aes-thetics of editing.

An editor from England works in a slightly different manner than an editor in the United States. First of all, their table setup looks different. Rather than working with a pair of rewinds on their table they have a rewind only on the right side of the table. On the left they have something called a *horse*, a rack onto which the editor can slip many rolls of film which can then feed into the synchronizer. On either side of the synchronizer a large hole has been cut into the table and bags (exactly like those in a trim barrel) are hung in them. The English editor does a lot more of his or her work at the synchronizer and, as a result, needs to have receptacles for the film on either side. As an assistant, you will find yourself continually searching the bottom of these bags for lost trims or rolls of film. Often, you will find something there.

The storing of trims and outs is also somewhat different. First of all, trims and outs are not separated (this situation also exists in many editing rooms in Hollywood) but are always kept together by code number. This is made easier by the eight-digit coding system in use there. As I mentioned briefly in the section of coding systems in Chapter 5, English editors use an eight-digit coding block on a Moy coding machine. The numbers look something like 123D5678. This is a particularly good coding system because of the way that takes are slated in England. Instead of using scene numbers and setup letters (such as Scene 12A, take 3), the English system begins with slate number one on the first day of shooting and continues sequentially each time a new setup is done. Thus, if a film shoots twenty setups on the first day of shooting they would be Slates 1 through 20 (such as Slate 15, take 2). The next day, they would pick up with Slate 21. In this system there is no relationship between slate number and the scene number but that is always evident from the lined script.

Each take is spot coded, as were the musical playbacks. For Slate 35, take 3, A camera, the slate mark would be coded 035A3000. If the next printed take is Slate 36, take 1, A camera, the slate mark would be coded 036A1000. If there was also a second camera printed on that take (or a B camera, as it is called) it would be coded 036B1000. This requires special attention during the coding process since each take must be coded by itself. In fact, on *Fame*, we hired an apprentice who did very little else besides coding the dailies and putting away trims.

There is one big advantage to this process and that is that since

the code number and the slate number are the same, one will immediately lead you to the other. If the editor wants to see another take
on Slate 34 all you do is march to the place where Slate 34 is kept
and you will immediately see what is there. There is no need to
look for a code number first. It is therefore easier if you do *not* separate the trims and the outs since the editor will be calling for them
in the same way—by the slate number.

On the cinetab for a film shot in this manner I usually put the
scene number that the scene is for (I also enter this information in
the logbook). I put it up in the top part of the cinetab.

There are other differences in the English system. Trims and
outs are not stored in white two-piece boxes but in 1000-foot film
cans. A notation as to what is inside is put onto the outside of the
can using paper tape. Often, there are no cinetabs. Instead, a square
piece of tape is taped on the top of the roll of film as it sits in the
can. This tape contains the information normally found on the cinetab. On *Fame*, I found this method to be less helpful to me than a
cinetab so I decided to use cinetabs anyway. Once again, everyone
adapts the systems to their own use.

8

CUTTING AWAY

At some point, usually just as you think that you won't be able to handle any more dailies, the shooting will stop. The producers will have a wrap party, the requests from the set for frame clips or special dailies screenings will end, the early-morning laboratory delivery problems will cease and the focus of the film will shift to the editing room—right where you are.

It's a rather strange feeling to suddenly be in the spotlight. During the shooting you find that the editing room people are often the last to know about many things—changes in dailies screenings times, adjustments in the shooting schedule, and many other items. The director is, if not exactly a stranger, seen very rarely. You, Wendy, and Philip have been developing a (hopefully) smooth working relationship.

Now, everything is going to be different. Adam will be coming to the editing room a lot more often (some directors, like Milos Forman, are in the editing room all the time; others, like Alan Parker, rarely visit it) and this will change your routine. Dailies will stop and this will change your routine. The editing will get more intense and this will change your routine.

Balancing the Cut Reels

As Wendy has been cutting *Silent Night, Silent Cowboy* she has been accumulating individual cut scenes. After a while she will have accumulated enough consecutive scenes to build them all together into a reel. Very often she will be building these reels as she cuts. Sometimes you will notice that, because of the order in which she has had to cut the scenes, there are now several consecutive scenes which have not yet been edited together. She may want to cut them together herself or she may ask you to do it. As the scenes go together onto the projection reels there are several things to keep in mind.

As usual, the head and the tail of each reel should be leadered. The leader should look something like Figure 8.1 (the example given here is for picture only). Once again, use red ink for track and black for picture.

The next thing to remember is the time limitation. Reels should, once again, not exceed 1000 feet except under special circumstances. However, they should be larger than 700 feet to give the projectionist enough time to thread up the next reel. I like to leave the reels at about 800 feet. As the film is recut scenes may be rearranged or lengthened. Leaving 200 feet on each reel gives you room to add footage at a later date without totally reordering the reels.

This determination of reel length and content is called *balancing the reels* and it will become quite important later on in the editing process. For now, however, it is most important to balance the film in a way to help expedite the handling of it in the editing and projection rooms.

Another thing to remember when you balance the reels is something called *changeovers*. These are the circles that you sometimes see in the upper right-hand corner of the screen. They are cues for the projectionist so he'll know exactly when to make the changeover from the reel on one projector to the reel on the other (projection rooms have two projectors). There are two sets of circles that you will see on the screen. The first set (on screen the *set* actually appears as a single circle, but in order to make it visible to the human eye it is actually a single circle appearing in the same spot on four succeeding frames) cues the projectionist to begin running the other projector though not to turn on its light. It is called the *motor cue* since it cues the starting of the second projector's motor. The second set is called the *changeover cue* and signals the projectionist to turn the picture and sound *off* on the first projector at the exact same moment that he turns the picture and sound *on* on the second one, containing the new reel.

Human reflexes being what they are, it would be impossible for the projectionist to make the changeover exactly from the last frame of one reel to the very first frame of the next. The adopted standard is to give the projectionist one second from the changeover

FIGURE 8.1 Head leader for cut picture and track.

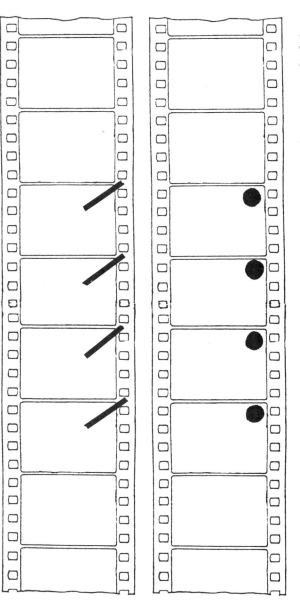

A

B

FIGURE 8.2 Two types of changeovers. In method A a grease pencil mark is drawn. In method B a small stick-on dot is placed on the film. In either case you must make sure that the mark extends well past the 1.85 cutoff so that the projectionist will be able to see it during projection.

cue to the end of the reel "just in case he misses it." Reaction time is supposed to be approximately two-thirds of a second. The extra time is for slower projectionists.

In reality, projectionists are normally a careless lot and you will rarely have a screening with perfect changeovers, so it is wise to plan ahead for these eventualities. I try to put changeovers in places where a missed half second will not be so crucial—commonly reel changes come in between scenes. I try to choose a place where the outgoing scene has a few seconds of pause at its end and the incoming scene has no dialogue in its first few seconds. It is also helpful if the incoming scene has a very different sound quality than the outgoing one (louder/softer, interior/exterior).

Then, after the reel balance has been decided, you can mark the changeovers. Since the balance will be changing a lot before the reels are *locked* (finished, with no more cutting to be done) it is important that these changeover marks be very . . . well . . . changeable. Some assistants use grease pencil to make a slash mark extending from the upper right-hand corner of the frame a short way into the frame itself (see Figure 8.2). Others like to punch out little dots (with a hole puncher) from a roll of paper tape. These dots can then be stuck onto the frame but easily removed when necessary. This method looks the neatest and has the advantage of looking more like the standard changeover marks (which are hollow circles). If you ever go into a screening room with a projectionist who is only used to projecting finished films these circular changeovers will be more recognizable to him. This will lower the possibility of an embarrassing mistake during a screening. Always make sure that your marks extend far enough into the frame to be seen, even if you are projecting in a 1.85 screen ratio.

There is a standard for where the changeover marks (whatever kind you use) go on the film (see Figure 8.3).

You need only mark your picture for changeovers. Visible cue marks would make little sense on the track.

As more and more reels are built up Wendy and Adam will want to screen the film more often in a screening room than on an editing machine. It will be up to you, as the assistant, to book these screenings. For that reason it is very helpful if you know as many screening rooms in town as possible and the relative merits and demerits of each.

11 FEET

24 FRAMES

Silent Night, Silent Cowboy
—Continuity (6·20·84)—

Reel #	Scenes	LFOA
1	1 – 26	930.07
2	27 – 35PT	944.05
3	35PT – 52	904.03
4	54 – 72	994.02
5	73 – 85	934.15
6	86 – 102PT	993.09
7	102PT – 113	955.11
8	114 – 130	973.07
9	132 – 156	943.04
10	160 – 181	978.03

(LENGTH 9432.12)
TIME–(1:44:48.5)
— INCLUDES HEAD & TAIL CREDITS —

FIGURE 8.4 A reel breakdown. The length of the film is the total of all of the reels minus the academy leaders (subtracting 11.15 from each LFOA will give the lengths of each individual reel).

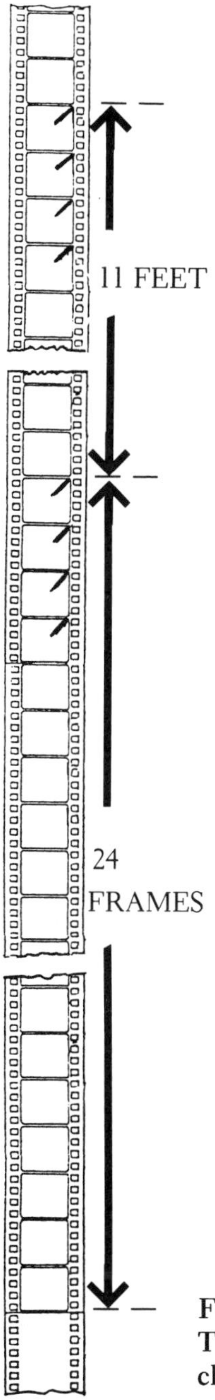

FIGURE 8.3 The placement of changeover marks. The motor cue begins 12½ feet before the LFOA. The changeover cue comes 1½ feet (one second) before it.

In a studio situation in Hollywood, you will usually be assigned a screening room to go to. However, even here it is helpful to know which rooms and which projectionists are better than others.

Keeping Track

As the film begins to take shape you will want to keep a list of just what scenes are included on each screening reel. This list is called the *reel breakdown* or *reel continuity* (see Figure 8.4). On it you will list the sequential reel numbers, the scene numbers included on that reel, and the *LFOA*. These initials stand for "last frame of action," which is the footage (from the 0'00 start mark) up to and including the last frame of picture before the tail leader begins. At the bottom of the sheet the total length of the film in both length and time is given. Note that, since the LFOA includes the academy leader, in order to find out the length of the film you must subtract 11'15 from each reel.

Some assistants also like to make a slightly more complicated reel continuity. An example of this one is shown in Figure 8.5 and we can see that it includes the short scene descriptions as well as the scene numbers. Each scene takes its own line. This makes the list rather difficult to refer to quickly but its comprehensiveness will often come in very handy.

Once you've determined the footages of each reel you should determine the length of the complete film in minutes. Add up the lengths of all of the reels (picture lengths, not LFOAs) then use a footage/time chart (see Appendices), a reddy-eddy, or a calculator to convert to time.

One of the uses for this kind of continuity comes after rough-cut screenings. After the film has been assembled into its first full cut it is customary (nay, it is necessary) to take it into a screening room and see just how well it plays "on the big silver" (as one director is wont to call it). This first cut will very often include every-*thing* that was shot and so it will seem overly long and quite boring to almost everyone.

First-cut screenings are always very tense moments for every-one involved in the film editing process. Directors often get very insecure or irritable. Editors begin to worry about minutiae like the number of people who will be coming to the screening. Usually, no one wants the producer around because this is where all of the film's worst faults will be all too visible.

As an assistant you can minimize some of the craziness by making sure that the film is in proper shape for projection. Be sure that the changeovers are on every reel (except, obviously, the last one) and in the proper places. Make sure that the head and tail leaders are properly labeled so that the reels go up in their proper order. Before the screening thoroughly clean the film with Ecco (being careful not to wipe off any of Wendy's marks for optical effects—which we will discuss more later). This is a rather painstaking and disagreeable task that involves soaking a Webril wipe with Ecco and running the film through it v-e-r-r-r-y slowly. Running it through slowly allows the Ecco enough time to evaporate off the film before it is wound up on the right rewind. If it is wound up too fast the Ecco will leave streak marks on the film that are almost worse than the dirt that it removed. When you are finished cleaning the film with Ecco, rewind it back to the head through a velvet to buff it up. Clean the track with a velvet (no Ecco, please, as it will dissolve the track).

Then pack up all of the reels in order into some sort of packing cartons and get them to the screening room. Bring along a copy of your reel breakdown and the length of the film (everyone will want to know how long the picture runs).

After the screening there is bound to be a meeting between Adam and Wendy. During the meeting you should be listening to what everyone feels are the film's major strengths and weaknesses. Take careful notes as to the proposed changes. These will include what scenes should be dropped from the film, what alternate takes need to be gotten, what scenes need to be moved to different places in the film, what sequences need to have major recutting done on them, and a host of other questions. All of these points require work from you to prepare for the director and editor. Be sure that you know what it is they want done, and when they want it.

It is wise, at this point, if the film has the budget to do so, to strike what is called a *slop print* or a *black and white dupe* of the entire film. This is a black and white copy of the picture and a track dupe of the soundtrack which will be stored as a reference. Sometimes, in recutting, a scene will get worse rather than better. It is helpful to have a record of the way the scene was *before* it was recut so that it will be easier to reconstruct properly. On *Four Friends*

```
                                August 10, 1984


       "S I L E N T    N I G H T ,    S I L E N T    C O W B O Y"

                       --- Reel Breakdown ---



Reel One                           Reel Three

  1 - Credit Montage               35 - ABBY/SEAN at SEAN's - Part 2
  2 - On The Set                   36 - "I Can't Get Out Of Bed"
  4 - Backstage                    37 - Phone Call Home
  5 - Driving Home                 39-42 - Going Home
  6 - ABBY's Empty Room            44 - ABBY Sits In Front Of His Home
  7 - Driving To Work              45 - The Family Inside
  8 - "Did The Zoom Look Okay?"    46 - ABBY Returns
  9 - Parking Lot                  47 - Birthday Party
 10 - ABBY At Home                 48 - ABBY Back To L.A.
 11 - "Mr. DeMille"                49 - ABBY's Still Empty Room
 12 - The Hot Dog Stand            50 - SEAN And BOB Talk
 17 - ABBY Meets SEAN              52 - The Three Party
 18 - ABBY And SEAN at ABBY's
 19 - "Jimmy The Baby"
 20 - COWBOY/DIRECTOR Fight        Reel Four
 22 - Lunch With GENIE
 23 - "The Rushes Are a Disaster"  54 - Driving To Work Happy
 24 - Parking Lot - Rewrites       55 - Redo The Bar Fight
 25 - Phone Call From GENIE        56 - DIRECTOR Is Happy
 26 - At The Restaurant            57 - Parking Lot Happy
                                   58 - BOB & ABBY at "La Bar"
                                   59 - "La Bar" Backstage
                                   60 - ABBY Writes - Night
Reel Two                           61 - ABBY Writes - Day
                                   62 - ABBY, MICHAEL, URI Talk
 27 - ABBY & DIRECTOR Have It Out  63 - "Great Dailies!!"
 28 - ABBY Wanders Around          64 - ABBY & SEAN At Mexican Restaurant
 30 - ABBY On Sunset Blvd.         65 - ABBY Writes With SEAN
 31 - Dream Montage                66 - SEAN Tries To Sleep
 32 - ABBY In The Hills            67 - Drive To Baseball Game
 33 - OPTICAL -- L.A. At Night     68 - Outside Ballpark
 34 - "Can I Make A Nuisance Of    69 - Baseball Game
       Myself?"                    70 - In The Stands
 35 - ABBY/SEAN at SEAN's-Part 1   72 - Return From the Ballgame
```

FIGURE 8.5   A continuity reel breakdown. Those scene numbers
missing from the list were either not shot or cut from the film during
editing.

we struck a three-quarter-inch videocassette of the film rather than
go to the expense of making a film dupe. Though the videocassette
is not as easy to compare to later on, we felt that the video was all
that was needed at that point in the film, since everyone knew that
the film was not going to return to that rough-cut stage. It was
merely a record of the film's continuity with *all* of its scenes rather
than a record of the cutting of individual scenes.

9

RECUTTING AWAY

After the first cut is made, critiqued, and recritiqued it will then be time to begin recutting the film. There are some editors and directors who love this part of the film; there are others who despise it. For, at one time, it encapsulates everything that makes editing what it is—attention to the minutest detail while still paying attention to the whole film.

On *Four Friends* the director and editors continually experimented with the order of different scenes. The editors would reedit the film for a week and then screen for the director. Then they would return to the editing room, work for another week, and go back to the screening room for another screening. The process went on for months.

After every screening there would be intense discussions about the relative weight we were attaching to a given character, a given scene, or a given action. "It moved slow in this part," someone would say, and if there was agreement on the feeling everyone would try to figure out why the sequence moved slowly and what could best be done to help the situation.

As an assistant editor you have to keep track of all of these suggestions and prepare to carry them out. I keep a spiral notebook with each page a new date, listing everything to be done that day and everything that was done on that day (rarely the same). Meeting notes, special addresses, or other pertinent information are kept in it as well. This helps me to plan what it is I'm going to have to do to prepare for the editor. It is also helpful to have an erasable calendar posted prominently on the wall.

Lifts

The first type of recut that you are liable to face is called a *lift*. A lift is, simply, a scene (or major portion of a scene) which is being dropped *in its entirety* from the film. Often a director will want to see how the film will play without a scene. You will then *lift* the scene from the film.

Lifts that are created in the film are never broken down and returned to the trims unless Wendy specifically requests it (in which case they really wouldn't be lifts at all, merely trims). They are stored and logged as lifts and saved for the time when the entire lift or pieces from it may need to be used again.

This system is not as elegant as it may seem on the surface. For one thing, it means that there are four places where picture may be found—in the outs, in the trims, in the cut, or in the lifts. You will need a way of locating specific code numbers in the lifts, and this necessitates another log. This log, which we will (predictably enough) call the *lift log,* is not very difficult to maintain. It consists of large index cards on which all of the code numbers (both picture and track) included in the lift are written (see Figure 9.1). These numbers (the head and tail codes of each cut in the lift) are taken directly from the film while it is in the synchronizer.

In the example shown, for Scene 27, "ABBY and the DIRECTOR have it out" (this is from your scene description chart), we can see that the lift is made up of seven picture cuts and five track cuts (two picture cuts, numbers four and five, have *cheated track* running under them—that is, track from another shot, in this case the shot used in cut number three of the lift). We can see what the scene is and what each of the picture cuts actually are. We label this lift "lift 1."

This card should be put in an index file reserved for lifts filed in order of scene number. By the end of a film some large scenes may have as many as three or four sections pulled from them and filed as trims. If you cannot find a particular trim in its proper trim box you should check the lift log for all lifts for the scene that the trim is from.

The lift itself should be put into a box reserved for lifts. You should make up a cinetab for it (see Figure 9.2). Then label the outside of the box "LIFTS #1-," leaving room for the number of

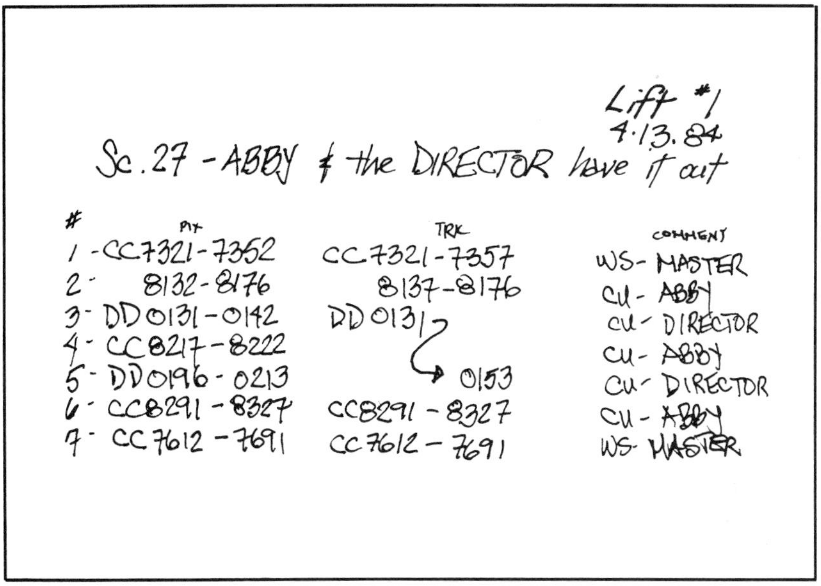

Lift #1
4.13.84

Sc. 27 - ABBY & the DIRECTOR have it out

#	PIX	TRK	COMMENT
1 -	CC7321-7352	CC7321-7357	WS- MASTER
2 -	8132-8176	8137-8176	CU- ABBY
3 -	DD0131-0142	DD0131 → 0153	CU- DIRECTOR
4 -	CC8217-8222		CU- ABBY
5 -	DD0196-0213		CU- DIRECTOR
6 -	CC8291-8327	CC8291-8327	CU- ABBY
7 -	CC7612-7691	CC7612-7691	WS- MASTER

FIGURE 9.1 A lift log card. Notice that for shots numbered 3 to 5 only one piece of track was used.

the last lift in the box (eventually you will probably have to have several boxes of lifts).

And that's all there is to lifts.

Complete Recuts

In some cases, everyone is so depressed by the way a particular scene turned out that it is felt that it is better to recut the scene from scratch, with no cut material to prejudice the editor. In this case, you will do exactly what you did not do in the case of the lifts—completely break down the scene, returning each piece to its virgin state as complete uncut takes—outs, and letting the editor start all over again.

In cases like this I feel it is very important to have a black and white dupe of the cut that you will be destroying. There are always cases where, after recutting the scene, someone feels that the old scene was better or that a combination of the two approaches would

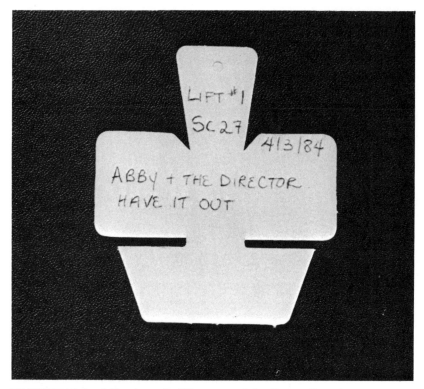

FIGURE 9.2   Lift cinetab. (Photograph by Janet Conn)

work better. At that stage it would be almost impossible to remember exactly how the original scene was cut. So I always make a black and white dupe in these cases.

The advantages of a dupe should be obvious. It is a record of how the scene was originally cut. In addition, when you order the dupe you should tell the lab that is making it to print through both edges. In this way your dupe will also have the edge and the key numbers copied onto it.

But how does one match up the track? When you make a track copy there is no way to print code numbers onto the new track. How can you get back to the old cut on the track?

To do this you will have to *hand-code* the track with the numbers. The easiest way to do this is as follows. Before you send the track in for duping (or *retransferring*), put a one-frame long beep tone on its head leader (you will remember to put head and tail leader on everything that you send out of the editing room, won't you?). There is a standard place for this—exactly three feet before the first frame. Then when the dupe track comes back from the sound transfer house you can listen to it, find the beep tone, and from there find the first frame of action. You should also, just as a matter of practice, check the two tracks—original and dupe—against each other to make sure that they are the same. You do this by listening for phasing as I described in Chapter 7 in the section on lining up playback music tracks.

Now you will have the original picture, the original track, and this dupe track all lined up in your synchronizer. Run them down together and every time that there is a picture or track cut mark it as shown in Figure 9.3. Where the picture and track are cut at the same spot mark the cut point with both red and black marks. On either side of each cut mark the first code number. Where the picture and track cuts do not come at the same spot mark each of them separately, again marking the code numbers that appear on either side of the cut. If you are in a rush, or if the cuts are coming rather close together, you can leave out the code number *preceding* the cut. But always mark the one following it.

Some people do not mark down the picture code numbers since there is already a picture dupe that marks the cuts. I find it helpful to have all of the information in the same place. But, if there is a lot of time pressure, I do without the picture code numbers if there is something more important that needs to be done. Once again, you should always be aware of the priorities in running an editing room.

With this set of dupes it is relatively easy to get back to the original cut picture and track if necessary. Simply put the dupe in the back two gangs of your synchronizer and match the cuts and code numbers on both the picture and the track in the first two gangs. After you have finished doing that you should check the picture against its dupe visually, and run the two tracks together to check them (using phasing).

Normal Recutting

By far the largest part of your recutting work, however, will lie somewhere between the extremes of completely recutting a scene, and completely discarding it.

FIGURE 9.3   Marking up dupe track. Black cut marks are made wherever picture cuts were made on the color picture. Red cut marks are made where track cuts were made on the work track. Code numbers are listed where helpful. At point A the picture and track cut at the same time. The last code number on the outgoing shot, before the cut, is EE6328. But the incoming shot used track cheated from another take than the picture, so both numbers are written down.

FIGURE 9.4   This sound effect begins at 152'10. An alternate method is to mark it at the next whole foot—153'00.

Before Wendy begins recutting each scene you should know which reel it appears on and give her that reel. You should know what scene number the scene is so you can examine the outs for it and let Wendy know, as she asks, just what is available and what is not. You should make yourself aware of any lifts that have already been made on the scene, if any.

Wendy will begin recutting and will almost immediately ask you for some footage. She will ask for it primarily in two different ways. If she wants to extend a shot that is in the film already she will look at the footage which is there and ask for either the head trim (if she wants to extend the top of the cut) or the tail trim (if she wants to extend the end). In both cases she will look at the number at the cut and ask for "the head (or tail) trim of CC8141." Since the trims are filed by code number all you have to do is to walk over to the box with the CC8000 trims in them, open it and look for the take which includes CC8141 in it. When you find it, you take it out of the box, remove the cinetab and the rubber band from the take and hang them on a pin on the top row of the trim barrel. You then unwind the take, remove the rubber band from around the top of the pieces of film (and hang that up with the other rubber band), and hang the pieces up on the row directly below the cinetab and rubber bands. Since the trims are in numerical order it should be a matter of seconds to find the proper trim and hand it to her. All of this should take about thirty seconds to accomplish if everything is moving right. In fact, some editors prefer to get their own trims if they know how everything is filed.

Obviously, the importance of making sure that every trim is filed properly cannot be stressed enough. Each time a trim is filed with the wrong take, or in the wrong box, or not put away at all (as sometimes happens if it falls into the bottom of a barrel) it takes up time while the editor is sitting around doing nothing except getting angry. The fewer mistakes the better. No mistakes is the ideal.

The other way that Wendy may ask for a trim is if she and Adam (or just Adam, let's be honest about who is calling the shots) feel that a take that she used for a piece of dialogue or a piece of action was not as good as it could have been. She may want to see the other takes or other angles shot of that part of the scene. In that case she will ask for "an alternate take to CC3121." Or, if she's already looked at the line script and knows what setup she needs she may ask for "an alternate take to 42A-4." If she asks for it in the first way all you have to do is look in the log book to see what take CC3121 comes from. "Ahha," you'd say. "Take 42A-4." A look at the log book will also tell you what other takes were shot for this setup. Write them down on a piece of paper or a piece of paper tape that you can stick to the back of your hand.

Then, check the outs boxes for Scene 42. Written on the outside will be a list of the takes for Scene 42. If you see another 42A there, take it out and give it to Wendy. Make sure that you immediately cover over the note on the outside of the box listing that take. If she decides not to use the out you can always remove the tape from the box, but if she does use it you will never have to go back and remove the number from the box at a later time (when you may have already forgotten just which take it was that you used from the outs). From that moment on, that take will be treated as a regular trim. Once cut, it will be filed as a trim, not as an out.

Sometimes, the alternate takes will not be in the out boxes but will be classified as trims because *other* parts of the take have been used in the film. In that case you will give the entire trim to Wendy so she can find the part that she needs (if you've been following the editing perhaps you can do it).

The two other places that you might find a trim are the lifts and, a few times, in the cut itself. Sometimes the editor has used the exact part of a shot that she needs for a trim in another part of the scene (as a reaction shot, perhaps). What usually happens in this case is that you run around in a small panic for a bit because you can't find the trim in any of the places you've looked and you dread spending time going through all of the takes in the movie looking for a misfiled trim. Then you ask Wendy if she could have used it anywhere else in the film. She will either answer an embarrassed "yes" and go on editing or she will say "no" and go and check the footage and give you a doubly embarrassed "yes" in a few moments.

Unfortunately, there are times when the dreaded does happen: the trim has been misplaced and you do have to look in all of the takes of the film to find it. There are some common mistakes that people make that might save you some time in searching.

First, check all of the other takes of that same setup. Then, if you still haven't found the take, look in takes with code numbers that are similar. Eights sometimes look like zeroes on inked code numbers, especially after a few months of wear and tear. The letter *E* looks like the letter *F* (which is why I never use both in any one coding system). The letter *B* might be confused with the letter *R*. Check for reversals of numbers—CC4253 might be filed as CC4523.

If the entire take is missing, the search becomes a little easier since all you have to do is to check the boxes for the errant take. Also be aware that another person (another editor, if you have one, or a sound or music editor if you have one of them on) might also be working on that scene and have the take.

Questions! Questions! Questions!

All during the reediting of the film you will be faced with questions you have to answer. Many of them will deal with organization—how should we code this reprint, how should we log in this scratch mix, how should we handle this optical? All of these questions will have to be dealt with with some degree of foresight. For, in much the same way that you have attempted to create a system that will function all the way through the movie, you must learn how to deal with those exceptions to the system without ruining your system or creating even more work for you and your system.

Let's examine these exceptions one at a time. During the course of editing, Wendy or you or someone will most assuredly rip a piece of film or soundtrack, or put a gouge in the film to such a degree that the piece is no longer acceptable either because it would be too distracting to look at or because it won't go through a projector without trouble.

You will need to order another print of that piece of film or soundtrack and be able to integrate it into the system. The best way to do that is to reprint the entire take from which the ripped piece came.

In your logbook (see Figure 5.2) you can see a list of all of the takes that were on the first two dailies rolls. Let's say that the piece that Wendy ripped had the code number AA1352. A quick look in the code book tells us that this comes from 10D-3. This will be the only piece with that code number since that's the way the system works (nice, isn't it?). The information in the log will also tell us that the take (1) was shot on October 7, 1983; (2) was from lab roll number one; (3) was from camera roll number one; (4) had the code numbers AA1321-1378; and (5) had the latent edge numbers F13X64247 through F13X64304.

This gives you all of the information that you need to reorder the take from the lab. Tell them that you want a reprint of take 10D-3, shot 10-7-83, lab roll number 1, key numbers F13X64247-64304. Tell them you would like it at the same timing lights as before. That's all you have to do (except to make sure that they deliver it on time). If you were ordering the track reprint (sometimes called the retransfer) of this take you would tell the sound transfer house that you wanted a retransfer of take 10D-3, shot 10-7-83, from sound roll number 1.

When you get the reprint back from the lab you have to code it exactly as you did the first print. The best way of doing this is to get the trims of that take out from the trim box and line up the new and the old prints in the synchronizer. Copy all the marks (slates, identifications, etc.) onto the new take. Add about ten feet of leader to the head of the reprint then find the first code number on the old take (it will be AA1321) and mark where it would fail on the reprint. Then set your footage counter to 0'00 at that frame and proceed to *back up* one full foot. This should put you into the leader you've just added. On that leader, in marker, mark that frame. Then, just as you set up your dailies reels for coding, mark that frame for spot coding with its first number being AA1320 (that is, one foot before the first code number that you want to print on the film).

There is a very good reason for backing up the one foot. Many coding machines do not print the first number or, if they do, it is smudged and difficult to read. In this way you will get readable numbers all the way through the take.

When you get the take back from coding you are going to completely replace the old print with the new one. Once again, get the trims from that take down from their box. In the synchronizer, line up the new and old prints. Then roll forward until you get to the first place where there is a piece of film missing on the old print. This is where there is either something in the cut work picture or in a lift. Cut your new print in exactly the same spot and hang the two head trims (old and new) on separate pins in a barrel.

Then find the next trim and line it up against the new print in the synchronizer. Cut the reprint at exactly the same point that the old trim begins. The piece that you've just cut off will be a piece that is being used (either in the cut work picture or in a lift). For now, hold it aside on its own pin, clearly marked as "New Print— In Cut." This way you won't confuse it with any part of the old print.

Continue on in this manner, replacing all of the pieces in the trims with the reprint. When you have finished you should have three pins of material—the first will be the trims from the old print, the second will be the matching trims from the new print, and the third will be those pieces destined for the cut. Make sure that each of the three is clearly marked.

Now take the cut work picture for the scene that you are replacing (in this case, you would take the reel that contained Scene 10 on it) and roll it down in the synchronizer until you get to a cut which comes from 10D-3 (you will be able to check this with the code numbers but you should have a very good idea of what it looks like and be able to spot it by eye). Choose the proper piece of reprint from the third pin and line it up against the cut work picture. The first frame of that piece on the reprint should exactly coincide with a cut in the work picture (where the old print begins). If it does not you have made a mistake somewhere along the line and you must go back and figure out where.

But, if all is well (and there is no reason to think that it won't be), you will find that the new reprint will exactly replace the old print frame to frame. In that case, carefully undo the splice in the cut work picture, remove the old print, and replace it exactly with the new reprint making sure that all code and key numbers still line up in exactly the same way that they used to.

When this is done hang the old print up on a fourth pin and continue with the replacement process until all of your new reprint pieces are used up. If you finish your scene without using up all of the pieces check to make sure that you haven't skipped a piece in the work print. If you find that you haven't then check to see if there is a lift from that scene and, if there is, replace the old print in the lift with the new reprint. If you have checked all the trims, all of the lifts and still have a piece left over then you have made a mistake somewhere or there is a missing piece of film.

In that case there is only one piece of advice I can give you— FIND THE PIECE!

When you have finished replacing all of the pieces you will have ended up with three pins of film. The first holds the new reprint trims, the second the old trims, and the third is the old print which used to be in the cut or in the lifts. Wrap up the first pin and return *it* to the trims. Then combine the other two pins. You should find that all of the pieces of the old print should now go together sequentially, forming one complete take. When you have done this you know that you have found every piece of old print that exists.

Then you throw away the entire old print.

The reason you go through this long involved process is rather simple, though not immediately apparent. Despite your request for a reprint at the same timing lights as the first print, differences in the temperature of the water at the laboratory, slight differences in the lengths of time that various parts of the process take place, and many other minute differences will make the new reprint look slightly different than the old print. If Wendy ever wanted to extend a shot and cut part of the old print onto a part of the reprint the color would not match exactly. And this would be very distracting to look at. So, in order to have a consistent color balance throughout any one take you must make sure that all of the pieces of that take are from the same printing of that take.

Scratch Mixes

When Wendy and Adam screen the film there may be sections where more than one sound is happening at the same time (there is a dialogue between two characters while a scene is being shot in the background, for instance) or places where they would like to hear temporary music under dialogue.

Many of these things are left until the end of the movie, when a sound editor will correct everything in preparation for the final film mix (or dub, as they say on the West Coast and in England). But sometimes there will be things that they want done for earlier screenings (either for themselves or for producers/distributors/etc.). Then you will have to *scratch mix* the movie.

Understanding the process of scratch mixing requires that you understand the process of film mixing, which is too large a subject for this book. But let me give a brief explanation that should suffice for now.

When a movie is being shot the sound behind any given piece of dialogue will almost surely not match the sound behind any other piece of dialogue, even if that second piece is just the reverse angle on the same scene. If there is a scene of two people talking, and the director has covered it in a wide-shot master, a closer two-shot, and close-ups on each of the people talking, the chances that all of these four camera setups will have the same background sound is very slim. This is not the fault of the sound recordist but is a simple function of differing microphone placements as well as (for films shot on location) the uncontrollability of the background outside of camera range.

Now, when Wendy cuts these angles together there is going to be a different background sound every time she changes the take she is using. Those kinds of changes are all right when you are cutting a movie but in a movie theatre a regular audience would be distracted by them, since they are used to smooth backgrounds. A dialogue editor is brought on to correct these *bumps* (as the points where the background changes are called).

This dialogue editor will *split the dialogue tracks*, which simply means that he or she will split apart the dialogue onto three or more synchronously running tracks so that each sound can be controlled separately, with a separate volume control and equalizer. In that way, when the tracks are combined back into one whole track at the film mix any disagreeable differences can be evened out by the dialogue mixer.

Now, of course, nothing is as easy as all that. The dialogue editor must do a lot of trickery with these tracks in order to prepare them properly for the dialogue mixer. But that is much too complicated for us to deal with here and now. That must be left for another book.

Another task of a sound editor is to add sound effects to the soundtrack. In order to have the utmost control of the dialogue sections in both the editing and the mixing, dialogue is shot with as few extra noises as possible. Phone rings, radios playing, guns shooting, etc., are all left out during the shooting, to be added in the final mix. But it is just those kind of things that can help a story along. So, before some screenings, Wendy and Adam may want to add those kinds of sounds (along with some music) to give them some rough idea about how the film plays.

Usually there is no sound editor on the film at this time so it will fall to Wendy, you, and Philip to prepare for this mix. Since this will be a mix just to give everyone a rough idea of the film, the mix will be done very fast and without much finesse. For that reason it is often called a *rough, scratch,* or *slop* mix. Dialogue is almost never split in these mixes. The usual purpose is to add a few sound effects to make the film more intelligible, and to try out some sample music.

Music is usually lifted off of phonograph records. Sound effects are available at many sound houses or from sound effects records. You will usually call up the effects house, or go there for an hour or two, and audition some effects. You will tell them, "I need a very loud door slam, two different types of horse hoofbeats, a series of gunshots, and a few phone rings," and they will be able to give them all to you in a short period of time transferred directly onto 35mm film (or 16mm, if that is your need). You should always make a note of the effects numbers of every effect (all reputable sound libraries have their effects catalogued in some manner) so that, in the likely event that Adam falls in love with one of the effects the sound editor will later on be able to go back and get additional prints of the same effect if needed.

Then, you should have all of the scratch effects and music coded. I like to code the effects with the prefix code FX1000 and up, and the music with the code MX1000 and up. Any effects which you are going to be using from the wild track will already be coded so you don't have to worry about coding them.

Start two new sections in your logbook—one for the scratch effects and one for the scratch music. List each effect by its code numbers, origin (effects house), catalogue number, date transferred, and description of effect. Make up cinetabs that list the code number and description on the front and origin and catalogue number on the reverse. List each piece of music by its code numbers, origin, date, and title. Make up cinetabs that list the code numbers and title.

You then must do a little sound editing. Many editors like to do this themselves and many do not. In case they do, watch them closely to see how they do it. But in case they do not, I can offer only this brief explanation.

You will need a three-head Moviola (called a *console Moviola,* or a Moviola with an *add-a-plate*) or a flatbed with two sound heads and one picture head. Thread up the picture and sound at the start mark (on the Moviola you should put the cut work track on the outside sound head, leaving the center one free) and zero out the counter. Run down until you get to the place that you want to add an effect or music cue. Place the effect in the center sound head (or, on a flatbed, in the other sound head), disengage this head from the other ones, and run the effect or music cue until you get to the place in the sound that you want to line up with the place that you already are at in the cut reel. Engage all three heads and run them together. You will be able to hear both tracks (dialogue and effect, or dialogue and music) at the same time and get some idea of how they line up. If you need to change the relationship between the cut reel and the new piece, move the effect or music cue only. Never move just the picture or just the dialogue track as that will throw them out of sync.

Once you have a relationship that you are happy with, go back to the beginning of the effect or music and find a zero frame (if the effect begins at 152′10, go to 153′00). Now, with grease pencil, mark that frame on the cue (see Figure 9.4). On a piece of paper you should begin to make a cue sheet (see Figure 9.5). This cue sheet will list all of the elements for the scratch mix for this reel.

For this example (a portion of the cue sheet for reel 1) we can see that we have dialogue running during the entire reel. At 152.10 we have the effect that we just selected—which happens to be the sound of a horse whinnying. We also have some gunshots later on as well as two pieces of music. Let's analyze the cue sheet a little bit.

At the top of the cue sheet we have listed much of the same information as you put on the head leaders of reels—the name of the film and the reel number. We have also listed the date of the scratch mix.

Under that we have listed the mix elements (or *units*). After we cut all of the effects as described above they will all have footage numbers on them. We will then have to cut them into reels of fill at those exact numbers so that they can run on another machine in perfect sync with the dialogue track. Since only one effect can be on a reel at one time whenever we have more than one sound going on at a time we will need more than one reel. In this case we are going to need four reels. One of these reels will be your work track reel, which contains the dialogue. Another reel contains the music. And the remaining two reels contain effects we will need including the horse whinnies. When all of the elements are run together, in sync, the dialogue, effects, and music will be combined *mixed*

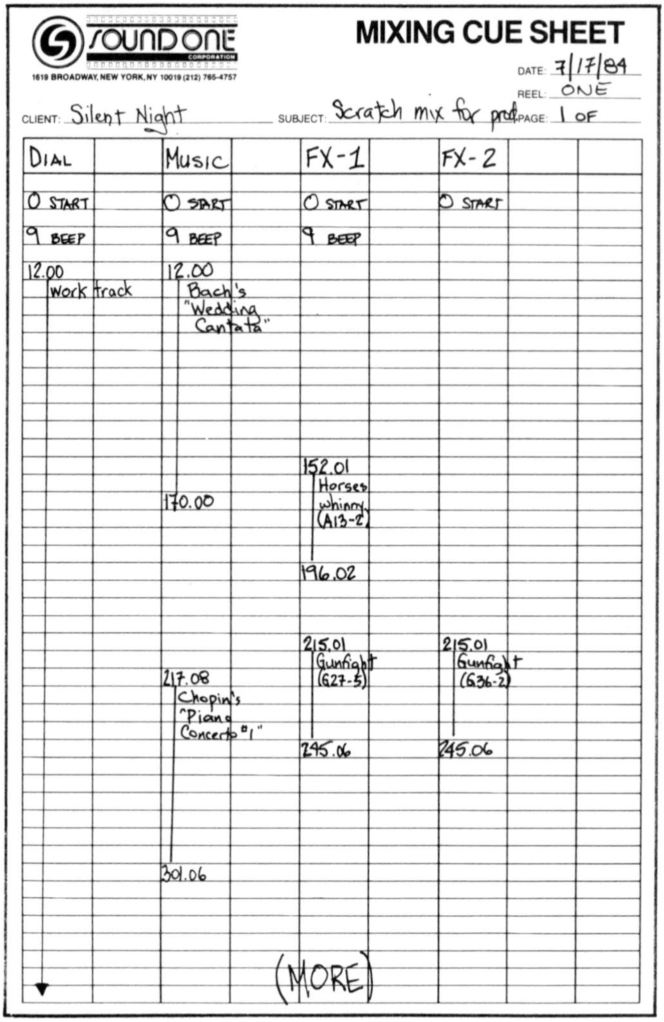

SOUND ONE CORPORATION
1619 BROADWAY, NEW YORK, NY 10019 (212) 765-4757

MIXING CUE SHEET

DATE: 7/17/84
REEL: ONE
CLIENT: Silent Night
SUBJECT: Scratch mix for prod.
PAGE: 1 OF

DIAL		MUSIC		FX-1		FX-2		
0 START		0 START		0 START		0 START		
9 BEEP		9 BEEP		9 BEEP				
12.00 Work track		12.00 Bach's "Wedding Cantata"						
		170.00		152.01 Horses whinny (A13-2)				
				196.02				
				215.01 Gunfight (627-5)		215.01 Gunfight (636-2)		
		217.08 Chopin's "Piano Concerto #1"						
				245.06		245.06		
		301.06						
				(MORE)				

FIGURE 9.5 A cue sheet for a scratch (temporary) mix.

together into one soundtrack for the screening.

On the first effects track (called FX-1, though it is sometimes called FX-A) we have put a beep at 9′00, the standard place for a beep (this is three feet before the first frame of action). This beep will transfer across during the mix and give you a way to line up the mix with the picture. Then, at 12 feet, a piece of music begins which lasts until 170 feet. The carat symbol at the end of line means that it is fading out. This is also noted by the initials FO.

Apparently the music is fading out into the sound of horses whinnying. The horses come in at 152'10 and last until 196'02 (during this entire time, the dialogue track has been running). Since the music, the horses, and the dialogue are all going on at the same time during the period from 152'10 to 170'00 we need three tracks to hold all of the elements.

Then, at 215'01 a gunfight breaks out and in order to attain the proper frenzy there will be two tracks of gunshots going at the same time. For that we need a second effects track. We might have put it on the music track but it is best to keep all of the music on its own track. In any case, the music returns again before the end of the gunfight (at 217'08) so we need all four tracks running at that time to handle everything that we want to do.

You can see, just from this simple explanation, that this process can get complicated very, very fast. In fact, for final mixes it is not uncommon to have forty or fifty tracks running for the same reel. On one film that I've heard about there were ninety-eight tracks!

Since this is just a scratch mix you are going to want to keep it as simple as possible while still getting the effects added that you need. On the average, five tracks is the most that you will need for these types of mixes.

When you go to the mix all of these four tracks will be lined up at their start marks and then run together. If everything has been lined up properly, when you get to 152'10 you should hear the horse whinnying while the dialogue and music are going on. The mixer will then set the relative levels of everything and mix them together. This process will continue for all of the reels of the film that need to have things added to them.

At the completion of the mix what you will want to take back to the editing room with you is a thirty-five millimeter stripe copy of the mix. A stripe copy is, simply, the type of track that you are used to dealing with—a strip of oxide on 35mm film with a balance stripe on the other edge (see Figure 4.14). Some studios can mix directly onto 35mm stripe, others must mix onto a 35mm four-track (a piece of soundtrack which is completely covered with oxide and onto which four separate tracks are recorded; because of this it is often called *full-coat*) and then make a transfer of that mix onto stripe. Regardless, when you are done you should end up with a 35mm stripe that you will code (I like to code it SA1000 for "scratch mix" and then to move through SB, SC, etc., as the need arises).

Log it in a section of your logbook devoted to scratch mixes. The mix can now be used instead of the dialogue/work track.

Some editors, in order to save money on 35mm stock, like to mix only that portion of the reel that needs mixing and then to cut that portion into the work track before the screening. I have never found this a particularly worthwhile way to save money since the amount of time needed to cut the mixes into the work track reels and remove them later (after the screening, when you will want the reels returned to normal) more than makes up for the increased cost in stock used. I like to mix the entire reel, even those sections which don't need mixing. For those areas, this "mix" amounts to nothing more than a straight transfer. But, after the mix is over, you end up with one complete track for the reel that will completely substitute for the unmixed reel. During subsequent scratch mixes, when you may not need to remix the horse whinny section but want to mix something else on the reel, I would simply use this mix as an element in the new mix.

After the mix is over the elements should be saved in their own section of the cutting room, plainly labeled as to what date they were used and what reel they come from. If those effects are ever needed again a look at the filed cue sheets will automatically lead you back to those exact reels. If Adam liked those horse whinnies, the sound editor will be able to use those exact ones for the final mix. To this end, it would be helpful if there was a mark on the horse whinny track which listed not only the footage (153' as we have already written) but the picture code number of the shot at that 153-foot mark. In that way we will always be able to find the exact sync point of the effect even though the reel may have been recut and rebalanced so many times that the footage count may be meaningless. This is a wise thing to put on every effect as you cut them as it will save the sound editor the time-consuming task of syncing up the effect later on; and attempting to match sounds from a clean effect and the mixed track is never easy.

There are many more fine points in the process of scratch mixing which you will only learn by watching and doing. Every editor and assistant has his or her own method. What you have just learned are only the basics.

10

OPTICALS

The act of making the impossible possible is one of the things that makes movie-going so attractive. Watching the Red Sea part or spaceships fly through space is an experience hard to find anywhere other than in a movie theatre.

Creating these fantastic effects, as well as a host of much less spectacular ones, falls under the category of making opticals. An optical can be as simple an effect as a scene fading out or as complicated as the space battles in *Star Wars*. All opticals, however, involve the manipulation of the film negative to create a new negative with some change in the original's image.

Simple Opticals

The four simplest, and most common, opticals used in film editing are the *fade-in, fade-out, dissolve,* and *superimposition*. In addition, the creation of titles is an optical effect. In 16mm these effects are not created optically (even though they may still be referred to as "optical effects" or just "effects"), they are created in the lab through a process called *A and B rolls*. In 35mm, however, these effects are created optically, albeit in a very analogous manner.

Let's say that, at the end of one scene in *Silent Night, Silent Cowboy* we wanted the image to fade to black. This is called a fade-out and it is accomplished by darkening the image gradually until we can see nothing but black. One way to accomplish this, of course, would be to do it in the camera, while we were shooting the scene. We would simply close the camera's aperture slowly while shooting the scene so that less and less light would be thrown on the negative. When we saw the dailies we would see the image get darker and darker until all we saw was black.

But if we changed our minds in the editing and wanted the fade-out to come two seconds later than we had determined during the shooting we would be unable to get that new image back onto the negative. By creating optical effects in the camera we force ourselves to accept *whatever* comes out of the camera, no matter how bad or inappropriate it is.

One solution, then, would be to wait until the last possible moment during the editing to do these effects. In that way we could have the people exposing our release print (i.e., the print that we will use for showing in theatres) to *stop down* the printing camera's aperture (*stopping down* is the process of closing the camera aperture so that it throws less light onto the film). In this way, we could tell the lab exactly where we wanted the fade-out to start and how long we wanted the fade to go on for before the frame was completely dark. We would preserve our original negative as well as all of our options until the very end.

In fact, this is exactly what is done in most 16mm films. After the negative is prepared for the lab (and we will see how to do that in a later chapter) the *lab* does all of the optical work based upon certain marks that you put on the workprint. The accepted marking for a fade-out is a long V whose length is the length of the desired fade-out; the open end is at the first frame of the fade and the point is at the last frame, as in Figure 10.1.

The marking for a fade-in, in which the image on the screen gradually emerges from complete black, is exactly the opposite—a V that grows from a single point. It is also helpful if you give the lab a list of all of these kinds of effects and their locations in the reels so that they can know where they are.

The optical dissolve is actually a combination of the fade-in and the fade-out. In it one image is fading out as the other is fading in. The effect on screen is of one image crossing into another. We say that one image "dissolves into" another. The manner in which this is effected is to run both images at the same time and to be fading one out at the same time you are fading the other in (see Figure 10.2).

The fourth type of optical—the superimposition—is actually an extension of the dissolve. In it two images are run together at the same time. If one of the characters in our film is reading a letter from another character and we want to show him thinking of that

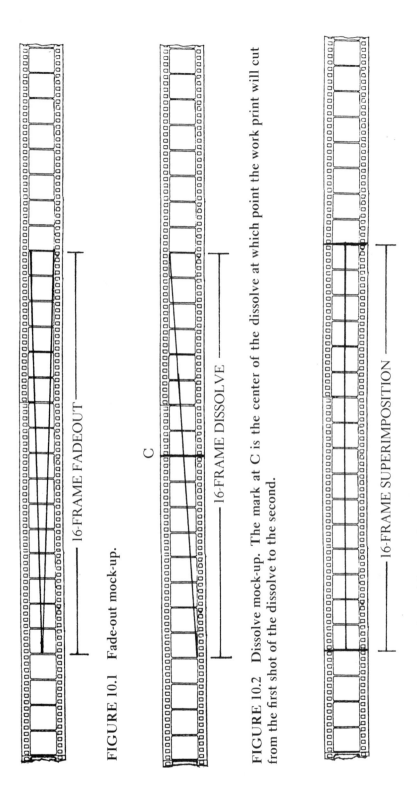

——————— 16-FRAME FADEOUT ———————

FIGURE 10.1   Fade-out mock-up.

C

——————— 16-FRAME DISSOLVE ———————

FIGURE 10.2   Dissolve mock-up.   The mark at C is the center of the dissolve at which point the work print will cut from the first shot of the dissolve to the second.

——————— 16-FRAME SUPERIMPOSITION ———————

FIGURE 10.3   Superimposition mock-up.

character we might want to show a picture of that other person superimposed over a close-up of him thinking. We would then run the close-up of him and the shot of the other character, exposing both at the same time. When projected, the end result would be that we would see both images—one right on top of the other (see Figure 10.3).

There are two major problems and restrictions in making opticals at the lab. The first is that it is extremely expensive. You may have to make many prints of your film so that it may play in many theatres simultaneously. If someone from the lab has to turn the printing camera aperture up or down every time you want an optical effect on every print, printing your film will be very expensive.

The second problem is that in the lab it is necessary to restrict the lengths of your opticals to some predetermined lengths and to keep them at certain distances from each other. This places certain restrictions on the editing of a film since it will be impossible to make, for instance, several quick dissolves in a row.

These problems are solved by not doing your opticals in the lab at all but in a place which is designed to do nothing but opticals—the optical house.

All of your opticals will be done in the optical house and will end up on a completely new negative. It is *this* negative, rather than the original negative that was shot on the set, that will be sent to the laboratory for making your release prints. In this way you will end up with one long strand of cut negative with all of the effects already incorporated into it. No one from the lab has to stand at the printing machine and create each effect. Each effect can be exactly the length and kind that you desire.

Let us follow one short scene from our movie through the optical house to see just how it works. In this scene we are watching a scene from the movie-within-the-movie when it freezes, and turns to black and white. We then find out that this frozen scene is actually a publicity photo that the director is looking at.

On the surface it sounds complicated. In fact, it *is* complicated. But this is how you would handle it.

In this case the editing room staff probably worked with the people on the set during the shooting. When the scene of the director looking at the photo was being prepared the art director may have asked for a frame clip of the scene to make into the photo. Wendy would have cut that movie-within-the-movie scene and chosen the frame where the freeze would be. You would have sent a frame or two of that shot to the art director who would have made it into a black and white photo to be used as a prop in the shooting of the director's scene.

When the scene was shot it began with a close-up of the black and white photo. The photo was then pulled away from the camera and we were able to see that the director had been holding it. The idea, therefore, would be to take the shot of the movie-within-the-movie, freeze the proper frame, and dissolve into the beginning of this shot of the black and white photo.

This complicated optical is actually three opticals. The first is the freeze frame. The second is the color turning into black and white (this is called color desaturation). The third is the dissolve from that into the live shot with the photo.

Wendy will have determined the exact frame where the freeze frame should begin, the length of time before it begins to desaturate, the length of time it takes to desaturate, the length of time before this image begins dissolving into the black and white photo, and the length of the dissolve. These five items determine how you will lay out the optical.

Let's say that these are the details of the optical:

1. freeze frame—marked with an X
2. length of time before desaturation—3 feet (2 seconds)
3. length of desaturation—6 feet (4 seconds)
4. length before dissolve—4.5 feet (3 seconds)
5. length of dissolve—6 feet (4 seconds)

The way that Wendy, or you, should have marked the workprint is shown in Figure 10.4.

You should make a list of all of the pieces of film involved in the optical. In this case, it is only two—the movie scene and the director's scene. From your logbook find the information that you would normally would give to the lab for a reprint order (that is, key numbers and take numbers, lab roll number, date shot). Now, before you do anything else order a *registration interpositive* (or *registration IP*) from the lab for these two scenes. A registration IP is a special interpositive which is a high-quality copy of the negative. It is an expensive item to make but it is a valuable one. In order for the optical to be made the negative will have to be removed from the lab and sent to the optical house. If anything happens to it—

```
                 Optical Number 1   --   Scenes 56/57

                                                          6' Handles

 Pt #    Footage      Key Number        Effect                  Comment

   1       0.00    E32X98533 + 11    Begin optical
   2      15.03    E32X98548 + 14    Freeze frame            Marked with "X"
   3      18.03    E32X98551 + 14    Begin 6' desaturation
   4      24.02    E32X98557 + 13    End 6' desaturation
  5a      28.11    E32X98562 + 06    Begin 6' dissolve       Outgoing piece
  5b      28.11    E26X46231 + 04    Begin 6' dissolve       Incoming piece
   6      31.11       -----          Center of dissolve      W/P cuts
  7a      34.11    E32X98568 + 05    End 6' dissolve         Outgoing piece
  7b      34.11    E26X46237 + 03    End 6' dissolve         Incoming piece
   8      55.05    E26X46259 + 14    End of optical
```

FIGURE 10.4 Optical layout sheet for our sample optical. The comment at point No. 6 means that this point comes at the place where the work print cuts from one shot to another.

either through loss or damage—you will never be able to use that shot in the final film. You will be able to use this IP instead of your original negative.

So, before any piece of negative leaves the lab make sure that you have some protection—strike a registration interpositive.

After the protection IP (as it is also called, for obvious reasons) is struck you should remove the involved scenes from the workprint so that you can prepare them for the optical house. Remove the entire cut on either side of the optical even if, for instance, the shot in the director's office goes on for twenty-five feet before it cuts to another shot. Put head and tail leaders on the removed workprint. In the cut workprint reel where you removed the footage, replace the extracted footage with the exact same length of white leader so that the reel may be run in sync with the track. Mark on the white leader exactly who removed the footage, when it was removed, and why (this will help anyone else looking for information about that section of the film).

Now take the removed workprint and put it in the synchronizer. Let us say that our optical house wants the first frame of picture to be considered 0′00. Zero out your synchronizer at the first frame of picture and begin a sheet of paper which will be your *optical layout sheet*. The purpose of this log will be to communicate directly to the optical house what you want the optical to look like. This paper will supplement the workprint which you will also show to the optical house.

Your optical layout sheet (see Figure 10.5) should contain a col-

```
            Titles for "Silent Night, Silent Cowboy"


 Note:    Each card should last a total of six feet, including fade
 out and fade in except as noted.

 | Pt #  |    Ftg    |    Title
 ----------------------------------------------------------------
    1       12.00      Logo begins
    2       57.00      End of logo.   Beginning of black.
    3       72.00      Title # 1 in ("An Adam Free Film")
    4       78.00      Title # 1 out
    5       79.08      Title # 2 in ("Silent Night, Silent Cowboy")
    6       88.08      Title # 2 out
    7       90.00      Title # 3 in ("Starring Carol Lestial")
    8       96.00      Title # 3 out
    9       97.08      Title # 4 in ("Michael Stellar")
   10      103.08      Title # 4 out
   11      105.00      Title # 5 in ("Enid Gaseous")
   12      111.00      Title # 5 out
   13      112.08      Title # 6 in ("and Bill Willy as 'Doc' ")
   14      116.08      Title # 6 out
   15      118.00      Title # 7 in ("With....")
   16      124.00      Title # 7 out
   17      125.08      Title # 8 in ("Casting...")
   18      131.08      Title # 8 out
   19      133.00      Title # 9 in ("Director of Photography...")
   20      139.00      Title # 9 out
   21      140.08      Title # 10 in ("Editor...")
   22      146.08      Title # 10 out
   23      148.00      Title # 11 ("Written by...")
   24      154.00      Title # 11 out

                      (more)
```

FIGURE 10.5 Title layout sheet.

umn for the footage, key number, effect wanted, and comments. I have also included a column at the beginning called "Point Number" which counts off the number of instructions I'm giving to the optical house. This will make it easier to talk to the optical house over the phone later on. All you will have to say is, "For point number 3 I want you to . . . etc." instead of, "You know, the point where the desaturation begins."

The information for the first cue point is rather simple. It is point number 1, at 0'00. It is described as "Beginning of optical." The key number can be found by finding the frame with the key number on it (if the number is spread between two frames choose the one in which the number ends and counting backward to the first frame of the optical. In this case it comes five frames before the key number F32X98534. Since there are sixteen frames to a foot this frame is also equivalent to being eleven frames after F32X98533. The key number is, therefore, F32X98533+11. Key numbers are usually expressed as positive numbers, that is frames *after* a given number. In addition, I usually mark on the layout sheet exactly where the frame comes in the key number. In this case it comes between the three and the two of the prefix F32X.

It is also a good practice to ask for a few extra frames both before and after the optical "just in case." This is called the *handle*. A normal handle is either six or eight frames. That is what the designation "six-frame handles" means at the top of the layout sheet.

Then, run down on the synchronizer until you reach the next point of reference. This will be the frame marked for the beginning of the freeze frame. Note the footage and key number. On your layout sheet you will mark down this information for point number two. Also mark down that you want a freeze-frame optical. You might also want to note that the frame is marked on the workprint with an X.

Run down until you reach the next point. This will be the beginning of the desaturation. Note the footage and key number and mark these down on your layout sheet for point number three. Note on the sheet the length of the optical that you want, in this instance, "Begin six-foot desaturation."

Your next point should be the end of the desaturation optical, *not* the beginning of the dissolve. All points of reference should be noted, both on the film and on your layout sheet.

When you are done with all of the optical reference points you should pick up the original negative at the lab and bring it (along with your workprint and layout sheets) to the optical house. There you should sit down with the person who will be supervising your optical and show him or her exactly what you want. Some opticals are simpler than others. Straight fades or dissolves are common opticals that your optical house can probably do without much consultation. Always, however, explain the more complex opticals such as this—optical number one.

After you've explained the optical to the supervisor you will leave all of your materials at the optical house. Make sure that you have copies of all of your layout sheets on file at the editing room. When they have completed the optical, which may take as few as two days or as long as one or two weeks depending upon the optical's complexity, you (or Philip) should pick up the materials from them. This will include the marked-up workprint that you supplied them along with an optical print, which is a viewable print of the optical that they have made for you. This print is made from an optical negative, just as your workprint is made from a camera negative. If the optical turns out to be perfect then send the negative to the lab to be stored along with the original camera negative. If the optical turns out to need more work then you should mark the can that the bad optical was in "NG-DNU" (for "no good/do not use") and either keep it in the editing room or send it to the lab like that. Leave the original negative for the optical at the optical house until you are sure that the optical is finished. Then, return it to the lab.

Once the completed optical is in the editing room check to make sure that it looks all right. This involves screening it on the Moviola (and in a screening room if possible) as well as running it through the synchronizer along with the marked-up workprint. Since the optical is shot on its own negative it will have its own key numbers and they will bear no relationship to the key numbers on the cut workprint. To give you a reference back to your workprint some optical houses scratch onto the negative, along the edge, a key number so that you may easily line up the completed optical with the cut workprint.

Some optical houses, however, do not provide this service. In this case there is no way to line up the optical against the workprint other than by eye matching. This is a tedious and often difficult process that involves finding at least one frame where you can get a precise match between the optical and the cut workprint. Good things to look for are frames where characters enter or exit the frame, frames where two objects hit one another, frames where light bulbs go on or off (be careful about these since they usually include two or three frames where the light level is gradually increasing), and the like. Find three different sync points, then line one of them up and see if the other two points also line up. If they do, then you know that you have found proper sync.

Once you have the optical lined up and have marked where the first and last frames are then you should code the optical (unless you've coded it before you lined it up). I generally reserve the prefix code OP for opticals. Naturally, you should enter the complete information about the optical—optical number, codes, key numbers, scenes involved, description of optical, date made, et al.—into a section in your logbook reserved for opticals.

When the optical is lined up and coded you can cut it into the cut workprint reel where the original shot was (there should be white leader there now). Then, you, Wendy, and Adam (and Philip if he is invited to participate in such things) should screen the film to check for several items. The first is that the optical is correct. It is possible that, even though the optical house followed all of your instructions correctly, the optical seems wrong when viewed on the screen. This can happen for several reasons. First, it is possible that Wendy miscalculated some of the footage. If this is the case you must completely remake the optical. Second, even with the materials available today, it is not always possible to control opticals precisely. Long fades or dissolves suffer the most from this since the degree to which the optical negative will *gradually* fade in or out is not predictable. For that reason, a long fade will not always seem gradual. There is virtually nothing that can be done about this problem with the negative stock available today except to try and avoid very long fades or to redo the optical and hope for better results.

Another thing you will be looking for, as a further check that you have lined up and cut the optical in correctly, is sync of the picture against the track. This will be the first time that you will have seen the optical with a soundtrack.

You will also want to check that the color of the optical does not vary too badly from the nonoptical shots in the same scene. Do not worry too much about some color drift. Slight variations in color are always correctable in the laboratory at the end of the film. But major variations may not be correctable.

A final word about the quality of opticals. Since the optical is made from a *negative* made from the *original negative* (it is therefore called *second-generation*) its quality will be slightly worse than the quality of the surrounding nonoptical material. You will notice an increase in the graininess of the image and the colors may be a bit more contrasty. Some shots degrade worse than other shots—lighter shots show the effects worse than darker, for instance. This is an unavoidable by-product of making an optical. Care in making the optical can minimize this problem. Some films, such as *Body Heat* and *Modern Problems*, did their optical dissolves in the lab using A and B rolling rather than in an optical house. If a scene is to contain many opticals intercut with original negative, many editors like to make the entire section (even those parts of the scene which would not normally be opticals) an optical. In that way the entire scene will be of the same quality. Even though it is of a lesser quality than the original negative, it will be less noticeable than the intercutting of good and less good material.

If the optical is not approved and must be redone you would send the workprint (along with another copy of the layout sheet) back to the optical house. If the optical is to be changed you would give it a new optical number and make a new layout sheet for it, then go over to the optical house and talk them through it again. However, if the optical is approved then you should have Philip bring the optical negative and the original negative (which he will pick up from the optical house) back to the lab so that they may store it with the rest of the original negative.

Store the original cut workprint and the trims from the optical print in a box marked with the optical number description, scene number, and code numbers. I like to use a different colored tape on the side of this box so that you can easily see which section of the trims is devoted to opticals. In fact, I like to use a different color for lifts, rough mixes, and scratch music as well. In this way it is faster to get to any one particular box that you might need and the chances of misfiling a box go down as well. One final note about these colors. Some people overdo the color system—until it can finally become more complicated to remember what color is what than it would be to find the materials mixed in with other footage. Usually, a color for trims/outs (white tape), opticals (yellow), scratch mixes (red), and, if there is a lot of it, music (blue) are enough for any film.

Titles

A special kind of optical work is the creation of titles (or credits) for the head and tail of the film. Though credits usually are not done until the very end of the film (on some films, in fact, the credits are so late in coming that they arrive only days before the opening of the movie) we will consider them here with the other opticals.

Titles come in two forms—either *on black* or *supered*. The first kind (such as the kind seen in Woody Allen's films) involves lettering on a plain background. The background may be colored, black, or white, and the lettering may be any color at all. The second kind of titles are those which are superimposed over a scene from the film. There are combinations of the two, such as in *Four*

Friends when the titles began on a plain background but were superimposed over the first scene after about half of them had completed.

There are several companies which design title sequences for movies. Sometimes they simply design the typestyle (along with the advertising department of the company that is going to distribute the film). At other times they design elaborate title sequences which are almost little movies in themselves. The Pink Panther and James Bond titles sequences are two of the latter type.

You will get a list of credits from the producer's office. These will include a breakdown of all of the credits which will go at the beginning of the film as well as at the end. It will show which people will share space on the screen (or *share a card* as it is called) and which get *single card credits*. Some directors', writers', or stars' contracts require that their names be no smaller than a certain percentage of the title of the film so this list will also show the relative sizes of the credits.

Wendy, the director, and the producer will also determine whether they wish the end titles to be a crawl, cards, or a combination of the two. These terms refer to the manner in which the mass of names at the end of the film will be displayed. Some films roll the credits up on the screen slowly (this is called a *crawl*), others present them as cards which fade in and out sequentially. Other films combine the two approaches. Once this approach has been decided on you will be able to determine how the end titles will fall out on the screen. If the names are to be on cards then they will have to be divided up logically (usually by job category in descending order of importance) without making the individual names so small as to be unreadable. If the names are to be on a crawl then it may be wise to separate job categories with an extra few lines of space to increase the readability.

Once all of these questions have been solved then you need to have the type prepared for the title cards. A typestyle will have to be selected. The director should do this, with the editor making sure that he is selecting a typestyle that is readable.

Then you have to go to the typesetter with the list to have the type set up for shooting. If you have a title designer then that person will take care of this. Sometimes your optical house will have an arrangement with a type house and so your optical supervisor will be able to handle the technical details for you. But in some cases this will not be possible. In that case you will go to the typesetter and go over the list of the names with him or her to make sure that it is all readable. You should discuss with this person exactly how you would like the titles to appear on screen.

Once the typesetter has the list he will begin laying out the type and printing it. Typically, this will take several days. While he or she is doing that there is one other piece of title material which you will be needing that you can get now if you haven't already. That is the main title logo.

Every distribution company has its own logo. Twentieth Century-Fox has the large letters with the meandering klieg lights. M-G-M has Leo the Lion. Columbia has the friendly torch lady. Warner Bros. has the colored letter W's zooming all over the screen. These are all opticals which have already been created by the individual company's advertising departments. You should get a print and a negative of that logo as early on in the cutting of the film as possible and cut it onto the head of reel one just as it will appear in the film. It is important to cut it on before the sound editor begins working because it will affect the length of the reel. When you get the print and negative treat it as an optical, giving it an optical number and coding it with the OP prefix. Then, just as you would with an optical, keep the print in its own optical box and send the negative to the lab to be stored with the rest of your negative.

When the typesetter has finished his or her job you will receive a printed list of all of the titles in the way that they will look when shot. You and the producer should very carefully check each name and title to make sure that everything has been spelled correctly and that no names have been left out.

If everything is not perfect (and it rarely is) then the typesetter must redo the list. If you have any other changes in the titles list, now is the time to bring them up as the list is going to have to be redone anyway. But if everything is perfect then you should have the typesetter send a clean copy of all of the titles to the optical house.

Like any other optical the optical house will need a layout sheet and a workprint mock-up. The most common way of mocking up titles on the workprint is to put a piece of white paper tape on the film indicating which title card is going where on the film. Let me explain a little further.

If you are having plain head title cards then you would make the mock-up on a long piece of white leader. Assuming that the titles came directly after the distributor's logo you would cut a piece of white leader onto the end of the logo. Then you would roll down a predetermined length until you wanted the first title to fade in. This predetermined length is a purely aesthetic decision and should be made by Wendy and Adam. Let's say that *Silent Night* is going to have ten seconds of black before the first title (which will say "An Adam Free Film") fades in. That is the equivalent of fifteen feet. Let us also say that the distributor's logo is forty-five feet long (thirty seconds). So the logo would begin at 12'00, the black before the titles would begin at 57'00, and the beginning of the fade-in of title card 1 would be at 72'00.

If the titles were to be supered onto an existing scene the process is very much the same except that instead of writing with magic marker on white leader you would be making your optical marks with grease pencil and your identification notations with magic marker on a piece of white paper tape which you would attach to the film at the proper place.

Once all of this has been determined then the optical house makes a *hi-con* of the titles. Hi-con stands for *high contrast* and it is a very sharp black and white negative that they will use for superimposing onto the picture negative. Certain decisions must be made about this time as to how you want the titles to appear. These involve the color of the lettering, the type of lettering (in order to increase readability many titles are made with *drop shadow* which is merely an extension of the letters at the bottom and to the right of each letter), and the color and treatment of the background. In *Four Friends*, when the background scene faded up behind the already running credits it came in first out of focus and then sharpened up. All of this was created at the optical house. Once again, these are artistic decisions which Adam and Wendy will make together.

All of these instructions must be communicated to the people at the optical house in as unambiguous a manner as possible. Title creation is a costly process and any mistakes that necessitate a redoing of the credits will be very expensive and unwelcome.

Special Opticals

Another kind of optical getting very popular nowadays really deserves an entire book all to itself—the special effects optical. These occur quite frequently in science-fiction movies or historical films where scenes must be recreated in the optical house that would have cost too much to shoot live if they could have been shot at all. The complexity of these types of opticals is so great that it makes the examples that I gave at the beginning of this chapter seem as easy as breathing. Some of the opticals in the *Star Wars* movies combine as many as eight or nine separate pieces of film and in *Return of the Jedi* there were almost nine hundred complete opticals. On such jobs the assistant editor rarely supervises these opticals. The job is given to either a postproduction editor or an optical effects supervisor. The assistant is involved in communicating the editor's needs to the optical people and vice versa.

But even with all of those complexities one fact about opticals still remains. Optical creation is a process of manipulating the original negative (or negatives) to create a new one. All involve laying out of the effects. There is no mystery to the process, though there is great artistry. The idea is not to be intimidated, but to realize that it is all "playing with film" and understandable.

11

PREPARING FOR SOUND

After many months of cutting and recutting the day will come when the film is nearly finished. Now, the movie *should* be turned over to a sound crew who will prepare the film's soundtrack for the final film mix (or dub).

Things never seem to work out this smoothly. Studio time is usually booked for the mix many months before the film is ready to be handed over to the sound crew. Often a film has a release date planned well in advance of its opening and that date sets the postproduction schedule rather than the postproduction needs of the film itself. As a result, it's rare nowadays that a film is actually *locked* when it is turned over to the sound crew.

Locking a film means simply to finish cutting it. It doesn't mean you're finished working on it, it just means that the picture edits are not going to change. I have only worked on one film— *Network*—that didn't have any picture reediting during the sound editing phase.

So, as you may imagine, one of the things that you will have to be very aware of as you prepare to turn the film over to the sound department is how to transmit recuts to them as you make them.

Handing Over Materials

On most films, a black and white dupe print is made of the film for the sound department since you will not want to be giving up your color picture to them to work on. There will be many things that you will have to do with the color print as we shall shortly see. In fact, on films with a decent budget, several black and white dupes are made to be split between the different sound editing tasks. These divisions are sound effects editing, looping editing, dialogue editing/splitting, foley editing, and music editing. On most films these tasks overlap so it would not be necessary to get a separate dupe for each category. On *Four Friends* we made five black and white dupes—one for the sound effects editor, two for the looping editor, one for the music editor, and one *screening dupe*. This screening dupe was used as the master dupe.

Before you even think of making the dupes there is one thing which is very important. Not only does the film have to be as close to locked as possible but the reel balance has to be quite final. Because of the mechanics of sound editing (where each reel may have as many as fifty mix elements with matching cue sheets) it will be far more difficult and time-consuming to make changes in the balancing *after* the reels have been sound edited than *before*.

Balancing for final release is very similar to balancing for your earlier screenings with one welcome exception—films are distributed on 2000-foot reels not on the 1000-foot reels you've been working on. So a reel change from an odd to an even reel (such as three to four) will actually not exist in the distributed version. This cuts down the number of problems by about one-half so it is a welcome change.

This does not mean that you should ignore those odd-to-even reel changeovers. Because your film will still be mixed in 1000-foot rolls it is often more convenient to put reel changes at places where you will not have any kind of continuous sound—such as a police siren or music. The even-to-odd changeovers (such as from reel two to reel three), which will be *projection changeovers* in most theatres, should never come in places where you will want to have music running. Because of the realities of film projection in theatres there is no way that a reel change could be made without losing some of the end and some of the beginning of each reel. Though this is not usually noticeable in parts of the film where there is no dialogue, it is always noticeable (even to the layman) if it interrupts a piece of music. Knowing this, composers who are instructed to write music bridging reels either bring their music to a stop one second before the end of a reel and don't begin it again for one second after it, or they bring it into a sustained hold for that length of time. Neither solution is perfectly satisfactory and so it is advisable to balance your reels so that true projection changeovers will come where there will be no music.

Another difference with this kind of balancing is in reel length.

While it may have been all right to include a few undersized or oversized reels as you were cutting it is not good form to do so now. I try to keep each reel at about 900 to 950 feet. When this is not possible I make sure that the *double reels* (which is what the *combination* of odd and even reels for release is called) run about 1800 to 1900 feet. If it is necessary for one reel to run 1000 feet I try and make sure that the next one runs no more than 900. The reason for this comes from the economics of lab work. Rolls of print film come in 2000-feet lots. If a double reel comes in at about that length there is no problem. If it is too large they must attach another piece of film to the printing reel and that is not only an extra cost but may sometimes lead to problems in projection. If the double reel is too small, however, there will be an awful lot of print film wasted which the distributor will have to pay for anyway. Plus, reels much over 950 feet are difficult to work with on the editing table and on the mixing stage. Properly balanced reels take this as well as the needs of the distributor into account. Once the reels have been properly balanced then you can send them out to a lab to be duped.

Sometimes, some reels of the film will be locked and others will not. In that case you should only make dupes of the reels that are locked. However, this is not always a good idea. On *Rollover*, on which I was the music editor, I needed *all* of the reels to give music timings to the composer, Michael Small, so that he would have enough time to write his music. I wanted to get him those timings even though there was a possibility that they might change. If they did change, I felt, they probably would change only in some parts of the music cues and would not change enough to throw his timings off too badly.

Let's say that Adam and Wendy have finished all of the reels except for the editing of one particularly troublesome scene in reel 6 (for some reason, every film has one or two problem scenes which either don't get solved until the very last minute or, more often than not, never really get solved; but they are always fiddled with until the end of the final film mix). You could leave reel 6 behind and dupe the remaining eleven reels or you could dupe everything and know that you are going to make changes on one scene in reel 6. My preference would be the latter one, since the sound editors would at least be able to work with the rest of the reel.

At the same time you should be sending out the reels of track to be duped. Before you do so, replace any piece of temp music with work track tone or fill. In this way the sound editors will be able to listen to their choices of effects against a clean work track, not one encumbered with scratch music. It will also be possible for the music to be recorded and cut in with a clean dialogue track as a reference.

In fact, almost all scratch mixes should be removed from the work track and replaced with the appropriate piece of work track (which should have been filed with the scratch mix elements). Your goal should be to hand over to the sound and music editors the following elements:

1. a black and white picture dupe
2. a dupe track of work track
3. the cut work track (to the dialogue editor)
4. all of the elements used in scratch mixes
5. the appropriate paperwork

You will be removing the scratch mixes from your work track to be duped for the sound department, but you will still want to have a mixed track, both for any future recutting as well as for any kind of screenings that you may be giving before the final mix is completed. Since you will be giving up your original soundtrack for dialogue editing, you will need one soundtrack for your own use and this track should be the mixed track.

This is one big advantage to having scratch mixed the film in complete reels rather than in sections which were then cut into the work track. Your latest mixed reels should be fairly current. If not you can easily construct one from them or make a quick sound dupe for them. If, however, you mixed only sections of the reels then you should make one complete dupe of the film before you remove any of the mixes. This dupe should be marked up with codes as I've explained before. The dupes that you make for the sound editors need not be marked.

After you get the picture and track dupes back they should be coded. This will enable the editors to keep the picture and track in sync as well as making it easier to do conformations later on in the sound editing process. Though the picture dupe will have the printed-through key and code numbers the sound track will not have any other code numbers on it, so this coding is essential.

I code each dupe with its own special prefix. Music dupes for reel 1 will be coded beginning MX1000 at the start mark. Reel 6 would be coded MX6000 and reel 10 MX0000. Since this, as well as most movies, run over ten reels I would code reel 11 MY1000 and reel 12 MY2000. I'd code the screening dupe with the prefix codes SX and SY. The effects dupes would be coded FX and FY. The only variation on this system is for the looping department which will often have two dupes struck for it. I code them LX and LY for the first set and LV and LW for the second set. The exact letters you use are not important since they are really only for identification and sync. But I have found that this system easily identifies both the editorial category and the reel.

You, as the assistant editor, will be the sound department's point of contact with the picture department. It is your responsibility to keep them informed of every change made in the film and in the schedule. I cannot stress enough that I consider this one of the assistant editor's most important jobs at this point in the film. It is all too easy for the sound department to be isolated from the picture-making process. But changes in schedule affect them at least as much as they will affect you. They should know about them and, in fact, be consulted about them *before* they are made. Sometimes your requirements will conflict with theirs. You, or Wendy, will have to make a decision as to which to change.

Because you will be the interface you should set up some of the systems for that interaction (in consultation, of course, with the supervising sound editor). Code them in an organized manner and let everyone know what your system is. When you head and tail leader the dupes do it uniformly. The way I work that system is as follows.

I will assign each dupe/department a color for their dupe. The normal color assignment I use is green for effects, blue for music, red for the first looping dupe and orange for the second, white for the work track (you should already have done this, of course), silver or some other really classy color for the screening dupe and, finally, yellow if there is need for a foley dupe (don't worry about what the word "foley" means; you'll find out in the next chapter). On this tape I write the name of the film, the type of dupe (music/looping/etc.), the date of the dupe (VERY IMPORTANT!!), the reel number (I make this very big so it can be seen from a distance), the "pix" or "trk" designation, and the word "HEADS." For the tail leader I put everything in the opposite order and instead of writing "FX DUPE" I would write "DUPE FX." In this way there is just one extra clue to me as to whether a reel on a shelf is heads or tails out.

The black and white picture dupe will already have an academy leader on it (duped from the color one on your work picture). Leave this on. Because of the relative thicknesses of color film versus black and white film a focus setting for one will not work on the other. If you were to cut a color academy leader onto the head of a black and white reel, a projectionist would not be able to focus properly on the leader. So cut your picture head leader onto the black and white academy a little before the start mark.

You should cut the tail leader onto the dupes at the last frame of action. In addition, mark a tail sync mark on the leader. There are two systems for doing this. One is to mark it exactly one foot after the last frame of action. The other is to mark it on the first whole foot (i.e., the first zero frame) after the LFOA. In other words, if reel 6 is 932'07 in length then the tail sync would be at 933'00. If reel 7 was 917'15, however, the tail sync would be not at 918'00 but at 919'00 (since the tail sync mark would overlap back into the picture area). The advantage of the first method is that any conformations do not require a new tail sync mark. The advantage of the second is that it is a more widely used standard and makes the placement of a reel in the Moviola or synchronizer just a little less prone to error. I've worked with both systems and both work just fine.

These are the primary tasks that will confront you as a picture assistant interfacing with the sound department. You will also have to answer many questions about where certain material came from, if there are alternates that were not used for picture but might be good for sound, exactly what things Adam liked in the scratch mixes, etc., etc., etc. You are the person who has been on the film for the longest time in an organizational capacity. You can answer all kinds of "Where can I get . . . ?" questions. If you are bright you will also be able to help them on the "Why was it done like this?" questions. You will function as the focal point for their questions.

In addition, put a tail beep mark three feet after the LFOA. Many people don't do this but I find it useful.

When the dupes have been leadered and coded then you can give them to the sound department. At the same time that you do that, however, you should also hand over some other items as well. Every sound editor should get a complete crew list with home phone numbers. Sound editing often involves a lot of late-night

Silent Night, Silent Cowboy
— Continuity   (8·8·84) —

Reel #	Scenes	LFOA	TAIL SYNC
1	1-26	930.07	931
2	27-35 PT	944.05	945
3	35 PT-52	904.03	905
4	54-72	994.02	995
5	73-85	934.15	936
6	86-102 PT	993.09	994
7	102 PT-113	955.11	956
8	114-130	973.07	974
9	132-156	943.04	944
10	160-181	978.03	979

(LENGTH — 9432.12)

— INCLUDES HEAD & TAIL CREDITS —

FIGURE 11.1   A reel breakdown for the sound department. Note that for reels with LFOAs on the fourteenth or fifteenth frame (e.g., reel 5) the tail sync is not the next whole foot but the second whole foot. This is done to leave enough room for the tail sync tape markings to be put on the tail leaders without overlapping into the picture area of the last frame or two. Some assistants prefer another system, which is to make all tail syncs fall one foot after the LFOA (931'07 for reel 1).

work and there will be questions that only you or another member of the picture editing crew can answer. They should know how to reach everyone. You should also submit a complete reel list to them. As shown in Figure 11.1 this list should contain the reel number, scene numbers contained on the reel, length of reel, and the tail sync. The total running time is also helpful though not necessary. As with any changeable list that you distribute you should put a date on it so that any subsequent lists will not be confused with the earlier ones. I've seen some films where reel lengths changed so often that the assistant editor began writing the hour as well as the date on his LFOA lists!

The sound department should also receive a photocopy of the lined script (with lined notes) and your logbook. They will often need this information as they go back into original quarter-inch tapes for sound retransfers and it will be inconvenient for everyone if they have to use yours.

As mentioned, you will give the sound editors your original work tracks. As they prepare the film's tracks for the final mix they will want to split the dialogue tracks to treat them for the best possible sound quality. This is nearly always done with the original tracks. Some sound editors, primarily in Hollywood, replace every piece of original track with fresh track by reprinting every take used in the film, recoding it, and having the dialogue editor cut these prints rather than the originals. This is supposed to increase the quality of the final track. I don't disagree that it may do so. I don't think however, that it is a precaution that is either cheap or necessary in all cases. Most editors use the original tracks to split with.

Conformations

In case you go back to the scene for recutting after a dupe has been struck you will then have the unenviable task of telling the sound and music editors that you have made changes in the picture and that they must *conform their dupes.* Conformation is the process by which all dupes are brought into agreement with the color work picture. The process is never a particularly happy one but is made even more depressing when the sound elements for the mix have already been built. If there are seventy tracks for one reel (let us say), making a simple one-foot addition or removal requires making that change on seventy tracks. I've seen directors make changes in the film up until the end of a film mix, completely oblivious to the chaos they were causing. It is crazy, but it is done very, very often.

For that reason, some very clear and good systems for communicating these changes must be arrived at. In all cases it is the assistant's job to make sure that the correct conformations are transmitted to the sound and music editors *as rapidly as possible.* You will be very busy in these final weeks making sure that the picture editing moves smoothly. There will be a temptation to regard the sound crew and their needs as a burden. But at this stage of the film editing process they are the major factor in terms of time, energy, money, and process. Without them the film would not be able to be projected in the theatres and their schedule is improbable enough without you making it impossible.

Transmitting the conformations should be your first priority after the conformations have been made. At the end of every day of cutting I transmit to the supervising sound editor (as well as the music editor) exactly what portions of the film were recut that day, even if the cut has not been completed yet. In this way he or she can plan the disbursement of work for the sound crew.

As soon as a scene has been recut and approved you should take the new reel and put it up against your screening dupe in your synchronizer. By comparing the two you will be able to tell exactly what has been done to the film. By having a black and white dupe of your own, as well as the color picture, you always have total information on the film, since the color picture will tell you what Adam and Wendy want with the film and the black and white dupe will tell you what everyone else *thinks* they want with the film. There should never be a discrepancy between the two.

The next step in processing conformations is a little tricky but essential. You are going to want to provide a black and white dupe of the changed sections of the film to all of the sound crew so that they will be able to have a completely current dupe of the film. There are two ways of doing this. The first is to recall all of the black and white dupes and recut them to match the color picture. The second is to provide the sound crew with all of the materials necessary to make the changes themselves.

The normal procedure followed is the second for two very good reasons. The flow of a sound editor's work is so defined that it may be very difficult for him/her to part with the black and white dupe for the time necessary to make the conformations. If, however, the editors are provided with the tools to make the changes themselves they can make them when it is convenient for them. This helps smooth out the sound editing process. The other reason is that many sound editors put odd marks all over their dupes that clue them in various ways. Some of these marks may be important to transfer over from the old dupe to the new one, whereas other marks may be unnecessary. Only the sound editor will know this, and you could seriously disrupt the editor's process by making the conformations for him or her. So, the editors will make the changes themselves on *Silent Night*.

In order to correctly convey to them just what the changes are you will have to supply them with two, possibly three, things. The first is a precise list of all changes. The second is a black and white dupe of any material that they will have to add to their dupe. The possible third is your black and white screening dupe so that they may follow it if necessary.

Let's examine these in more detail. The first task that you will have is determing just which sections you will have to dupe. I usually use two guidelines. First, any new material added that the editors would not already have must be duped. Second, any material which has been recut or rearranged so drastically as to make it very complicated to explain and to recut what should be duped. In this way, rather than recutting their black and white dupes all they will have to do is remove one part of their dupes and replace it with the new piece.

When you have determined exactly which sections of the picture need to be duped pull them out of the color work picture. Put leaders on the head and tail of them as well as short (one-foot) slugs in between each one. Number each one by the reel number and the consecutive number of the change within the reel. Do the same for the track that needs to be duped.

When the dupes come back you should have them coded. Make no attempt to code each conformation separately or each reel of these conformations separately. Merely code each set of dupes with the proper prefix code for the department for which it is intended. Since the last codes you used for the music department were MY2000 (for reel 12, music dupe) code this conformation MY3000. Note in your conformation log, which you will begin keeping, that MY3000 are music conformations for such and such a date. Code all of the dupes with the proper prefix (FY, SY, etc.) and then the numbers 3000. In this way not only will all of the dupes coded with a letter followed by Y3000 come from the same date's conformations but they all line up with each other.

When the new dupes come back from coding run them down together in the synchronizer and mark where the beginning and end of every conformation is on the track. Then cut them all apart so that you end up with one pin on your barrel for each conformation.

Now take your screening dupe and your color picture and line them up in the synchronizer. Run them down together until you get to where your first change will be (whether it be an addition or deletion). Note the footage and exactly what the change is. For instance, in Figure 11.2 we see that at 121'07/08 we need to remove 21'05 of both picture and track. This is conformation one on this reel. The next conformation is the removal of 2'02 of picture only at 230'10. The next one is the removal of the matching amount of track at 231'05 to bring the picture and track back into sync. Conformation number four is an addition. At 356'13 the editors must add the 34'07 of picture and track that you are supplying them. And so on.

At each conformation point make the conformation yourself in your black and white screening dupe. Make sure that all of your footages are correct. For this, it is helpful to have a second synchronizer to measure lengths added or removed. You should hang up all of the pieces that you remove, hanging all of the conformations for any one reel on one pin. Mark, with grease pencil or on a piece of white tape attached to the top of the removals, exactly which conformation number it is and what length it is. Also, as you are making the changes in your own reels, keep one white box for each dupe open nearby. After you have made change number four, for instance, mark the reel number and the conformation number four on the top of each of the new dupes. Flange each up separately so that they are heads out and put them into their proper boxes (FX dupes into the effects editor box, MX dupes into the music editor box). In this way, when you are done each editor will have his or her own box of conformations plainly marked as to reel number and conformation number. This will make life much easier for you and for them.

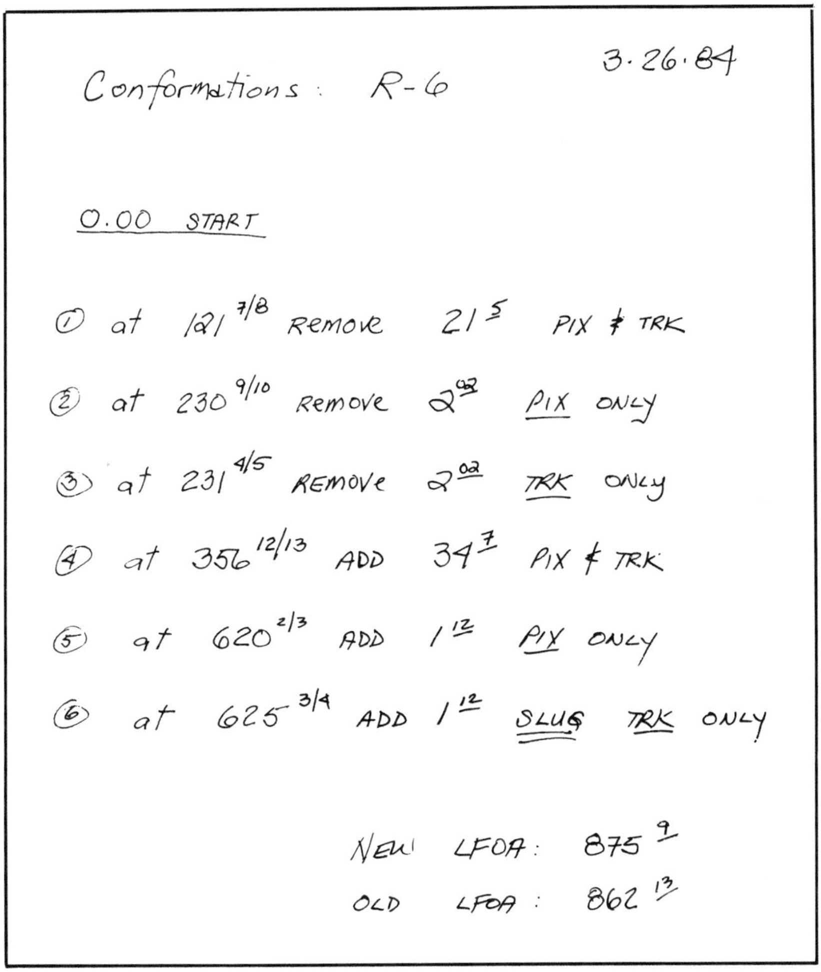

Conformations : R-6   3·26·84

0.00 START

① at 121 $^{7/8}$ REMOVE 21 ^{5} PIX ≠ TRK

② at 230 $^{9/10}$ REMOVE 2 ^{03} PIX ONLY

③ at 231 $^{4/5}$ REMOVE 2 ^{02} TRK ONLY

④ at 356 $^{12/13}$ ADD 34 ^{7} PIX ≠ TRK

⑤ at 620 $^{2/3}$ ADD 1 ^{12} PIX ONLY

⑥ at 625 $^{3/4}$ ADD 1 ^{12} SLUG TRK ONLY

NEW LFOA : 875 ^{9}

OLD LFOA : 862 ^{13}

FIGURE 11.2 A conformation sheet. For changes four and five, picture should be supplied to the sound department with the numbers "4" and "5" written on them. The term *slug trk* means that one foot and twelve frames of fill leader should be added at 625.03/04.

When you are finished with all of the conformations for any one reel run down to the end of the reel and get the new LFOA. Make sure that it is the same on your color work picture and black and white screening dupe. Do the same for all of the reels that have conformations in them. The new LFOA must be listed on the conformation sheet so the sound editors making their own conformations will be able to check that they have made them all properly.

When you are finished, make copies of all of your conformation sheets (use separate conformation sheets for each reel as different sound editors may be editing different reels)—one for each set of dupes. Then get the boxes of conformations and the conformation sheets to each editor immediately.

When this is done, and the inevitable questions asked by the sound editors and answered by you, you will be ready to clean up after yourself. Have Philip box up all of the conformations you made to your screening dupe. Have him flange up and cinetab each reel's conformations by themselves and then box up the conformations for that date together. Future conformations can be added to the same box so long as the box doesn't get too crowded and so long as a notation of which date's conformations are in the box is made on the outside of the box.

Then, correct your LFOA list and reel breakdown if you haven't already done so. Generally, I make new copies of this list only when there are drastic changes in the reel breakdown. Otherwise I tell the sound editing crew to make the LFOA corrections themselves from the LFOAs noted on the conformation sheets. Keep the conformation sheets in one place. I file them by date and then by reel number within that category. I can tell you for sure that at some point during the sound editing things will get just confused enough for you to want to find out what exactly it was that you did on such and such a date. It will be very handy for you to have these sheets filed safely away.

These are the primary tasks that will confront you as a picture assistant interfacing with the sound department. You will also have to answer many questions about where certain material came from, if there are alternates that were not used for picture but might be good for sound, exactly what things Adam liked in the scratch mixes, etc., etc., etc. You are the person who has been on the film for the longest time in an organizational capacity. You can answer all kinds of "Where can I get...?" questions. If you are bright you will also be able to help them on the "Why was it done like this?" questions. You will function as the focal point for their questions.

12

SOUND EDITING

There are various facets to sound editing—*dialogue splitting, sound effects editing, looping,* and *foleys.* Dialogue splitting is the process that was described in Chapter 9 that places pieces of dialogue that need to be treated separately in the film mix on separate tracks to allow for the film mixer to mix from one to the other and create a seamless dialogue track. Sound effects editing is the process by which the sound editor adds the sound effects necessary to make a soundtrack sound real (almost all traffic, background, and special noises in a film's soundtrack are usually added by a sound effects editor). Looping is the process of rerecording lines of dialogue which will replace or add to lines that are already in the film. Foley editing is the process of recording and adding specific sound effects which need to be done exactly in reference to the picture. Most body movement falls in this category, such as footsteps or various specific sounds of people's clothes. Many of these types of sound editing have similar systems, though some of them do not.

Similarities to Picture Editing

To a large degree, every sound editor and sound assistant must fit within the system that you, as the assistant picture editor, have devised for the picture editing. There are countless ways the two departments overlap. The first and most obvious overlap is your code numbers. The code numbers on both your color picture and the black and white dupes all refer to your logbook and, therefore, to your system. The sound department has to find original quarter-inch tapes from these codes and, unless you want to spend all of your time finding bits of information for them, your logbook and system had better be in order enough for them to find what they need.

In fact, any time that the sound department either takes material from you or creates new material they have to make sure that it fits into your system. You will want to make sure that material that they create but which you do not want confused with your material (this will usually happen when they make extra soundtrack prints) is coded so that it can't be confused with the original track.

This applies even more if you are doing your own sound editing, as often happens on low-budget jobs. You will want to make sure that you will not accidentally mix up two things that are not the same, such as a sound take and its reprint. When I was discussing reprints I made a big point of stressing that a track or picture reprint should *completely* replace the old take. In this way the old and new prints cannot get confused. Though sound editing often requires the editor have two or three or even more prints of the same take around simultaneously, he should never get confused about which is the original take.

On any film where there will be more than one sound editor there will almost always be more than one assistant sound editor.

Scene Title: Barroom Fight				Scene #: 8	
ADR/EPS	FOLEY	FX TO RECORD	PRE-RECORDED FX NAME	SOURCE	COMMENTS
Wild lines – fighters	Entire fight	Camera dolly	Chair smash		must be dull
Grunting – fighters	JAMES walking onto set after yelling "Cut!"		Camera noise		
A.D. whispering			Kleig lights – on/off	WT 1086	
Specific babble from crew members after fight	Crew members walking		Asstd Fx	WT 1087-9	
① Find an alternate "Cut!" from JAMES to replace sync line (noisy track) ② Idea of fight is to show how stagey and unreal the live/sync sound is: DO NOT make the fight sound like a finished, effected scene. Make the sound after the fight sound more "real" than the fight itself.					
③ Check all wild tracks. Wendy remembers good sound.					

FIGURE 12.1   A sound editor's note sheet. In this case, Charles has listed those items he will need for this scene as well as Adam's and Wendy's comments from their meetings.

Each editor needs his or her own assistant as we shall soon see. In the case where there are multiple assistants it is necessary to assign one assistant to the position of supervising assistant. This is not as complicated as it sounds, as the supervising sound editor's assistant is normally the person assigned the supervising assistant job. It will be this supervising assistant who will set up all of the sound editing systems to be used by the sound editors and assistants.

In addition, there should be at least one and normally two apprentice sound editors. Everyone will be generating an incredible numbers of trims and since the assistants are busy at other tasks, the apprentice can do these trims as well as the hundreds of other minor tasks necessitated by an impending mix. These apprentices will not be assigned to any particular editor or assistant but will be doing work for everyone in the sound department, directed by the supervising assistant.

Sound Effects Editing

In New York and many Hollywood low-budget editing rooms an individual sound editor is assigned a reel in a film (or, more likely, four or five reels in each film). He or she will be responsible for all of the sound work (except the looping) in that reel.

In other Hollywood situations, there are editors hired for the dialogue editing, other editors hired for the sound effects editing, and still another editor hired for foleys. In this case, there are various pluses and minuses to doing the job. It is certainly more efficient for one person to be doing only one job. Often, foleys take time away from sound effects editing that can hardly be spared in the rush to get to a mix. In addition, this enables an editor who is very good in one facet of sound editing to specialize in it.

However, there are also some problems with this way of doing things. Assembly-line sound editing leaves the editors feeling uninvolved, and the more people are involved with the film they are working on the more they'll give that little extra effort. If an editor is doing all of the sound work on any given reel then he or she will feel more of a sense of the film as a whole and, therefore, more involvement. It would be lovely, of course, if one sound editor could do all of the work on the entire film, but there is never enough time to do a top-notch professional job with a solitary sound editor though this is often how a low-budget film works. As a result, more than one editor must be brought on.

We will discuss each task individually as if different editors were performing each one, though ultimately it doesn't really matter to the assistant. He or she should be familiar with *all* of the necessary skills.

When the supervising editor and assistant first come on the film they will be charged with many tasks, not the least of which will be developing a sound effects library. But the first task that they have is to screen the film. They should try and get to know it as well as they can, for it is only then that they will be able to get the sense of the film necessary to do an effective and creative sound editing job.

They should first screen the film in a screening room so that they can hear exactly what the tracks are like. It would be helpful to screen the film in a screening room that the editor knows fairly well so that he or she has a reference point while listening. After this the editor and the assistant should begin to screen the film either on a flatbed, Moviola, or video machine so that they can analyze the film scene by scene. As they screen each reel they should be taking notes on exactly what the needs of each scene are.

Figure 12.1 is a sample sound editor's note sheet. Some supervising sound editors use these to list every single thing needed to be done with each scene. At the top is listed the scene title (this is gotten from the reel breakdown) and scene number. Each scene gets its own page which is then inserted into a master book in the order that it appears in the film. Dividers can be placed between reels so that it is easy to find scenes on any given reel of the film. If the film is reedited so the order changes it will be a simple matter to rearrange the order of these sheets.

Underneath this header is a series of five columns. In the column marked "dubbing" the editor should list all possible candidates for looping. This list will not be definite at this time but it will serve to remind the sound editor of any potential problems.

Under "foley" the editor will list all effects needed to be foleyed. The final three columns are for effects. In these columns the editor will list the effects that he or she thinks will be necessary to have in the scene. From his or her experience it should be fairly obvious what effects can be bought from a sound effects library and which will need to be recorded especially for the film. In discussions with Wendy or you the sound editor should be told what effects were added to the scratch tracks by you and which effects need to be replaced or must be kept from those scratch mixes. All of this will be noted in these columns (the "source" column will be the name and number of the effect as catalogued at the sound effects house; it therefore cannot be listed now).

At the very bottom of the sheet is a section for notes. Many of the scenes will have notes that can't be exactly translated into one of the five columns at the top of the page. Adam will say that he wants the scene to "feel festive." The sound editor should write this down. If Wendy says, "this scene will almost certainly be recut before next month," the editor should write this down along with the date.

The lists on these sheets will grow as the sound editor gets more and more ideas for the film. Each time an editor looks at the film he or she may get better ideas for the design of the soundtrack. This will mean changes or additions to these sheets. The assistant should keep these notes up to date.

At the earliest opportunity the sound editor should sit down with Adam and Wendy and go through the entire film asking detailed questions about what should go into every scene and what is definitely not necessary. The sound assistant should be there taking plenty of notes. It is not uncommon for a director to know very little about sound. Sound editors learn, after a while, to know just what directions to pay attention to and which to ignore. Sometimes a director will say that he or she won't need a certain effect which the editor feels very strongly *will* be helpful. If the editor is smart, he will do the effect even though the director has said it is not necessary.

So, let's say that you have hired Charles Heap and Liz Deare as supervising sound editor and assistant. They've just gone through the film with Adam, Wendy, and you for special instructions. There is another screening which would be helpful at this stage and that is a looping screening. If possible it is nice to have the looping editor there at this screening. This screening is held at a mixing studio where the best quality sound can be heard. Every reel is meticulously examined. Any lines which the sound or looping editor feel need to be looped should be mentioned here. Possible candidates are lines which are obliterated by some unwanted sound (background sounds, another actor/actress talking, radio interference, etc.), lines on which the director wants to change the reading, lines that the sound editor feels may be problematic for splitting tracks, lines that must be added to help the story line (these lines are usually off-screen lines, that is, coming from a character not shown on screen), or lines needed for the television version of the film.

At the end of all of these screenings Charles and Liz will have accumulated enough notes to write a book and enough work to keep them occupied for quite a while. They can then begin to plan their sound editing task.

One of their biggest jobs is building a sound effects library. There are many stock effects libraries and all of them have tens of thousands of individual effects on tape. Charles will, after going through all of the notes that Liz and he have been accumulating since they first started working on the film, figure out just what effects they need for the film. He will then have Liz reserve a block of time at a sound effects house for listening and transferring of effects. Six hours a day of listening is enough to drive any grown person insane so many editors prefer to listen for no more than five or six hours, broken up by a lunch break, and then to work in the editing room for the remainder of the day on other necessary tasks. This will of course be a matter of preference for the individual editor.

Liz should set up these sessions as soon as possible and then begin to set up her own library. All of the effects will be transferred onto 35mm film (or 16mm if that is the film gauge you are working in). Liz will buy a large quantity of 35mm sound stock and precode it before these sessions at the effects house.

Every assistant has his or her own coding system. About the only real requirement is that none of the numbers duplicate any of the picture department's numbers. In fact, you (as the picture assistant) should assign Liz the codes that she will use so that there is no possible confusion. A common setup is to let her use all of the codes with the F code (such as FA, FB, etc.). She would begin coding the first roll of stock for transfer FA1000, then FA2000, all the way up through FA0000. This would be followed by FB1000 and so on.

At the first sesssion Charlie (but because we're working with him, let's call him Chuck) will sit down with the sound effects house librarian and discuss his needs. They will then begin listening to effects.

Let's say that one of the categories that he will need is traffic. In one scene of the film there is a traffic jam. In another there is someone standing alone on the street at night with only one or two cars going by. In yet a third scene, Abby is in his apartment which is near a moderately busy street. Each slightly different sound will require a different effect. On many television shows there are certain standard sounds. Kojak's police car is one particular sound effect, to be used every time Telly Savalas is driving. The car siren is also one particular sound. In much the same way, Chuck will want to use similar sounds for similar locations and times of day, but he will try to use different sounds for all other cases. It wouldn't do to have every bit of traffic sound the same.

At either the head or the tail of every transferred sound effect the transfer person will attach a piece of paper tape to the mag which will list the exact number of the sound effect. Since every house has its own system these numbers will look different from house to house but this number is very important. If you ever need more of one particular sound at a later stage you will be able to order the exact same effect by this number. Chuck will also be keeping a list of these numbers with short descriptions on a separate sheet of paper. This sheet will eventually be transcribed onto a log sheet by Liz (as I will describe later).

At the end of the first day Chuck's sound effects sheet might look something like this:

C13-5	Medium day traffic, no horns
C11-2	Heavy traffic, many horns, type 1
C11-2	Heavy traffic, many horns, type 2
C23-5a	Distant traffic, day—for Abby's room
C09-1	Light traffic, night, a few horns
C09-5	Light traffic, night, on wet street
C15-2	Single car-by
C15-5	Car approaches and stops short, 2X
C15-6	Car slows down and goes by
C15-9	Revving engine—sports car, MG
C16-23	Engine idle—Rolls-Royce

This is just a short sample of the kinds of effects that Chuck might get for traffic. And, yes, they really do get that specific.

After the day's transfers have been done Liz will get several rolls of 35mm mag which she will begin to break down. Each sound

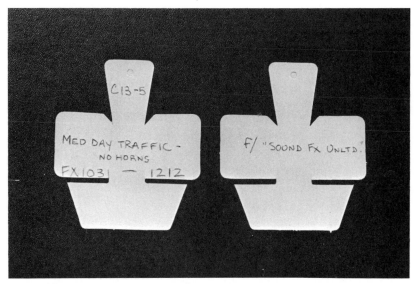

FIGURE 12.2   The front and the back of a sound effect's trim tab.
The effect was bought from a sound effects house called Sound FX
Unltd. This company gave it the number C13-5. This information will
facilitate the reordering of this effect if more is needed. (Photograph
by Janet Conn)

CODE NUMBERS	SOURCE	CAT.	FX#	DESCRIPTION	COMMENTS
FX 1031 - 1212	Sound FX Unltd	Traffic	C13-5	Med. day traffic. No horns	
1213 - 1347	"	"	C11-2	Hwy traffic, many horns, #1	
1348 - 1452	"	"	C11-2	Hwy traffic, many horns, #2	
1453 - 1601	"	"	C29-8	Distant day traffic	For ABBY's room
1602 - 1726	"	"	C9-1	Light night traffic - few horns	
1727 - 1832	"	"	C9-5	Light night traffic - wet street	For scene 28
1833 - 1872	"	Cars	C15-2	Single car-by	
1873 - 1956	"	"	C15-5	Car approaches & stops short - 2x	
1957 - 2036	"	"	C15-6	Car slows down & goes by	
2037 - 2072	"	"	C15-9	Revving engine - MG	
2073 - 2127	"	"	C16-28	Engine idle - Rolls Royce	
2128 - 2196	"	Chairs	F7-13	Chair smashes - single	For Sc. 8
2197 - 2256	"	"	F7-21	Chair smashes - many	For Sc. 8
2257 - 2341	"	Camera	C2-3	Camera noise - Type #1	For all on-set scenes
2342 - 2410	"	"	C2-4	Camera noise - Type #2	"
2411 - 2472	"	"	C3-7	Camera magazine on/off	"
2473 - 2521	"	Lights	E17-2	Kleig lights - hum	"
2522 - 2567	"	"	E17-5	Kleig lights - on/off	"
2568 - 2598	"	"	E17-12	Brutes - on/off	"
2599 - 2662	"	"	E17-19	Lights - hum. Increasing volume	"

FIGURE 12.3   A page from a sound effects logbook. Note the simi-
larity of the information to the trim tab (Fig. 12.2).

effect should be separated out, just as the wild track was. Each gets its own cinetab and its own line in a sound effects logbook (see Figures 12.2 and 12.3). The cinetab will list, on its face, the code number and a short description of the sound effect. In addition it is helpful to list, in the top part, the category that the particular effect belongs in. In the effects above, for instance, it might be wise to separate these effects into two categories—cars and traffic. This is because each effect will be used slightly differently. The traffic effects will be used as a general background while the car effects will be used to match specific things that are on the screen. On the back of the cinetab Liz will list the sound effects house that the effect was purchased from and its number.

On the effects log sheet much of the same type of information is listed. There is a column for "scene" which some sound editors find useful. Since some effects are used in many scenes it is not always helpful to list the scene number and, in fact, I rarely do. Instead, I list the set or location in the description. The original source is the effects house and number. The transfer remarks are for special notes. In many cases sound effects are "treated" in some special way. On one film I worked on we were trying to find a particularly eerie thunderstorm. Nothing that we were able to find seemed to work perfectly. Instead we took one of the better storms and sped it up by 50 percent. This created precisely the effect we wanted. The fact that the effect was sped up by 50 percent was noted in the transfer remarks column and on the back of the cinetab. In this way, any effect can be duplicated exactly or, if the original effect doesn't work, it can be changed. All that is necessary to know is exactly what was done in the first place.

As Liz breaks down each of these effects (or as one of the apprentices does so) they should be boxed by category. Each of the boxes should be labeled very plainly by its category. The usual practice is to put a piece of green tape (or whatever color the FX department has been assigned) down the center of one side of the box and write the film name on the tape followed by the category in large letters spreading the height of the box (see Figure 12.4).

At the end of the effects sessions the sound department will have accumulated quite a number of shelves of effects. Some films have several racks full of effects.

Sometimes effects cannot be obtained from any sound effects house. These will have to be recorded specifically for the scene. On

FIGURE 12.4   A sound effects box. The legend is written over green tape, to signify effects. (Photograph by Janet Conn)

another film I worked on we could not locate a specific sound effect for a modern elevator door closing. We had to record one ourselves. Almost any film will have effects that need to be recorded especially for the film. Either a sound recordist or the sound editor takes a Nagra (or some comparable quarter-inch portable tape recorder) and goes out and records them.

Let's say that, for our film, Chuck cannot find various sound effects of movie making—a film crane rising and lowering, klieg lights coming on, fake-sounding gunshots, and many more. Liz would try and organize a recording session for these things. She might call people who were shooting a film and see if she could get permission to record a few effects one day. Or she might make arrangements with a film equipment rental house to do the same thing. Then, after ascertaining that the booked day was fine with Chuck, she would rent the equipment for Chuck or hire a sound recordist. On the day of the recording she might go to the set with Chuck and take thorough notes of exactly what it is that he is recording. Before each effect Chuck would announce a voice slate into the microphone such as, "This is sound effect number two, Chapman crane rising slowly." He would then record the effect.

After the day's session the tape would be given to your sound house for a transfer. Liz should make sure that a proper sound report is included just as one was submitted with every roll from

the dailies shooting. It will also save some time if Liz submits the
required amount of precoded 35mm stock with the tape so that the
transfers may be made onto it. In this way the track will not have
to be sent out for coding when the transfers come back. Some editors like to leave the quarter-inch tape with the sound house, others
like to keep it in the editing room with them. After the transfers
have been done they will arrive back at the editing room. Liz or an
apprentice will break them down just as was done for the library
effects. The only difference is that in the logbook column for "original source" and on the back of the cinetab the sound roll number
and effect number should be written instead of the sound effects
house. In this case, for instance, the back of the designation would
be SR#1 (for sound roll number one), effect 2. The front would say
"Chapman crane rising slowly" with the code numbers and category listed as usual.

Editing Sound Effects

Before any of these effects can be edited Chuck will have to
have the proper equipment. A console Moviola (one with a picture
head and two sound heads) will be necessary along with a synchronizer with sound heads on all four gangs. He will also need a sound
box (amplifier) that can accept and separately control four different
sound inputs.

Chuck will be editing these sound effects much as described in
the section on scratch mixing in Chapter 9. He will run the black
and white dupe and its track on the two outside gangs of the console
Moviola. The middle gang is where he will try out all of the sound
effects. He will be able to shift the position of the effect he is trying
out against the picture to see where the most accurate and pleasing
position for the effect should be. Then, when he has decided on the
proper placement, he will do two things—the first will be to put a
footage on the sound effect he wants cut in identifying which track
it is to be put on and at what point, the second will be to enter it
onto his cue sheets (see Figure 12.5). Chuck will then hang the
effect on a pin reserved for all of the effects in that mix element.

After Chuck has finished cutting the effects for a reel he will
give both the barrel with the effects, and the temp cue sheets, to

Liz. Often, if the apprentices are experienced enough, they will end up *building the tracks*. Otherwise, Liz will do it.

Building the tracks consists of taking all the little pieces of track which Chuck has cut for the effects and putting them in their proper places in the elements. The basic philosophy of mixing is quite simple. Every sound that has to be separately controlled should be on its own element so that it will come into the mixing board on a separate volume control knob. Its level (as well as its sound quality) can then be controlled without affecting any of the other sounds. The way that this is accomplished is to have a large number of reels (called *elements* or *units*) made up of fill. They will all have a start mark and can all be run together, just as you can gang up four tracks at one time in your synchronizer. Every time that you want to hear a sound you will cut it in precisely the right place into one of these elements. Leading up to it will be fill, and leading away from it will also be fill. But at the point where the effect needs to be heard, that effect will be cut into the tracks so that it can be played back through the mixing board. If five effects need to be heard at the same time (in a thunderstorm, for instance, one might want to hear rain, thunder, wind, cars passing on a wet street, and dripping water) then each must be put on its own element. The more complicated the scene, the more elements will be used.

There are many subtleties involved in deciding how to apportion the effects on the elements. Let us say that in the above-mentioned rainstorm we cut from inside a car parked in the rain, to outside the car. Every time we cut from inside to outside all of the above-mentioned effects would get louder. But if the characters inside the car were having a fight, that dialogue would get softer when we went outside. Also, the sound of the windshield wipers would change when we went outside the car. This gives us seven elements which must change at precisely the same time and on a single frame. This is rather difficult to do, so the sound editor does something called *splitting for perspective* which simply means that at the exact frame where we cut from the inside of the car to the outside the seven effects that were running get cut and moved onto seven other tracks. In this way the mixer can set levels and tone controls separately for the inside elements (on one set of seven tracks) and the outside elements (on another set of seven tracks). When we cut back inside the car again the editor would move all of the sound effects back to the first set of tracks since the old set of levels and tone controls would apply. In this way the mixer wouldn't have to change anything at the cut to outside. Voilà! You've saved everyone a lot of very expensive time at the mix (and, in 1982, mixing time was going for upwards of $400 hour).

When Liz gets these pieces of sound and the temp cue sheet she will have to build the tracks that will eventually be used in the mix. Everything must be cut into these reels exactly right so that an effect supposed to come in at 145'08 comes in at exactly 145'08. Time lost at the mix looking for misplaced pieces of track wastes money and disrupts the creative flow of mixing.

All of the elements must have leaders on them, since they will be leaving the editing rooms and going to the mixing studio where many other films are working. However, it is not necessary to make up scores of white leaders for every reel on the film. The elements can be leadered with fill.

The leaders, of course, should be written in red ink on the color of tape assigned to the particular category of track that it is. In this case, it would be green (for effects). Cut a frame of the 1000-cycle tone in at exactly 9'00 (from the 0'00 start mark) on the first element of each category. In our case, this would be on FX-1 (or FX-A, depending on what system you choose for identifying your elements; New York convention is to use letters, everyone else seems to prefer numbers).

Looking at Figure 12.5, the cue sheet, we can see that the first effect that needs to be cut in is a car idle on element one at 12'00. Liz, or the apprentice, will put up the black and white dupe for reel seven in the first gang of her synchronizer and then three rolls of fill in the next three gangs. She will leader these rolls as FX-1, FX-2, and FX-3 of reel 7. After about ten feet of blank leader, for the thread-up, she will put start marks on all three elements. Then she will zero out the counter and begin to roll down.

At 12'00 on the first track (which is normally the second gang) she will make a cut and put in the car idle effect which Chuck should have hung on the FX-1 pin and put a footage on. She will do this by marking the 12'00 frame line on the fill and then rolling it out to the left of the synchronizer (make *all* cuts to the left of the synchronizer since that is *before* it goes into the synchronizer and the footage counter). She will cut the fill there and then splice the effect onto the piece of film going through the synchronizer. This

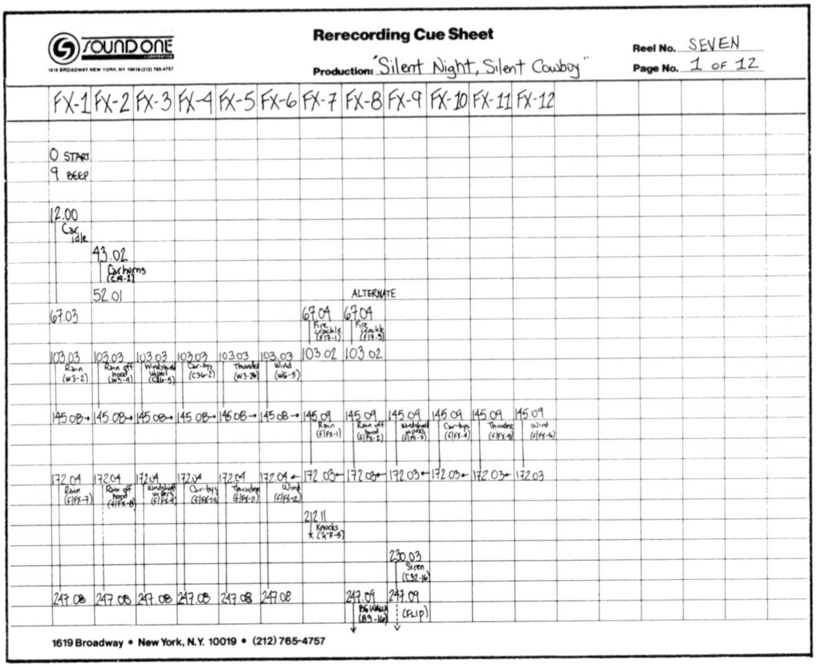

FIGURE 12.5 Part of a cue sheet. This cue sheet is missing all of the dialogue and music tracks. Note the splits at 145'08 and again at 172'03.

completes cutting the head of the effect in. While she is rolling down to the next location for an effect she will listen to the effect that she's just cut in. In this way she can verify that she has cut in the proper effect. Rolling down to about 43'00 she will stop and look for the car horn effect which should be hanging on the FX-2 pin. This effect, since it does not cut in at exactly 43'00, may be marked in either of two ways (see Figure 12.6). The exact footage (43'02) may be marked on it or a box may be drawn at the spot where 44' 00 will fall. In the first case all she would do is make a cut at 43'02 and cut in the effect, just as she did with the effect at 12'00 on the FX-1 track. In the second case, however, she would roll down to 44' 00, place the track on top of the fill in gang number two, aligning the track's sprocket holes with the sprockets of the gang, and then carefully roll back to the beginning of the effect while holding the track down against the fill and the gang.

If you've been following this explanation so far you will have figured out that Liz will now be running the black and white dupe in the first gang of the synchronizer, two pieces of track through the

FIGURE 12.6 There are two ways of marking sound effects. In one (A), the footage of the first frame is written on the effect. In the other (B), the next whole number frame is marked on the track.

FIGURE 12.7 Tail syncs are marked on the first zero frame after the LFOA unless it would be the first frame after the LFOA. Then it is the second zero frame. In this case, the LFOA was 955'11. The tail sync is marked at 956 feet.

FIGURE 12.8 This streamer extends for one-half of a second to the frame with the X in it. Most often, streamers are three feet (two seconds) or longer.

next two gangs, and one complete roll of fill in the back gang. The two effects will not be attached to anything at their tail. The first two rolls of fill will also not be connected on the feed side.

As she approaches 52'01 she will slow down and stop. The end of the effect on FX-2 is coming up. She can then attach the end of this effect to the second roll of fill which is on the left rewind. At 67'03 she will do the same for the effect on FX-1.

The next two effects (at 67'04 on FX-7 and FX-8) cannot be cut in just yet because Liz only has FX-1 through 3 up on the synchronizer now. The next effects that she can cut in are at 103'03 on all of her tracks.

In the case of these effects, which will be split off for perspective at 145'08/09, Chuck probably did not make the cuts at that point on the effects themselves. Instead, he ran them long, for the length that they will appear on all of the tracks (which, in this case, runs from 103'03, through the perspective split at 145'08, through the next perspective split at 172'03 and until the end of the effects at 247'08). It will be up to Liz to make the splits at the proper places.

At this point she should make the cut herself, referring to the footage count on the sheet and black and white dupe running in gang number one. The fact that so many tracks begin and end at this point makes it almost certain that there should be a change of location at this point. If the footage count does not come at the point in the picture where there is a location change then this is a good time for Liz to ask Chuck if the footages are correct. In fact, every time she cuts in an effect she should look to see if it makes any sense in reference to the picture. Obviously there will be many things that she won't be able to judge by looking at the picture in the synchronizer. But since she knows the film, there will be some that she can. The best assistants keep a lookout for any oddity and, if they can't figure out the solution to the oddity, ask their editors. Safety is a lot better than trying to look knowledgeable and having something ridiculous come up at the mix.

After Liz makes the cuts in the long effects (which she will do at 145'08) she should mark the tail trim of the effect and hang it with the rest of the effects for FX-7, FX-8, and FX-9.

There are three little kinks in the cutting of the tracks listed on this temp cue sheet. The first will come when Liz gets down to 172'04 and is ready to cut in the *continuation* of the rain effects that are split off from FX-7 through FX-12. To do this she needs to find the proper frame in the middle of these effects. She would take the piece from FX-7 at 145'09 (which is, in this case, the piece that she cut from the earlier FX-1 piece), put it in another synchronizer at 145'09 and roll down to 172'04. She will then mark the track there and cut it at this frame line (172'03/04). She should then mark the tail piece as FX-1 at 172'04. She can do this with the pieces she will need for FX-2 and FX-3 as well. Then, she can hang the head pieces back up in the barrel on their pins and cut the tail pieces into their proper tracks.

I should mention here one little wrinkle that some sound editors like to throw into split tracks such as these. If the people who line up the tracks at the mix for the playback do not line them up at precisely the same exact point some gaps might be created. For instance, at 145'08/09, if FX-1 was lined up just a tad early and FX-7 was lined up just a tad late then the rain sound might disappear for as much as a sprocket (depending on just how off each track was). In order to avoid this occurrence many editors like to put a one-sprocket overlap in their tracks at splits. In this case the FX-1 element would run out one sprocket past 145'08/09 even though the effect on FX-7 would still begin exactly on the frame line. If this is what Chuck wants then Liz must take this into account as she is building the tracks. Let us assume, however, that Chuck feels that such a precaution is not necessary.

A second little kink occurs on FX-7 at 212'11 where the temp cue sheet lists *knocks*. You may notice that there is no end footage listed. Instead, there is a little X. This is placed there to note that the effect is of very short duration. This makes it very obvious to the mixer who will not have to look at the actual numbers to see how long the effect runs. The third little kink comes on FX-9 at 230'03 where the cue sheet calls for a siren to begin. Normally this siren would stop at the scene change at 247'08/09. However, Chuck was unsure whether it might not be a good idea to continue the effect for a little bit under the beginning of the next scene (where there is a crowd walla—which is simply a crowd in the background talking indistinguishably). At the scene split, therefore, he wants to *flip* the track. The sound effect would be cut at the proper point but instead of attaching the tail of the effect to the fill it would be attached back to itself with the continuation of the effect flipped over. On playback the sound of this effect would disappear as the head would be riding over the back of the track (which should have no sound on it). When the track runs out altogether then it would be spliced back onto the fill, making sure that the fill would continue to ride with its base side toward the mixer's playback head.

The advantage of flipping this piece of track is that if the director decides at the mix that he does want the scream to extend into the crowd walla it can be flipped back to its proper orientation with only a few minutes' lost time. If Adam does not like the idea then nothing need be done at all, since a piece of flipped track acts just like a piece of fill—it has no sound on it.

After all of the effects for these three elements have been cut in and Liz is down at the tail of the reel she will make sure that all of the LFOAs match the LFOA listed in the reel breakdown. I also like to physically make a cut in the fill at the LFOA frame line and then resplice the pieces back together again. This makes the LFOA very easy to see.

After this, the tail syncs should be marked as shown in Figure 12.7 and then the reels wound down for an additional thirty feet beyond these tail syncs. In addition, white leader should be added to the end of the black and white dupe so that it also extends out about thirty feet beyond the tail sync (try and make all of the reels run out at the same time). This extra thirty feet is called the *run-out* and is there because the machines which play back these elements at the film mix often take quite a bit of time to slow down to a stop. If the film mixer doesn't hit the stop button until ten feet or so after the end of the LFOA (which is, after all, only about six seconds) then it would be likely that the reels would run out past the end. This extra thirty feet at the end of every reel should be enough to ensure that this doesn't happen.

Tail leaders should then be taped onto the end of the reels. The dupe can then be rewound and the process repeated with FX-4, FX-5, and FX-6. When those reels are completed then the next three reels are done and then the next three until all twelve elements have been cut in.

At some point it would be a wise idea to run these built reels on the Moviola (obviously, you would not be able to do more than two at a time) against the picture to make sure that everything is cut together properly.

Often, there are adjustments to be made to the track. There are two kinds of changes that are common. The first comes from the addition or deletion of effects. If you must delete an effect it is best just to flip it out, rather than to physically remove it from the tracks. This way, if Chuck changes his mind *again* and wants the effect back in, it is a simple matter. If an effect is to be added Liz should roll down to that spot on the proper element (always rolling down against the black and white dupe) and mark the fill in the same way that she would for any piece of track to be cut in. However, if Liz just cut in the new effect (which was, say, three feet long) without doing anything else then she would be adding three feet in length to the entire reel from that point on. To compensate for the new footage, she must remove an equal amount of fill before the next sound effect occurs. The best place to remove it from is from the exact place where she is cutting in the new effect.

The second type of adjustment Liz will be making is the conformation. You, as the picture assistant, will provide detailed lists of all the conformations. Liz should first conform the black and white dupe and put a piece of tape on the head leader of each conformed element and dupe listing the date of the conformation. Chuck will then go through all of these conformations and determine exactly which sound effects are affected by them. For instance, if the scene in the car was shortened (let us say by exactly two feet at 120'03/04) then it will be necessary to delete two feet of all of the sounds going at that time. The sound changes will not always come at the same footage as the conformation so Liz and Chuck should determine exactly how he wants to approach each change. Then she should make them. On elements which have only fill running at the conformation point it will only be necessary to delete the proper amount of footage to make the conformation (or add fill if the conformation is an addition).

If the conformation is an addition it might be necessary to obtain new sound for some of the areas of the film. Chuck will do this (or instruct Liz *very thoroughly* on how to do it) and Liz will end up with new pieces to add to the elements.

On the conformation sheet supplied to her she should list every element involved in the reel. As she makes the conformation in each element she should check off that the conformation has been done. Obviously, a simple conformation in the picture department turns into a much more time-consuming conformation in the sound department after reels are built.

There are two other types of sound effects tracks which Liz

may be dealing with. These are *goodies* and *loops*. Goodies are effects which Chuck decided not to cut in, but which he wants available in case he needs to cut them in at the mix. Goodies are placed into their own white box, which is marked "GOODIES for reel 7" (or whatever reel it is) on one side. On the top of the box, or on a sheet of paper inside the box, a list of all the goodies in the box is kept. This list should contain all of the effects, along with the footage where it should be cut in. If there is any conformation at all, these footages should be changed.

There might also be a separate box for loops. Loops are effects which are so general that it does not matter if they repeat after ten seconds or so. Room tone is commonly treated as a loop since it doesn't really matter where it falls in the scene—it should all sound the same. These loops are filed by number and labeled on the top of the box or on a separate sheet of paper by scene and description. Often an editor will make an *analysis loop* which is a loop of a particular sound that needs to be treated. Some sounds, like hums or air conditioners, need to be filtered out of the soundtrack or they would be too annoying for an audience. But they appear only in the background of scenes and it would be very difficult for the mixer to fool around with his equalizers over the few seconds that the sound is present by itself. In this case, Chuck would make a loop of just the sound that needs to be filtered out. This could be run until the mixer discovers the proper settings to filter out the unwanted sound. This analysis loop is then filed away. It is not meant to be used in the final soundtrack. It is only a tool to get a better mix.

Foley Editing

Often a scene which has been shot does not have the proper types of body movement for the feeling that one intends to convey. A scene in which a person walks across a creaky wooden floor or down a cavernous passageway may have been shot without any sound at all. If sound was taken with the shot, the footsteps might not have the proper sound. In addition, scenes in which the dialogue is being replaced by looping will have absolutely no background sounds at all to them since all of the original background will be thrown out at the same time that the original dialogue is. The sound editor cuts in backgrounds and specific effects to help in all of these cases but there are many cases where a needed effect cannot be found in an effects library.

You have already seen that some effects may have to be recorded especially for the scene. In many cases this is done on location (on *Apocalypse Now*, for instance, the supervising sound editor spent weeks recording military aircraft) but what happens if you need to put in those footsteps down the cavernous hallway? How would you do that? One choice would be to actually go to a cavernous hallway and record someone walking down it. But this approach has two problems to it. The first is the uncontrollable nature of the resulting sound. It may be too echoey. While it is always possible to add echo to a sound during the mix it is almost impossible to take the echo out. So, if the sound you got by recording the footsteps in a big hallway had too much echo in it for Adam, you would be in a bad fix. The second problem is that, on location, you would have very little way to exactly mime the pace of the actor's or actress's footsteps.

Fortunately, there is an easier way (you knew there would be, didn't you?). It's called *foleying*.

A foley is, basically, any kind of body movement effect obtained in a studio. A foley studio is a recording studio which has the ability to play back the picture and sound while you watch them and mimic the action on the screen. In the case of our actor walking down the hallway, the scene would be projected and Chuck (or Liz) would mimic the way the actor walks on the screen. These footsteps would be recorded. Later on, they would be cut into perfect sync in the editing room (it is almost impossible to get these sounds 100 percent accurate on the foley stage).

Foley stages are interesting places. They are usually large rooms with a number of surfaces to walk on. There may be a section of the floor which is dirt, another which is polished wooden floor, another which is brick, another which is tile, a fifth which is hollow wood, and so on. The foley stage gives the sound editor most of the possibilities necessary to recreate footsteps in the studio.

There are tricks that editors get to simulate some sounds. People walking in snow or sand are duplicated by having the editor walk his *fingers* through a bowl of soap flakes. Some sounds can be duplicated without actually recreating the action. For instance, it may be necessary to do the sound effect of someone taking off his pants. This sound is easily gotten by holding the sleeve of a jacket up to the microphone and pulling it inside out.

Liz must prepare the film before it goes to the foley stage. First, she and Chuck should decide which things are to be foleyed. This is a decision which should not be taken lightly. Foleys are not very time-consuming to create but they are very time-consuming to cut into the film. If a scene does not really need foleying then by all means do not foley it. Many foleys are eventually not used in the film anyway. I've seen some editors foley practically everything in a film. This seems wasteful to me. But if there is any doubt as to whether a scene should be foleyed, then it is wiser to take the time to foley it and cut it in than to show up at the mix without the proper sounds.

After Liz has determined exactly what things need to be foleyed she should *streamer* the reel. Streamers are long lines which, when projected, slowly cross the screen from left to right. They are used to warn a person making the foleys that a foley is coming up soon. If Liz is doing the foleys (and it is not uncommon to find an assistant editor doing it) she would watch for the streamer to appear. As soon as it hits the right side of the screen she would know to begin the foley.

These streamers are put on the film in the editing room before the session. On a Moviola a frame is chosen where the foley is to begin and a mark is made there and three feet before that frame. The dupe is laid down on a table and a long three-foot line is drawn with grease pencil (see Figure 12.8) from the top of the film at the three-foot mark to the bottom of the film at the first frame of the foley. When projected this will appear as a two-second line crossing from left to right on the screen.

It is not necessary to streamer every single foley that is to be done. If there is a scene with five characters all dancing and each character needs to be foleyed, it is only really important to streamer the first character unless there is some difficult cue point for the beginning of another.

Streamers should be used to help the foley maker find the cue for the foley. If some other visual on the screen can do the same thing, it is not necessary to streamer it.

If there are several characters in a scene who need to be streamered then it is sometimes helpful to make the streamer lines in two different colors of grease pencil or to make them go in opposite directions on the screen (one going left to right, another going right to left).

Foleys are recorded on three-stripe (or full-coat) 35mm track whether your film is in 35mm or 16mm. This gives you three passes at any given spot on the film. In that way you can do a foley twice or three times if you are unsure of it. Or, if there is a scene with a lot of characters in it, one or two of them can be done together on one channel of the three-stripe, another one or two can be done on the B channel, and still more can be done on the C channel. In this way you can achieve an entire crowd using only a few people on the foley stage. Later on, each of the channels of the three-stripe will be transferred to its own coded 35mm (or 16mm) track. It is this track that the editor will cut, not the three-stripe. That will remain at the foley stage's transfer room until it is no longer needed.

It is helpful to have someone taking notes at these foley sessions. In that way when you get the transfers to cut in (and we will get to that very shortly) you will know exactly what to do (see Figure 12.9).

Let us say that Liz has prepared all of the reels that she needs. She then brings them to the foley studio where either she or some other people will actually do the foleys. In London and in some places in Los Angeles, some groups of people are so good at doing foleys that they do only that. They move so fast and are so accurate that they often save the production more than the cost of their salaries. But let us say that Liz and a few others are doing the foleys, not these pros. They begin a reel. Let's say the first foley is not until 125 feet. Rather than wasting 125 feet of three-stripe material they will disengage the recording machine from the projector, roll down to about 100 feet and then lock the two of them up. When they roll forward they will be ready to record the foley.

It is possible that this foley may require more than three passes, if it is a large fight scene for instance. In this case, after making the first three passes (and filling up all three channels on the three-stripe) the film would be stopped and the recorder again disengaged from the projector. Then the projector would be rolled back to the beginning of the scene and locked in again. When they roll forward again they will be recording on a new area of the three-stripe and Liz will be able to get up to six passes of the same area of the film.

It is helpful if someone voice-slates these foleys so that it is easy

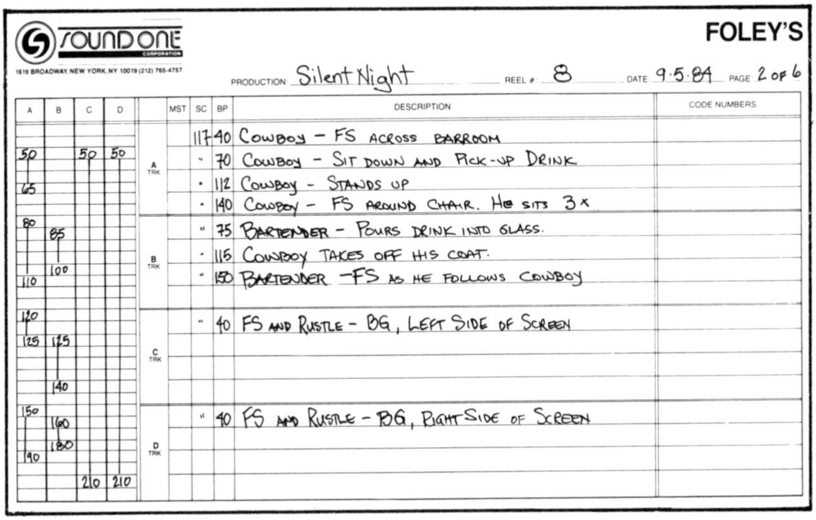

SOUND ONE CORPORATION
1619 BROADWAY, NEW YORK, NY 10019 (212) 765-4757

FOLEY'S

PRODUCTION Silent Night REEL #: 8 DATE 9·5·84 PAGE 2 of 6

A: 50, 65, 80, 110, 120, 125, 150, 190
B: 85, 100, 125, 140, 160, 180
C: 50, 210
D: 50, 210

TRK	MST	SC	BP	DESCRIPTION	CODE NUMBERS
A TRK		117	40	Cowboy – FS across barroom	
		"	70	Cowboy – Sit down and Pick-up Drink	
		"	112	Cowboy – Stands up	
		"	140	Cowboy – FS around chair. He sits 3x	
B TRK		"	75	Bartender – Pours drink into glass.	
		"	115	Cowboy takes off his coat.	
		"	150	Bartender –FS as he follows cowboy	
C TRK		"	40	FS and Rustle – BG, Left Side of Screen	
D TRK		"	40	FS and Rustle – BG, Right Side of Screen	

FIGURE 12.9 A page from a foley log. The four columns on the left represent the four channels on the full-coat mag that the foleys are being recorded onto. The footages marked show where foleys were recorded on those tracks. Each foley has a beep laid down before it in order to facilitate locating its proper position against picture. That footage is listed under the "BP" column. The description tells just what the foley is (You'd be surprised just how much one set of footsteps sounds like another). "FS" means footsteps. "BG" refers to background characters. Rather than taking the time to foley each background character separately, they are often done four or five at a time. (Courtesy Sound Corp.)

to identify what set of footsteps goes with what picture later on in the editing room (you'd be surprised how much one set of footsteps sounds like another on a Moviola). Liz should call out "Reel 7, foley at 125 feet, take 1" on the first pass and then increase the take number as each new channel is used.

So, let us say that Liz has done the foleys. She will now get (from the foley transfer house) three rolls of 35mm sound film for each roll of foleys that she made. Every one will have some foleys on them and some blank space. After coding them she can, on a log sheet, write down the starting and ending code numbers for the foley along with the date recorded, the foley three-stripe number, the reel and footage it was designed for. In this way, reprints can be ordered very easily from the three-stripe. The reels do not have to be broken down into individual foleys unless Chuck requests it. Normally, the foleys can be cut off of the large 1000-foot rolls.

Then Chuck, or whoever is cutting the foleys, sits down with the dupe on his Moviola and begins fitting the foley to the picture much as he would any other effect. Foley cutting is an extremely tedious process, since every footstep must be cut in exactly right. Most foleys will require some moving around from the position that they were recorded in. This involves either removing some track from between two foleys or adding little bits of fill to lengthen the time between them.

After the foleys are cut Liz will end up with a number of long strands of track, with footages marked on them along with the element that they are assigned to. The foleys should then be built into reels in the same way that the effects are.

Preparing for the Mix

If *Silent Night* is like most other films, the tracks will be being built no more than one day before they are to be mixed. After they are built it is a good idea to check them in the Moviola against the picture dupe. Then someone with good handwriting should recopy the cue sheets so that they are neat and orderly. All footages at the same point (within half a foot or so) are lined up with one another on the cue sheets.

Often, the film mix is done in the same building or on the same studio lot where the editing rooms are. In this case, it is a simple matter to ship everything over to the mix. But in many cases this is not so: The editing rooms are far removed from the film mix. In this case it is necessary to set up a little editing room at the mixing stage and to bring all essential trims and outs to the mix with the elements (production tracks as well as looping and effects trims).

13

DIALOGUE AND LOOPING EDITING

There is, of course, a lot more to preparing for a mix than dealing with the sound effects problems. The major problem on most films is the condition of the dialogue tracks. Some tracks might have so much extraneous noise on them that they would be completely unusable while other tracks have sporadic noises on them that make sections of the tracks unacceptable. And other tracks, while having no generally unacceptable portions on them, have backgrounds that sound slightly different from camera setup to camera setup, thus making cutting from one to the other noticeable. Each of these problems can be handled in the process of dialogue and looping editing.

In editing situations where one sound editor will handle multiple functions it is common for this person to do both the dialogue and effects editing but not the looping editing. However, since both dialogue and looping editing attack the same problems we will deal with them together here.

Let us take these three problems just mentioned in reverse order.

Dialogue Splitting

In Scene 11 (see Figure 4.5) there is a scene between Abby and his neighbor Bob in Abby's bedroom. Many different kinds of shots were done of the scene (this is called *coverage*), including shots of Abby, shots of Bob, and shots of the two of them. Because of the direction the camera was pointing during each shot the microphone had to be facing different portions of the set during each setup. This means that there will be subtle differences in the sound quality that might become evident when cut together. Correcting this is a fairly simple matter for a mixer—he simply uses different equalization (see Chapter 15 for more details about this), echo, and volume settings on each of the two shots. To do this he needs to have each shot's sound on a separate track element. In addition, to help make the point of the transition less apparent he will want to *segue* from one to the other. A segue is a sort of audio dissolve in which one sound fades up through another sound, as that second sound is fading out. You hear segues all of the time on the radio when the announcer will fade from one song into another.

But in order to accomplish this segue the mixer will need to have a short overlap of the two sounds. That is, he will need about ten to sixteen frames where both sounds are running simultaneously. This is generally accomplished by putting *extensions* on each of the tracks.

To understand what extensions are look at Figure 13.1. In it we show two pieces of track one marked "Abby's Shot" and the other marked "Bob's Shot." These correspond to the two slightly different sounds from the two different setups. If the mixer were to mix the tracks like this there would be a change in the sound at the point where one ends and the other begins. This change, called a *bump*, would be slightly annoying to the audience.

Instead, Chuck or Liz would go through the entire take of Abby's shot and look for a short section where there was no noise, only background sound (this means there would only be general tone, no audible sound at all). They would remove this small section and attach it to the end of Abby's shot. They would then try and find a section of tone from the entire take of Bob's shot and attach it to the head of the dialogue piece on the second track. This would leave the tracks looking something like Figure 13.2. After the mixer had adjusted all of his settings so that the two tracks matched as best as they could then he would be able to run both together and one would automatically segue into the other.

Finding this tone is not as easy as it sounds. Often there are only six or seven frames that you can find where the actor or director isn't talking or where some crew person isn't moving some piece of equipment around. Immediately after the slate hits and before the director calls "action" or at the end of a take after the actor or

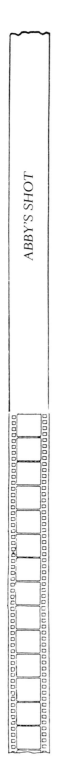

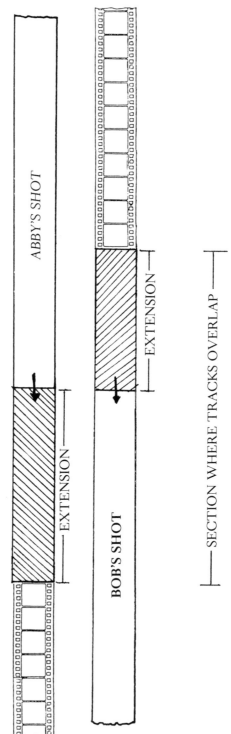

ABBY'S SHOT

BOB'S SHOT

FIGURE 13.1   A pair of dialogue tracks after splitting but before any extensions have been put on (the film portion on the tracks is soundtrack fill). If the sounds were to be mixed this way the mixer would have no capability to ease from one track into another.

ABBY'S SHOT

EXTENSION

EXTENSION

BOB'S SHOT

|— SECTION WHERE TRACKS OVERLAP —|

FIGURE 13.2   After extension, the tracks can be cross-faded during the overlapping section.

actress has finished but before the director calls "cut" are good places to look.

Often, if there isn't enough tone in one take, Chuck could try another take of the same setup. Another trick is to find about two feet of tone on one take, make it into a loop and then transfer twenty or thirty feet of it onto another piece of 35mm sound track. He would then use the tone from the loop rather than the original track for his extensions. If he cannot find two feet, he might make several transfers of the piece (he might have some transferred forward and some backward to help him cut them together) to make the length necessary.

Looking for these extensions is rather time-consuming and tedious and it is the kind of task that sound editors would prefer to give to their assistants rather than do themselves. Liz would most probably end up spending hours poring over takes and making loops, ending up with hundreds of tiny little trims in her barrel.

In the case where there is an isolated noise that Chuck wants to get rid of, these sounds can be cut out of the track. This of course produces a *hole*, a section of the track where the sound drops out. This hole is filled by putting tone from the take either on another track (which the mixer will then fade into and out of the scene to cover the hole) or cut directly into the track to replace the fill at the hole. Liz or Chuck would be very careful and listen to see if the tone inserted at the hole exactly matches the tone immediately before and after it. If not, they would cut the tone onto another track so that the mixer could treat it with extensions.

Looping

There are cases where these unwanted noises can come directly on top of a line of dialogue. In this case there is no way to remove the noise without also removing the line of dialogue. This type of case is treated very much like the third case of dialogue editing—where an entire scene is unusable because of lousy sound. The only way to cure these problems is with looping.

As I mentioned in the last chapter, looping is the process of rerecording words or lines that have been ruined in some way. The way in which this is done resembles the foley process because both are attempting to do the same thing—record some sound (either a foley or a looped line) directly in sync to a picture.

Looping got its name because lines used to be recorded by cutting them into a loop in which the line of dialogue would be followed by a piece of fill exactly the same length as the line. When this was made into a loop and played back the actor or actress would hear his or her line followed by a space. Then the line would repeat, then the space. And on and on. This would enable the actor or actress to repeat the line immediately after hearing it. This is what would be recorded.

Today, looping is no longer done with loops but in a process known either as *ADR (Automatic Dialogue Replacement)* or *EPS (Electronic Post Sync)*. The actor or actress faces the screen and hears, in a set of headphones, the dialogue immediately leading up to the line to be replaced. As the line approaches they see a streamer and hear three beeps. At the moment the streamer hits the right side of the screen they are to begin their line. The beeps are another clue to the timing.

This requires a certain amount of preparation on the part of the looping editor and assistant. The first order of business is obviously to decide which things need to be looped. This is usually done at a big screening with Chuck, Wendy, and Adam. The kinds of things that determine whether a line should be looped are whether there are extraneous noises over it, whether it is audible, whether it is comprehensible, and whether it is the reading that the director wants. Sometimes the director will want to change the performance of a line or even its wording.

Another reason for looping a line is to obtain a television line. This is an alternate wording of a line which does not contain an objectionable word that was in the original to be used in the "soft" or television version of the film.

Often it is necessary to record lines for off-screen or background characters that were not gotten on the set. In a scene where a lead character is talking to someone at a party the sound recordist would never want to mike the scene so that the background characters could be heard and disturb the lead's dialogue. In fact, in many cases the extras performing the parts of background partyers merely *mime* their conversation without actually saying anything. This gives the cleanest track possible for the lead character's dialogue. Later on, of course, the background chatter must be added, probably by a library sound effect of party walla.

After it has been determined just what lines need to be looped then the actors and actresses involved should be booked for looping sessions. This should be done by the producer since it involves calling agents and actors and actresses to determine their availability. The looping department should advise the producer's office of just how much time is needed with each actor or actress and give them a deadline for completion of the looping.

At this time the assistant looping editor would take one looping dupe and go through it, pulling out the sections that include the selected lines. Before doing this, however, it is important to plan ahead just how these pulled sections are going to be rebuilt into reels for projection in the looping studio. First, it must be understood how the looping process works. Usually, one actor or actress will come in and do all of his or her lines. Then the next person will come in and do all of his or her lines. In order to avoid time-consuming downtimes as reels are taken off the projector and other reels put on, it is helpful to have all of a single character's looped lines together on one reel (or a set of reels if there are to be a lot of looped lines). In *Star Wars*, for instance, all of Harrison Ford's scenes to be looped would have been on one set of reels and all of Carrie Fisher's would have been on another. Of course, there were scenes where both of them played together and would be working off the same dupe. If there are a lot of scenes like this then it is better to get another dupe and to make separate reels for each character with the duplicate scene. If there are, however, only one or two cases where this occurs, then it is not uncommon to unbuild the scene from Harrison Ford's *character reel* (as it is called) and build it into Carrie Fisher's.

Once all of the scenes have been pulled out of the looping dupe and rebuilt into character reels then the reels are given to the looping editor. The editor then proceeds by marking up exactly where he or she would want each loop to begin and where each would end. This is not as self-evident as it all sounds. Some actors and actresses get tired faster than others. It is often difficult to loop long lines and get good sync in all parts of the lines. On the other hand, it is unwise to break down the lines too much since that would break up the actor's or actress's concentration and create a stiff, unnatural rendition of each line. Some middle ground has to be found. A good looping editor will be able to make intelligent choices.

While the editor is marking up the character reels, he or she should also be making a *looping cue sheet* (see Figure 13.3) listing

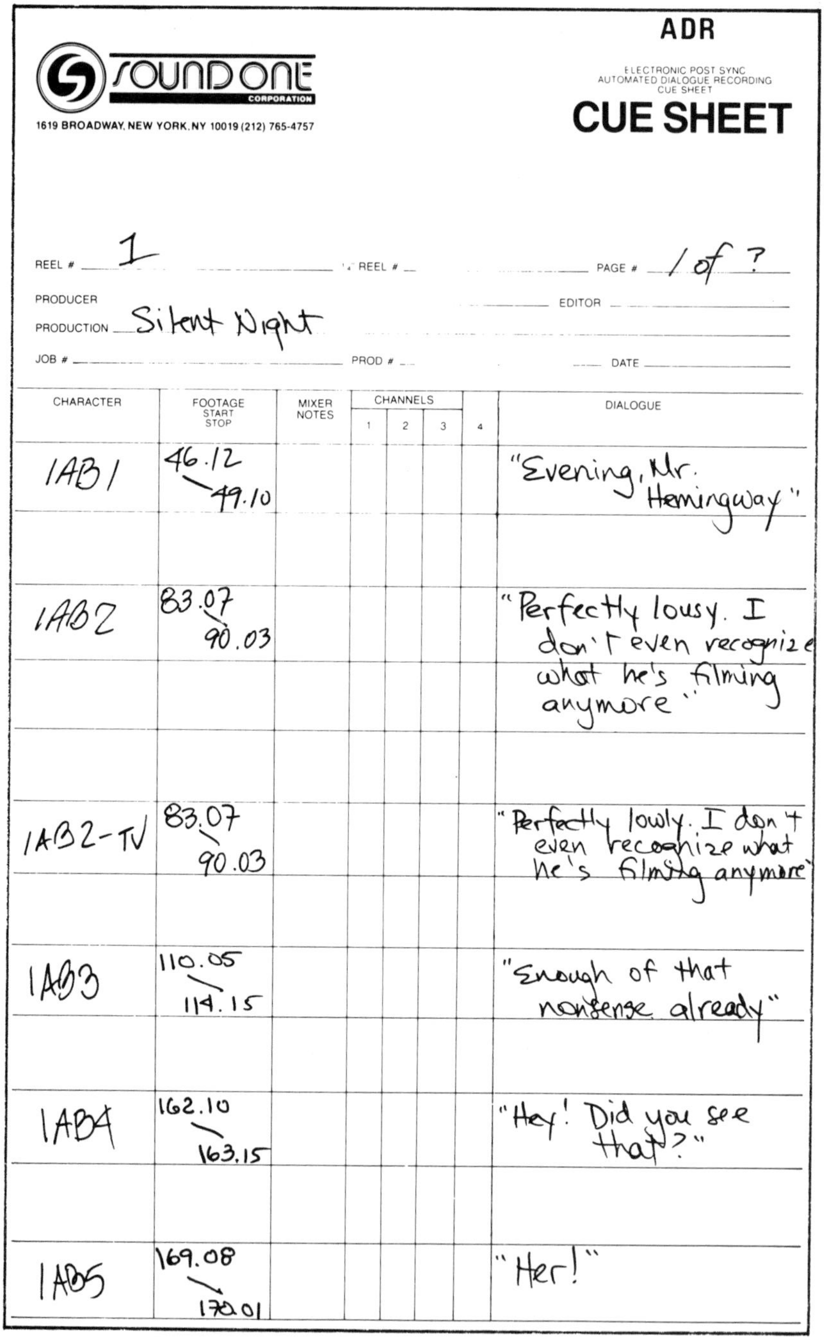

ADR

ELECTRONIC POST SYNC
AUTOMATED DIALOGUE RECORDING
CUE SHEET

CUE SHEET

SOUND ONE
CORPORATION
1619 BROADWAY, NEW YORK, NY 10019 (212) 765-4757

REEL # ___1___   REEL # ___   PAGE # ___1 of ?___

PRODUCER ___

PRODUCTION ___Silent Night___   EDITOR ___

JOB # ___   PROD # ___   DATE ___

CHARACTER	FOOTAGE START STOP	MIXER NOTES	CHANNELS				DIALOGUE
			1	2	3	4	
1AB1	46.12 / 49.10						"Evening, Mr. Hemingway"
1AB2	83.07 / 90.03						"Perfectly lousy. I don't even recognize what he's filming anymore"
1AB2-TV	83.07 / 90.03						"Perfectly lowly. I don't even recognize what he's filming anymore"
1AB3	110.05 / 114.15						"Enough of that nonsense already"
1AB4	162.10 / 163.15						"Hey! Did you see that?"
1AB5	169.08 / 170.01						"Her!"

FIGURE 13.3 A looping cue sheet. Each of the lines is given a unique number. (Courtesy Sound One Corp.)

each loop by a loop number, footage on the character reel, and the line to be done. Loop numbers are assigned by character, reel number, and sequential number of the loop. On the example given we see the looping for Abby's lines in Scene 10, which would fall on reel 1. The first line ("Evening Mister Hemingway") is given the number 1AB1 which stands for the Abby's (AB) first (the one at the end of the number) for reel number 1 (the number one before the letters "AB"). If this was the twentieth line on reel 3 for Abby the number would be 3AB20. If this was the first line for reel 10 it would be 10AB1. Other systems are also used. The crucial thing for any system, however, should be that it uniquely and quickly identify each character and reel number.

The footage listed on the cue sheet is normally the first modulation of sound of the line. Most ADR studios cannot use this number to set their equipment (when they set a footage on their machines the machine will automatically set the beeps so that the beeps lead up to a given footage; that setting also determines exactly where the machine will stop playing back the track to the actor or actress and where it will begin recording them). Most studios cannot use the exact first modulation since there are a few frames of time before the recorder completely kicks in. For that reason the studio will ask you to make all of your footages a certain number of frames before the first modulation. The exact number will vary but they usually run from four to six frames.

After the editor has finished with the character reels he or she gives them to an assistant. The assistant will then redo the sheets to conform to the correct footage (including the requested four- to six-frame advance) and, at the same time, mark streamers on the dupe to that frame. These streamers are placed on the film in exactly the same manner as foley streamers are. On the redone sheets the assistant should make sure that the line to be done is also listed completely and correctly. The assistant will also check any notes that he or she has to make sure that the looping editor has marked all of the lines that were requested to be looped. With all of the preparation involved in looping, it is important not to have to make any additions at the last moment.

These redone sheets can be made in two ways. One way is to have them typed in a slightly different form (see Figure 13.4A). This new form lists each line on its own page. The line is typed at the top of the form in very large letters so that it is easy for the

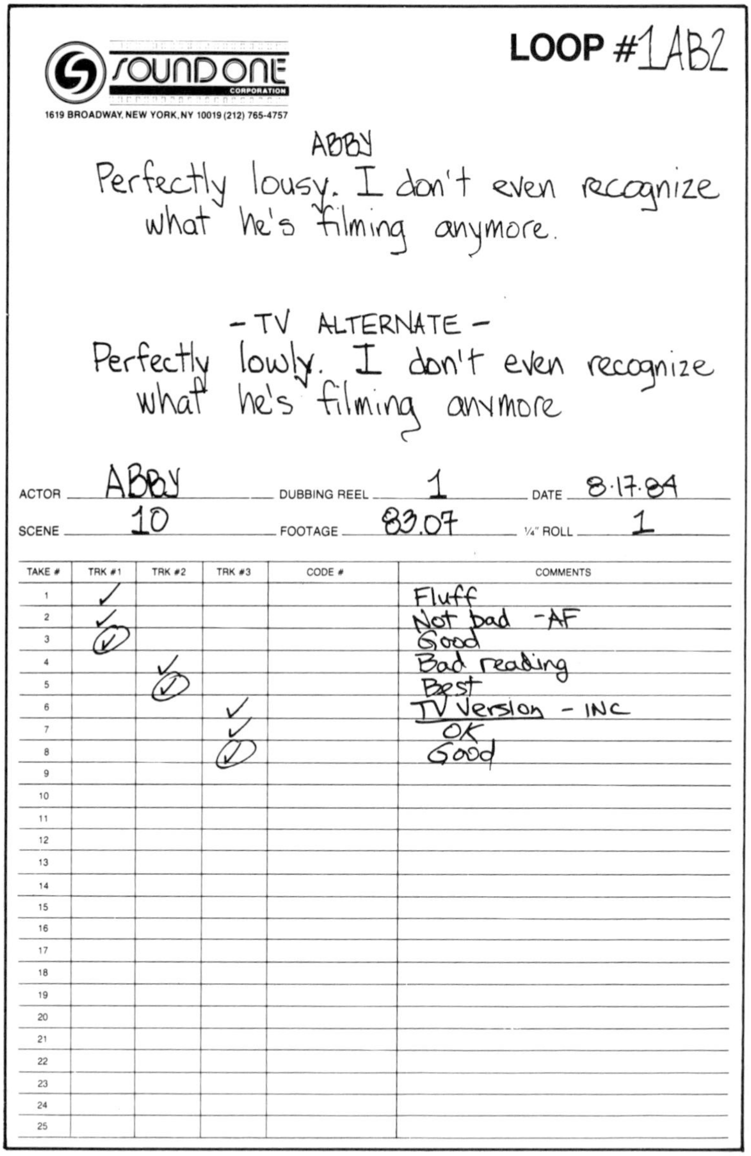

FIGURE 13.4 Two versions of finished looping cue sheets. In the first (A), each looped line is given its own page. At the session the information at the bottom of the sheet is filled in. In this case, Adam didn't like takes one and two enough to save them, so take three was the first saved take (on track one). Take five was the next saved take (on track two). In addition, the actor was also requested to give an alternate reading for a television ver-

ADR

SOUND ONE CORPORATION
1619 BROADWAY, NEW YORK, NY 10019 (212) 765-4757

ELECTRONIC POST SYNC
AUTOMATED DIALOGUE RECORDING
CUE SHEET

CUE SHEET

REEL # __ONE__   ¼" REEL # __1__   PAGE # __1 OF 7__

PRODUCER __Big Time Film Co.__   EDITOR __Geraldine Smith__

PRODUCTION __Silent Night, Silent Cowboy__

JOB # __—__   PROD # __   DATE __8·17·84__

CHARACTER	FOOTAGE START STOP	MIXER NOTES	CHANNELS				DIALOGUE
			1	2	3	4	
1AB1	46.12 / 49.10		②	③	⑤		"Evening Mister Hemingway"
1AB2	83.07 / 90.03			③	⑤	—	"Perfectly lousy. I don't even recognize what he's filming anymore."
1AB2-TV	83.07 / 90.03		—	—	—	⑧	"Perfectly lowly. I don't even recognize what he's filming anymore"

B

sion of the film. The third take (take eight) of the TV version was the best and was saved onto track three of the fullcoat. All eight takes were saved onto ¼-inch roll number one. The second version of the finished looping cue sheet (B) provides similar information for more than one loop. A disadvantage of this form is that the information on it is less complete. (Courtesy Sound One Corp.)

actor or actress to read in the looping studio. At the bottom is a form to take notes on at the session.

The other system is simply to type up the same looping cue sheet that we've already seen into a readable form (large type is used here too). This puts many looped lines on one page and may slightly complicate things for the actor or actress. It does, however, reduce the amount of paperwork involved (see Figure 13.4B).

The assistant should call the looping studio and make sure that they have the proper amount of stock for the session. Just as in the foley session, the looped lines will be recorded onto 35mm three-stripe or full-coat stock. In addition the lines will also be recorded onto quarter-inch magnetic tape. We will see why in just a minute.

On the day of the session, the assistant should show up a little early with the reels to be looped and give them to the projectionist and the sound people. A copy of the lines to be looped should be given to the looping editor, to the director, and to the actor or actress. The assistant should also retain a copy for his or her own notes.

The looping process works like this. The film is rolled and everyone listens to the dupe track. The engineer recording the lines announces a slate which goes onto the quarter-inch tape only. The slate will be something like "Loop 1AB7, Take 3." The actor, Abby in this case, watches the screen while listening to the track in his headphones. He sees the streamer and hears the beeps, then begins the line while watching the film, attempting to match his line to the lip movements on the screen, as well as trying to recreate the feeling of the scene (this is why the ADR/EPS system is nicer than the old looping system—he gets to see and hear the entire scene, which the assistant should have included in the character reel). The first take of the loop gets placed on channel A of the full-coat. If it is unacceptable (either for sync, acting, or because of a fluff) then take two is made on the same channel, wiping out the old one. However, the take is not erased on the quarter-inch tape. In this way, if a line doesn't work in the editing room or at the mix, there is always this backup to go to.

Once an acceptable take is done the director may want to do another one, either for safety or for a different reading. The director may like a reading on one but the sync is not good (the looping editor should be very active in advising the director just what is acceptable, what is passable, and what is good in terms of sync). In these cases, the take on channel A is saved and another take is made onto channel B.

At the bottom of the second type of looping cue sheet (see Figure 13.4) is a chart on which either the looping editor or assistant should be taking notes. In this example, Loop #1AB3 (Abby's third loop on reel 1) the first three takes went onto track 1, of which the second reading was "not bad" according to Adam but the third one was the best. The next two went onto channel B, where the best take was take 5. Track 3 was reserved for a television line of which take 8 was the best.

In addition to these lines, the director may request certain wild lines from the actor. This may be something that he wants to experiment with, or something for an off-screen line. Since there is no 35mm film to go by the line will be recorded only onto the quarter-inch tape. The assistant should make a note as to exactly where these wild lines are. The best way to do this is to keep a separate wild line log which lists each take of each wild line recorded, along with the quarter-inch reel number it was recorded on, the date it was recorded, where on the tape it was recorded (e.g., "After 3AB21"), and any other information on it (the scene it is for, where it is supposed to go in the scene, comments, etc.).

Cutting In the Looped Lines

After the day's looping the 35mm full-coats should be transferred to three separate 35mm stripes. Each of the three should be lined up, using the beep which was transferred from your head leader (you did remember to put a head leader with a beep at the nine-foot mark, didn't you?). They should then be coded in sync with each other. In the case of the first reel of Abby's looping I would code the transfers from the A channel 1AB1000, the B channel transfers for the same reel 1AB2000 and the C channel transfers 1AB3000. By a lucky coincidence, if you code the black and white dupe of Abby's first character reel 1AB0000, then (unless you did any moving around of the 35mm full-coat to accommodate lines which required saving more than three takes) all four things will line up which will help the looping editor cut the loops into the film.

All of the lines should be broken down after coding and flanged up with cinetabs. The lines should be logged in a logbook (there is also a column on the looping cue sheet for the code numbers). Then when the looping editor is ready to cut in the looping it will be a simple matter to give the editor all of the loops for the reel that he or she needs.

The looping editor is concerned with much the same sort of thing that the foley editor is concerned with. Even though the loops were recorded directly to picture there are always tiny adjustments which need to be made in order to make the line look exactly in sync. As the editor cuts the loops he or she will be marking the footage on the loops (the editor will be cutting to a second looping dupe, one which was never broken down at all and conforms exactly to the way the picture is cut) and hanging them in barrels and making scratch cue sheets, just as the foley and sound effects editors do. Later on these will either be built into their own reels or integrated into the split dialogue tracks. In either case, they will be entered onto the main cue sheets.

Any words or lines which are to be replaced by looped lines are physically removed from the dialogue tracks (where they are usually replaced by tone). They are shifted over to another set of tracks reserved exclusively for dialogue pieces removed for looped lines. These are generally called the X and Y tracks. There, the pieces sit ready to be used if Adam decides at the mix that he does not want to use a looped line but prefers the original better (this happens all the time; it is difficult to know whether a line is really superior to the original until the sound editor and mixer have done all of their clean-up work on it). For this reason the X and Y tracks should also be prepared just as if they were going to be used in the mix. This will involve inserting tone in between sections and removing unwanted noises that do not affect the dialogue.

Once all these things have been done then the tracks can be built just as effects tracks are built. Dialogue tracks are never integrated with effects tracks but are kept separate, though they are listed on the same cue sheet.

14

MUSIC EDITING

Eventually, as the film's editing is almost complete, Adam's thoughts will turn toward music—in particular, what kind of music would be exactly right for *Silent Night*.

Perhaps Adam will have decided that he wishes to work with the same composer that he's worked with on other films. Perhaps he will have decided that he wants no music, or to use pieces of already recorded music. Or perhaps he will have decided to take a chance on a new composer. But, if there is to be any type of music at all in the film there will have to be a music editor.

On many Hollywood low-budget and New York films, if there is to be very little music the picture editor functions as a quasi-music editor, primarily assisting the composer in getting his timings and then laying in the tracks (don't worry, we'll learn about these terms in a short while). But even if this is the case, there will always have to be someone functioning as a music editor. That is what this chapter is all about.

There is already a good book for the music editor which lays out many of the music editor tasks. *Music Editing for Motion Pictures*, by Milton Lustig, discusses many of the tasks that a music editor must perform and some of the techniques for editing music. I would recommend the book for those with a further interest in the subject.

Before the Scoring Session

The music editor faces two major tasks. The first is to prepare the composer so that he or she can write the music, and the second is to edit it to the film. To do the first he or she must know the film fairly well.

Let's say that you've hired Nate High to be your music editor and he has hired Betty Bound as his assistant. The first thing that they must do is to see the film as many times as they can. Then there must be a *spotting session*. A spotting session is usually held with the music editor and assistant, editor, and director. Spotting sessions can be held either in a projection room where the film can be run forward and backward, or in an editing room. The director will go through the film reel by reel explaining where he wants the music, what kind of music he wants and where he wants accents in the music. The composer will ask for *adjectives* so that he can better interpret just what it is the director wants musically. Meanwhile, Nate and Betty should be furiously taking notes.

Let's say that we are going to be spotting Scenes 8, 9, 10, and 11 (see Figure 4.5). You may remember that these are the scenes where Abby looks on at the shooting of a barroom fight. We then cut to the parking lot that evening as Abby, and the rest of the studio workers, leave work. Abby goes to his car, turns on his engine, and sits watching the cars leave. He then closes the side door (which he had left open) and leaves. We cut to Abby as he walks into his apartment, looks around, goes to get a drink and then, hearing a typewriter from the other room, exits and goes to his bedroom. There, at a desk, sits Bob, a neighbor. They begin talking.

Adam's idea for scoring this scene is that the music should begin in the barroom set, continue through the parking lot and into the apartment scene where it should go out.

Nate wants to know where in the apartment it will go out.

The composer suggests that it cross-fade (segue) into the sounds of the typewriter as Abby notices them.

They will all discuss the character of the music and when it should change.

When the spotting session is over Nate will have a list of where all of the music cues will begin and end in the film. Copies of this list should be given to the sound editors so that they know exactly where music is planned for the film (it will help them in the choice of effects and how they plan them out). It is then time to do the *music timing sheets* for the composer.

Nate will sit down with a dupe of the film and his and Betty's notes and go through the film marking the exact point where the music is to begin at each musical cue. Each music cue will be given a number much like the looping numbers. The fifth cue on reel two would be called 2M5 (other editors prefer to call it cue 205). Each cue will be given a title which is used for identification and copyright purposes.

Nate will go through the reels marking every potential accent point in every single musical cue. On a timing sheet (see Figure 14.1) he would list everything that the composer might ever want to accent musically. Normally, composers only use about 10 percent of this information but they rarely know ahead of time which 10 percent it will be so the music editor must detail practically everything. The sheet also includes the dialogue because it is very important that the composer's music not conflict with the dialogue.

You will also notice that the timing sheet lists the cues in terms of sequential time from the beginning of each cue. This figure is the only really useful figure for the composer. But there is another figure—the footage in the reel—which is important to the editor. Sometimes the editor will make a scratch timing sheet which will include the footages, though they are not retyped onto the final timing sheet (I use a small Apple computer at home and ask it to print out sheets either with or without footages depending upon my need). Most often, these timings (in minutes and seconds) can be taken directly off a second counter on the Moviola or flatbed which is zeroed out at the start of every cue. Sometimes, if such a counter is not available, it may be necessary to convert these footages to timings.

As the timing sheets are being made up and typed, copies are given to the composer. He or she will then write the music for each cue based on the numbers Nate has given. As the composer writes each cue he or she will determine a tempo (speed) for the piece. Rhythms in film are given not in metronome settings but in *clicks*. These are numbers that look something like this: 12/0 or 16/4. The click number represents the number of frames for each beat of music. Each frame is divided into eight parts, each corresponding to half of a sprocket. So a 12/0 click would mean that there were twelve frames for each beat of music (this is the equivalent of two beats of music each second or, for the musicians reading this, 120 beats per minute). A 16/4 click means that there are sixteen and one-half frames per beat (four-eighths of a frame is one-half of a frame).

All of this is important because, after the composer determines the click of each cue, the assistant will have to set up each cue with

```
                                           August 8, 1984

                 Cue 1M3 -- "Abby Meets Sean"

0:00.0           Begin cue as ABBY looks up, shock on his face.

0:02.6           Cut to SEAN.

0:05.2           Cut back to ABBY shaking his head.

0:10.7               BOB (o.s.): "Are you okay?"

0:15.2           Cut to SEAN.

0:19.8               She turns to look at us.

0:26.2           Cut to ABBY.

0:28.5               He quickly turns back to his hot dog.

0:35.0           Cut to BOB, looking around quizzically.  Something is
                 going  wrong with his friend and he has no idea   what
                 it is.

0:39.6               BOB: "Abby... "

0:44.2               BOB: (finishes) "... going crackers."

0:46.0           Cut to ABBY.  He looks at BOB.

0:52.1               ABBY: "It's okay."

0:55.7               He turns back to SEAN.

0:56.5               Shock!!!

1:01.2           Cut to his p.o.v.  SEAN is gone.

1:09.8           Cut back to ABBY.

1:12.3               End cue as ABBY bolts upright out of his seat.


                 Adam's notes:
                     "We  want to mislead the audience  into   thinking
                 that Abby is falling in love."
                     "Begin  schmaltzy  but change it at the  shot  of
                 BOB.  It should become funnier here."
                     "ABBY  is  insecure.   He needs BOB but he  can't
                 figure  out   why.   ABBY needs something after  his
                 terrible day -- BOB, SEAN, a new job -- he's just not
                 sure what that something is."
```

FIGURE 14.1   A timing sheet. The composer will use these timings
to determine exactly where his musical accents should fall. Adam's
notes are very important as they are a record of what he wanted the
music to be like.

streamers so that, during the recording session, the conductor will
be able to look at the film and see where the piece is to come in.
   Streamers are usually placed on the film at several places in the

music cue. The beginning and end of each cue is streamered so the composer can know when to start and finish. Any places inside the cue that the composer wants to accent will also be streamered. Finally, there will often be streamers leading up to the first *warning click* or *free click* before the piece begins.

When a cue is to be recorded to a click track (sometimes called an *electric metronome*) the conductor will need to hear some clicks before the cue begins so he can give the count-off to the musicians (this is the "and a-one . . . and a-two . . . and a-three . . ." that you often hear). The tempo at which the conductor gives the musicians these counts will determine the tempo at which the song is played. In addition, many of the musicians are fed this click track while they are playing. The click track is a repetitive dull clicking sound that is adjustable to the tempo needed.

The composer will tell Nate how many clicks are needed before the beginning of the music. All that is needed, then, is to determine the length (in feet and frames) for the required number of clicks/beats. When that is determined, a streamer can be placed on the film. When this is projected at the recording session this streamer will cue Nate to begin the click track generator.

Let me give an example. Let's say that cue 1M3 ("The Barroom Fight") is the musical cue to be streamered. The composer has written the piece in a 17/2 tempo and has requested eight free clicks. There is a book called *Project Tempo* which is also known as the *Click Track Book*. This lists, for most tempi, the footages for every beat from the first beat to the six-hundredth. For my own use, I have developed a computer program to do the same thing, a page of which is reproduced in Figure 14.2. This sample page lists the data for a 17/2 click.

To find the length of film needed for eight free clicks at 17/2 Betty needs to realize that if the first free click is the first beat then the first beat of the song would be on the ninth beat. She would then look for the length listed for beat number nine, which is eight feet, ten frames. She would then place the music dupe in the synchronizer so that the first frame of the song (which Nate should have previously marked) falls at 8'10. She would then roll back to 0'00. That will be the first frame of the clicks. She could then make a streamer three feet long leading up to this 0'00 frame.

Going into a recording session with the complete dupe of the movie is a fantastically time-consuming way of working; the music

The click is a 12/4					Metronome setting = 115.2				
0	**1**	**2**	**3**	**4**	**5**	**6**	**7**	**8**	**9**
0 0-00	0-0	0-12	1-9	2-5	3-2	3-14	4-11	5-7	6-4
00:00.00	0:0	0:.52	0:1.04	0:1.56	0:2.08	0:2.6	0:3.12	0:3.64	0:4.16
10 7-0	7-13	8-9	9-6	10-2	10-15	11-11	12-8	13-4	14-1
0:4.68	0:5.2	0:5.72	0:6.25	0:6.77	0:7.29	0:7.81	0:8.33	0:8.85	0:9.37
20 14-13	15-10	16-6	17-3	17-15	18-12	19-8	20-5	21-1	21-14
0:9.89	0:10.41	0:10.93	0:11.45	0:11.97	0:12.5	0:13.02	0:13.54	0:14.06	0:14.58
30 22-10	23-7	24-3	25-0	25-12	26-9	27-5	28-2	28-14	29-11
0:15.1	0:15.62	0:16.14	0:16.66	0:17.18	0:17.7	0:18.22	0:18.75	0:19.27	0:19.79
40 30-7	31-4	32-0	32-13	33-9	34-6	35-2	35-15	36-11	37-8
0:20.31	0:20.83	0:21.35	0:21.87	0:22.39	0:22.91	0:23.43	0:23.95	0:24.47	0:25
50 38-4	39-1	39-13	40-10	41-6	42-3	42-15	43-12	44-8	45-5
0:25.52	0:26.04	0:26.56	0:27.08	0:27.6	0:28.12	0:28.64	0:29.16	0:29.68	0:30.2
60 46-1	46-14	47-10	48-7	49-3	50-0	50-12	51-9	52-5	53-2
0:30.72	0:31.25	0:31.77	0:32.29	0:32.81	0:33.33	0:33.85	0:34.37	0:34.89	0:35.41
70 53-14	54-11	55-7	56-4	57-0	57-13	58-9	59-6	60-2	60-15
0:35.93	0:36.45	0:36.97	0:37.5	0:38.02	0:38.54	0:39.06	0:39.58	0:40.1	0:40.62
80 61-11	62-8	63-4	64-1	64-13	65-10	66-6	67-3	67-15	68-12
0:41.14	0:41.66	0:42.18	0:42.7	0:43.22	0:43.75	0:44.27	0:44.79	0:45.31	0:45.83
90 69-8	70-5	71-1	71-14	72-10	73-7	74-3	75-0	75-12	76-9
0:46.35	0:46.87	0:47.39	0:47.91	0:48.43	0:48.95	0:49.47	0:50	0:50.52	0:51.04
100 77-5	78-2	78-14	79-11	80-7	81-4	82-0	82-13	83-9	84-6
0:51.56	0:52.08	0:52.6	0:53.12	0:53.64	0:54.16	0:54.68	0:55.2	0:55.72	0:56.25
110 85-2	85-15	86-11	87-8	88-4	89-1	89-13	90-10	91-6	92-3
0:56.77	0:57.29	0:57.81	0:58.33	0:58.85	0:59.37	0:59.89	1:.41	1:.93	1:1.45
120 92-15	93-12	94-8	95-5	96-1	96-14	97-10	98-7	99-3	100-0
1:1.97	1:2.5	1:3.02	1:3.54	1:4.06	1:4.58	1:5.1	1:5.62	1:6.14	1:6.66
130 100-12	101-9	102-5	103-2	103-14	104-11	105-7	106-4	107-0	107-13
1:7.18	1:7.7	1:8.22	1:8.75	1:9.27	1:9.79	1:10.31	1:10.83	1:11.35	1:11.87
140 108-9	109-6	110-2	110-15	111-11	112-8	113-4	114-1	114-13	115-10
1:12.39	1:12.91	1:13.43	1:13.95	1:14.47	1:15	1:15.52	1:16.04	1:16.56	1:17.08
150 116-6	117-3	117-15	118-12	119-8	120-5	121-1	121-14	122-10	123-7
1:17.6	1:18.12	1:18.64	1:19.16	1:19.68	1:20.2	1:20.72	1:21.25	1:21.77	1:22.29
160 124-3	125-0	125-12	126-9	127-5	128-2	128-14	129-11	130-7	131-4
1:22.81	1:23.33	1:23.85	1:24.37	1:24.89	1:25.41	1:25.93	1:26.45	1:26.97	1:27.5
170 132-0	132-13	133-9	134-6	135-2	135-15	136-11	137-8	138-4	139-1
1:28.02	1:28.54	1:29.06	1:29.58	1:30.1	1:30.62	1:31.14	1:31.66	1:32.18	1:32.7
180 139-13	140-10	141-6	142-3	142-15	143-12	144-8	145-5	146-1	146-14
1:33.22	1:33.75	1:34.27	1:34.79	1:35.31	1:35.83	1:36.35	1:36.87	1:37.39	1:37.91
190 147-10	148-7	149-3	150-0	150-12	151-9	152-5	153-2	153-14	154-11
1:38.43	1:38.95	1:39.47	1:40	1:40.52	1:41.04	1:41.56	1:42.08	1:42.6	1:43.12
200 155-7	156-4	157-0	157-13	158-9	159-6	160-2	160-15	161-11	162-8
1:43.64	1:44.16	1:44.68	1:45.2	1:45.72	1:46.25	1:46.77	1:47.29	1:47.81	1:48.33
210 163-4	164-1	164-13	165-10	166-6	167-3	167-15	168-12	169-8	170-5
1:48.85	1:49.37	1:49.89	1:50.41	1:50.93	1:51.45	1:51.97	1:52.5	1:53.02	1:53.54
220 171-1	171-14	172-10	173-7	174-3	175-0	175-12	176-9	177-5	178-2
1:54.06	1:54.58	1:55.1	1:55.62	1:56.14	1:56.66	1:57.18	1:57.7	1:58.22	1:58.75
230 178-14	179-11	180-7	181-4	182-0	182-13	183-9	184-6	185-2	185-15
1:59.27	1:59.79	2:.31	2:.83	2:1.35	2:1.87	2:2.39	2:2.91	2:3.43	2:3.95
240 186-11	187-8	188-4	189-1	189-13	190-10	191-6	192-3	192-15	193-12
2:4.47	2:5	2:5.52	2:6.04	2:6.56	2:7.08	2:7.6	2:8.12	2:8.64	2:9.16

FIGURE 14.2   A page from a click track book. This page is for a 12/4 click. Both the footage and the time from the first click can be found. The length from the first beat to any other beat, say, the sixty-fifth, can be found by looking at the numbers at the intersection of the sixties row and the fives column. The top of the two numbers is the number of feet and frames from the first beat (50 feet, 0 frames). The numbers underneath it give the time (33.33 seconds). (Courtesy the author)

dupe should be broken apart so that only those sections that need to be scored go to the sessions. Because of the time needed to get

```
        "S I L E N T   N I G H T ,   S I L E N T   C O W B O Y"
                    Scoring Reel Sheets
                       Page 1 of 3


                                        Wednesday, September 12, 1984
                                        Evergreen Studios
                                        9:30am - 4:30pm (+1hr)


      #         Title            Start   Click  Free   Time        Comments


Scoring Reel # 1

1M1       Main Titles           30.00    Free   ---   1:13.2

1M3       Abby Meets Sean       171.10   16/2    4    1:12.3    Internal streamer
                                                                  at 56.5.

10M4      End Titles            312.06   Free   ---   2:13.0

3M1       Going Home            552.11   12/0    8    1:56.7    Don't use guide

3M2       Abby Returns          749.08   12/0    8    0:20.4

4M4       The Baseball Game     793.05   10/6    8    1:51.6


Scoring Reel # 2

5M7       The Shoot-Out         40.00    Free   ---   0:32.2    Alternates.
                                                                Use same pix
5M7alt    The Shoot-Out - alt   40.00    Free   ---   0:32.2     + trk

8M3       The Beach             112.12   16/4    4    2:17.2

6M2       Return to "La Bar"    337.09   Free   ---   1:52.3

4M3       Backstage @"La Bar"   560.03   Free   ---   1:47.6
```

FIGURE 14.3   A page from a scoring reel list. The footages are continuous footages within the scoring reels. Note that the cue titles are
usually the same as those on the detailed reel continuity (Fig. 8.5).

the projectors up to proper speed and the time necessary to make
the necessary slates, which we will discuss shortly, Betty should
remove about thirty feet more at the head of the cue than needs to
be recorded. About twenty feet before the beginning of the free
clicks she should mark a start mark on both the picture and track
dupes. This mark will give the projectionist an easy way to thread
up at the beginning of each cue every time there is another take or
a playback of that particular piece of music (and, believe me, there
will be plenty).

The reels that will be going to the scoring sessions should be
leadered properly and contain the cues in the order that they are to
be recorded (this is determined by the composer, the copyist, or the
arranger).

At the end of every musical cue, and before the leader slug, I also like to leave twenty or so feet of the dupe so that the picture won't cut off so abruptly as the music ends.

When all of the reels have been built then Betty should have a list of cues typed up (see Figure 14.3). This chart gives all the information that anyone at the recording sessions might need to set up the mechanics of the recording.

At the Scoring Session

On the day of the scoring session the assistant should get to the recording studio early. Copies of the scoring sheets should be given to all technical personnel.

Betty should have brought along with her the click track book, all of the timing sheets, the continuity for the movie, a stop watch, plenty of note paper, and a few editing room supplies (a splicer, splicing tape, a ruler, grease pencils, etc.) in case changes need to be made in the scoring reels. All of these things might come in very handy in case the session does not go exactly as planned.

From the recording studio Betty can get some track sheets. These are preprinted sheets like the one shown in Figure 14.4 onto which may be written exactly which instruments are being recorded onto which tracks of the recording tape.

Several recordings are made simultaneously. The first goes directly onto a 35mm piece of full-coat. The instruments are separated into three groups and each group is recorded onto a different channel. There is some leakage of one group onto the channels of other groups because they are all playing at the same time into open microphones. But this separation will enable the music engineer to have more control over the sound.

A second copy of the music is made onto a piece of half-inch recording tape, which has four tracks on it—one for a 60 hertz sync pulse and three for the three channels of music on the full-coat. The third recording is made onto twenty-four-track tape. This tape is two inches wide and it has twenty-four different tracks on it, so that, for instance, the string section can be split into violins, violas, cellos, and basses if the engineer desires. This gives the engineer much more flexibility in the recording of the music since many things can

EVERGREEN RECORDING STUDIOS	NAB ☒ 15 IPS ☐	MACHINE # _____	
4403 W MAGNOLIA BLVD / BURBANK CA 91505 / (213) 841-6800	DOLBY ☒ 30 IPS ☒	VSO# _____ FREQ. ___	FILE NUMBER
	MSTR EDITED BY _____	DATE _____	REEL # _____ OF ____

TITLE _Silent Night, Silent Cowboy - Cue 1M1_   MASTER # _6_   DATE _4·19·84_

ARTIST _Big Time Film Co._   STUDIO _A_   J.O. # _8352436_

PRODUCER _L. von Beethoven_   ENGINEER _R. Riccio_   ASST. _TLM_

- TRACK PLACEMENT -

1 Hi-Hat (4 COUNTS)	2 Bass GTR (DIR)	3 Bs DRM	4 SNARE
5	6	7	8
(L)——— DRUM KIT ——— (R)		12-STRING GTR	6-STRING GTR
9	10	11	12
(L)——— PIANO ——— (R)		ELEC. GTR (DIR) O/D - 4/26/84	LD. VOCAL O/D - 4/25/84
13 VOCAL - DBL O/D - 4/25/84	14 (L)——— FLUTES ——— (R) O/D - 4/27/84	15	16 HORNS O/D - 4/27/84
17 VLN I O/D - 4/27/84	18 VLN II O/D - 4/27/84	19 VLA O/D - 4/27/84	20 CELLI O/D - 4/27/84
21 Bs O/D - 4/27/84	22	23 SMPTE Code 01:07:12:10	24 60 Hz SYNC

COMMENT _Cue 1M1 - Main Titles_

                                        TK 6 ✓·2:16

Form 4403-4-79

FIGURE 14.4 A track sheet for cue 1M1. Two types of sync pulses were laid down—a normal 60-hertz sync pulse (on track 24) and a video SMPTE time code (on track 23). The number in box 23 is the actual time code existent on the track for the selected take (take six). The first ten tracks were recorded all at once (on April 19). The other tracks were added later (overdubbed), on the dates shown. One track has been left open for technical reasons. (Courtesy Evergreen Recording Studios)

be changed later and the original mix does not have to be precisely right.

On some films that I've worked on *(Hair, Fame, Rollover)* we made the original recordings solely on twenty-four-track tape and mixed down to fewer tracks later. If this is the case, however, there will be certain other problems. First, since the music will no longer be on sprocketed film there must be a way of making sure that the tape runs at exactly the right speed every time it is played, from recording all the way to the end of the film mixing process. This is accomplished in one of two ways—either through the use of a 60 hertz sync pulse (just as is placed on quarter-inch tape for sync) or through the use of the SMPTE Code described in the section on video editing in Chapter 17. Both forms of sync are acceptable but since we are in a transition period where both types of sync are used I prefer to put both on the tape, rather than risk the case where I would have to go to another studio where they do not use the one type of sync that I had chosen to be on the tape. I generally put the two sync pulses on tracks 23 and 24 of the tape.

The assignment of instruments to individual tracks should be listed on the track layout sheet by Betty. Each cue should get its own track sheet if they have different track layouts because of differing orchestrations.

When the first cue is ready to be recorded the picture is rolled. The engineer or the music editor will slate the take ("Cue 1M3, Slate 1"—slate numbers run sequentially from the first take until the end of all of the recording sessions, they should not be restarted for new cues, new tape reels, or new recording sessions) and everyone will look for the streamer. The music editor will have his finger poised over the click track generator machine ready for the streamer to hit the right side of the screen. As soon as it does Nate will press the button beginning the clicks. The conductor will count out the free clicks and then begin conducting the piece while keeping one eye on the film being projected.

During the cue, Nate and Betty should be keeping notes as to the positive and negative aspects of the take. There are often chair squeaks or misplayed notes that are difficult to hear from inside the recording studio but are quite noticeable in the control booth. A take should not be approved until everyone is sure that there are no such objectionable noises on the tape that cannot be mixed out later.

Either Betty or Nate should have also begun a stopwatch at the moment of the first note of music (most recording studios have their own digital stop watches that can be used). At the end of the take Betty should note in a sequential log the length of the piece along with any of the composer's or Nate's comments. The take will not be erased even though it may not be selected as the preferred take at the recording session, and the composer may want to listen to it later at the music mixing session.

At the end of the take the conductor or composer (who are often the same person) will decide immediately whether to do another take or to go on to the next due. If he or she decides to redo the cue Nate or Betty should immediately notify the projectionist who can reload the dupes at the start marks for that cue. If the composer decides to go on then he or she should listen to the take in the control room and discuss its merits technically with the engineer and Nate. If the take is approved then the projectionist should be notified not to return to the top of the cue but to roll down to the next one.

As more and more takes are recorded new reels of tape will be necessary. Betty should keep track of exactly what is on each reel of tape (there will be assistant engineers, sometimes called tape operators, to do this task but it is always very good to have your own notes to refer to).

Something else should be on the head of the first reel or at the tail of the last reel recorded on the first day: a set of alignment tones. These tones provide a standard for the relative recording levels on the tape. When the tape is subsequently played back these volume and equalization controls are set to these standards so the playback will be the same as it was when the tracks were recorded. There should be a middle, a high, and a low frequency tone recorded (usually 1000 hertz, 15,000 hertz and 100 hertz), about forty-five to sixty seconds of each is the norm. In addition, if the original tape was recorded in Dolby® (which it can be regardless of whether the film is to be released in Dolby format) a set of Dolby tones should be recorded.

On normal scored films it is necessary to come to the film mix with three, not twenty-four, tracks of music. If a separate three-track was recorded at the session Nate will use that one as his mix element (and use the half-inch tape as a backup for reprints). If no three-track was made, or if the composer doesn't like the mix on the three-track, then he or she will have to mix down the music.

The normal manner in which this is done is to mix down to

three channels of a four-track half-inch tape (the fourth channel will be used for the 60 hertz sync pulse). A normal mixdown arrangement is to separate the music into strings, rhythm section, and everything else. These three tracks are then transferred onto three-stripe 35mm track film.

Betty should, once again, keep accurate records of what is going onto each track of the mixdown and what mixes are on what half-inch tape reels. It is not uncommon to erase a mix which was no good and record over it. It is also not uncommon for a composer to want to mix down two recorded takes and to have the two cut together to produce one take. Sometimes, this cutting together is done with the recording tape (either with the original two-inch tape or the mixdown half-inch) and then only one take needs to be mixed. At other times, two complete mixes are done and Nate will cut the 35mm mags of those mixes together.

Back in the Editing Room

After all of the recording and mixing is over with, Nate and Betty will end up back in their editing room with a lot of 35mm track and all of the scoring reels. The scoring reels should be taken apart and returned to the music dupe reels from which they came. No marks should be removed from them since Nate will be able to use them to line the music up against the picture.

In addition, all of the 35mm track should be coded. In cases of simple scoring jobs it is not necessary to code each cue and take individually. Instead, each reel of music can be coded (MA1000, MA2000, etc.). When the reels come back from coding they should then be logged and given cinetabs which list the cue number, the name of the cue, and the codes.

The only time when a take must be coded specifically is in the case where there are several prints of the same recorded take (not different takes of the same cue). This can occur when three tracks proved to be too few for the mix, such as when a vocalist is singing with a band that's already on three tracks. In such cases both pieces of three-stripe should be coded so that they line up together in the proper manner. This is done in one of two ways. At the mixdown a short beep would be put across all of the tracks of the twenty-four-track tape (except the sync pulse tracks) before the song began but after the sync pulse was engaged. This beep would be on all of the mixdown tracks and could be used to line up the two mixdown three-stripes with each other.

The other way of lining up tracks is a bit more complicated. After the first mix has been done (that is, after most of the tracks have been mixed down to three tracks on the half-inch tape) then one of the elements that went into that mix is chosen and put onto an open track of the half-inch tape during the next mix. For instance, if there was no room for a vocalist on the first three-track, when it came time to do the second three-track mix you would actually only need one of the three tracks. Transfer the vocal onto track 1 and on track 3 put the drums. In this way, there would be drums on both the first and the second mix. You would not use the drums from the second mix in the film mix but Betty could use them to line up the drums on the first mix. This is done by listening for phasing as described in Chapter 7.

Nate will then cut the music tracks using the marks on his dupe picture. Betty is sure to end up with a lot of trims of music which are primarily head and tail pieces of the take, before and after the music. She will wrap everything up as trims. There may also be a few loop transfers that she will have to supervise and code but, overall, the difficult work for a music assistant does not happen during the editing but during the preparation for the recording session.

After the music tracks have been built (and they will be built in the same way as sound effects tracks) and the cue sheets prepared (some mixers prefer their music tracks listed on separate cue sheets, others want them on with the rest of the mix elements), all of the trims can be wrapped up and the tracks are ready to go to the mix.

Paperwork and Other Sundries

The music editor has one responsibility that the sound editors do not and that is to provide something called a *music cue sheet* to the music legal department of whatever film company the film is being made for. As shown in Figure 14.5 this legal form describes exactly how much of each cue is in the film, who wrote the music, and who owns the copyright. This information is necessary for the

Cue	Title	Footage	Timing	Vocal	Instr	Non-Vis	Visual	Composer	Publisher
	Reel One								
1M1	Main Titles	12 – 121½	1:13.2	X		X		Ludwig Kumposeur	—
1M2	The Parking Lot	352½ – 380½	0:18.6	X		X		Ludwig Kumposeur	—
1M3	Abby Meets Sean	510½ – 619	1:12.3		X	X		Ludwig Kumposeur	—
1M4	Jimmy The Baby	625½ – 703	0:45.2	X			X	Mickey Twilltone	Lotsa Music, Inc.
1M5	The Restaurant	736 – 900	1:22.7	X		X		Ludwig Kumposeur	—
	Reel Two								
2M2	Can I Make A Nuisance?	716 – 769	0:35.3	X		X		Ludwig Kumposeur	—
	Reel Three								
3M2	Abby Returns	422 – 483	0:90.6		X	X		Ludwig Kumposeur	—
3M3	Birthday Party	483 – 560½	0:51.6		X	X		Ludwig Kumposeur	—
3M4	The Three Friends Party	774½ – 904	1:26.2		X	X		Ludwig Kumposeur	—
			(MORE)						

FIGURE 14.5   A music cue sheet. The markings in the fifth and sixth columns tell whether the cue contained a vocal or whether it was entirely instrumental. The next two columns tell whether the cue was visual or nonvisual. When an actor or actress plays an instrument or sings part or all of the cue, the cue is considered visual (see 1M4, our bar song from Scene 19). Underscore is nonvisual.

musicians performing rights organizations both in the United States and abroad.

Getting this information is relatively easy if the movie is all scored material. If it is not then there should be someone who is assigned the task of researching the rights of the music before it is used. All music must either be out of copyright protection (this is sometimes called "free and clear" or "in the public domain") or it must be purchased for the use of the film.

As a music editor it may not be your job to make sure that all of these things have been cleared before the mix, but it is certainly in your interest to ascertain the information. If a piece is not cleared for your film you will find yourself replacing it at the last minute with something else.

In the case of the purchase of the rights to use an already recorded song, once the rights have been purchased then Nate and Betty must obtain from the record company that has the master tape (the original stereo tape from which the album was pressed) a copy of the song so that they can make a transfer from it onto 35mm film for use in the mix. When this tape is received it will not have a sync pulse on it (records don't need sync pulses since they have no picture to sync up to) and will almost certainly *not* sync up perfectly with the copy of the song which is already being used in the movie as a piece of scratch music. In some cases this will not matter at all but in other cases Nate will have to adjust the sync on the new tape (by transferring it to a tape while putting on a sync pulse and then varying the speed of a transfer off of the new tape). When the proper sync has been established, 35mm copies can be made for the mix. These are coded and treated like any other piece of music.

In the case of musicals with playback material, the situation will be much more complicated. In musicals, certain instruments that are on screen may need to be accented more than others. In that case they should be on their own tracks at that point in the film. This usually means that there are many more than three tracks of music going into the mix on a musical film. In such cases, all of the music tracks should be coded so they line up with each other and they should all run simultaneously except when that particular instrument (or vocalist) is not playing or singing. Then, Betty should cut out the track and replace it with fill. This will eliminate any unwanted noises from that portion of the song.

15

THE MIX

Finally, after many months of sound and music editing and way too many months of picture editing, *Silent Night, Silent Cowboy* will be ready to mix. Everybody will show up at the mixing (or dubbing, as it is called in Hollywood and London) stage. The editor, sound editor, music editor, and other assorted editorial personnel will all be there with the mixers—everyone except Adam, who will show up later.

In Hollywood there are usually three mixers—one each for dialogue, effects, and music. The dialogue rerecordist also functions as the supervisor of the team. In some situations, and almost everywhere outside of Hollywood, one mixer handles all three tasks. The procedure is usually as follows.

Often the dialogue tracks will come with six or seven elements (or units as they are also called), the music might be on a total of seven or eight channels, and there might be as many as fifty effects elements. This gives a total of nearly seventy separate channels of sound to be controlled individually. It not only would be too confusing to do that many at one time but there is no mixing board in the world that I am aware of that could handle that many tracks.

The solution to this problem is premixing (or predubbing) the individual sections. The dialogue premix takes all of the dialogue—split original tracks and looped lines—and combines them down to one three- or four-channel full-coat 35mm mag for each reel. In this way the tedious work of smoothing out the backgrounds and removing all of the annoying glitches in the tracks is handled by itself. There is often another full-coat reserved for the looped lines. This may not seem like much of a combination and, indeed, it isn't. The time that is spent in the dialogue premixes is usually spent on the tiny technical details necessary to get the smoothest dialogue sound possible.

The sound effects are also not combined into a few tracks. Usually they are reduced to no more than eight tracks (two four-channel 35mm mags) split in some intelligent way—general effects, specific effects for different characters, etc. Often some effects will not be mixed in to the premixes at all but held out so they may be run as separate elements in the final mix.

Scored music is generally not premixed at all since it has been premixed down to three tracks at the recording studio. Of course, on a musical film there would be plenty of need for a music premix, since music functions as importantly as dialogue in such a film (indeed, it often takes the place of dialogue).

During the premixes, Liz, the sound assistant, should be taking thorough notes on exactly what transpires at the mix. Any track elements which were not put into the premixes but will be needed in the final film mix should be noted so that they are not forgotten when the mix for that reel comes up. Effects which were in the tracks but omitted during the premixes should be plainly marked on the cue sheets (usually with heavy slashes through them). After the final mix is over, these effects will need to be flipped out so it is helpful to have them plainly marked.

When all of the premixes have been completed, the director joins the crew in the mixing room. Beginning with reel 1, all the elements will be combined into one soundtrack. Adam will be making decisions on the relative volumes of effects, music, and dialogue. He will be deciding if he likes the sound of someone's voice and, if he doesn't, how he wants it to change. He will be making decisions as to the texture of the film's sounds. The way that this is done is to play the various elements together. The mixer will struggle to get a pleasing sound and then everyone will begin discussing what they've just heard. Adam will ask for a little more door squeak at a certain point and a little less music. The film will be rolled backward until just before that point and the mix redone *just at that section.* This method of repairing the mix at certain sections is called *punching in* and the process by which the sections to be mixed are projected is called *rock and roll* (since you can move backward and forward in the film).

The process is a long and tedious one, requiring a lot of concentration on minute details. Typically, a ten- or twelve-reel film might take as long as six weeks to mix completely.

When I said above that the sounds were being mixed down to one soundtrack I was actually stretching the truth a bit. In actuality, the sounds are never really combined totally. The mix is made onto a piece of three-track full-coat 35mm mag. All of the mixed dialogue goes onto the first track, the music goes onto the second, and the effects onto the third. This mixed three-track is sometimes called the *D-M-E* as a result.

There are several reasons why this is done. The first is that it helps the rerecordist tremendously. If there is an effect which has to be redone he or she can just punch in the change on the effects channel of the mix, without touching the dialogue and music.

Another reason has to do with the creation of foreign versions of the film. After the completion of the film the distributor will want to release the movie in foreign countries as well as the United States. In countries where English is not the native language they will be creating a dubbed version of the film in which that country's native language will be dubbed into the film, replacing the English-language dialogue. Since the mix for the film was done so as to separate out all of the English dialogue onto the first channel of the D-M-E it will be a simple matter to remix the film. The foreign country is supplied with a transfer of this mix full-coat. This transfer is called an *M & E* or *foreign track*. The foreign distributors can then loop their dialogue and record over the English dialogue on the first channel.

There are, of course, certain complications to this approach. There will, naturally, be many sound effects which were part of the original dialogue recording of the film (people moving, chair squeaks, etc). When the dialogue channel is omitted from the mix these effects will also be eliminated. Obviously, someone will have to put them back in, either by effecting them or by foleying them. This can either be done by the company in the foreign country or by the sound editors in the United States after the completion of the regular mix (the *domestic version*).

Most sound editors try to build their elements knowing that this foreign version will eventually be made. They split off all of the effects on the dialogue track and put them on the effects tracks, filling in the resultant holes on the dialogue track with tone. Those effects that are marked with the dialogue and, thus, cannot be split off, are foleyed and cut into reels which can later be used in a foreign version mix.

It is this M & E which is part of the *delivery requirements,* those elements of the film that must be handed over to the film's distributor (see the next chapter for a more thorough discussion of this). Some companies would rather not invest in making a new M & E for the foreign, preferring instead to send the foreign distributors the domestic M & E. It is a rare case, however, where it is as easy for those in the foreign countries to make a good foreign M & E as cheaply as it can be done when the materials are all around— as they are when the original sound editors are still on the film. In any case, what kind of M & E the producer wants should be ascertained as early as possible.

After the mix has been completed, as I've mentioned, all of the track elements must be conformed to accurately reflect what was really mixed into the film's soundtrack. Occasionally, new sound effects will be added at the mix from tape cartridges owned by the mixing company. Copies of this effect must be gotten onto 35mm film and cut into the effects elements so that if the film must ever be remixed the sound elements will truly reflect the movie's soundtrack.

In the end, all of the sound effect trims and unused sound effects can be thrown away. All that really needs to be saved are the elements, the original tapes from the looping sessions, the half-inch four-track music mixdown tapes, the original two-inch music recording tapes, and a set of proper cue sheets.

You will be making an optical negative track off of this three-track D-M-E. The laboratory will make the soundtrack for the release prints with this optical negative (see the next chapter for more details). It is made by combining all three tracks into one. At the same time as this happens, it is wise to make a *mixed mag* in the same manner onto 35mm mag stock. This can be a soundtrack that you use for interlock screenings, if you ever need to screen one of the silent answer prints. It will also be of much better quality than the optical track.

16

TO THE ANSWER
PRINT—HO!

Much of what you will be doing to get the film ready for showing
to Real People (translate that as "paying audiences") will overlap
and be involved with what the sound and music editors are doing.
Now that we have seen exactly what the sound crew will be doing
during this period we can get back to what you will be struggling
to do—get the entire film finished on time.

On the Way to the End

There's a toast that many picture editing crews I've worked on
use whenever they are in the final throes of the editing of a picture.
At this time we've probably been on the film for nine or ten
months. We are preparing for the sound mix. The end of the film,
while actually quite close, still seems to be very far away. At times
like these, when we are clinking our glasses of wine (or whatever),
I usually hear someone say something like, "To the answer print!"
The answer print is what this chapter is all about.

The workprint that you have been cutting with for these many
months is, in a sense, nothing more than a blueprint for the actual
print of the film that audiences will see. With the amount of working and reworking that goes on during the editing of a film, cutting
the actual footage that would go out into the theatre would be ridiculous. Not only would that only provide you with one print of the
film but that print would be so chopped up that it would be dan-
gerous to run it continuously through the projectors. And, of course,
the sound is on a separate roll from the picture and very few theatres (other than screening rooms) can handle that sort of arrange-

ment. With all this in mind, you can understand that you are going to have to come up with a way of making clean, spliceless prints to release to the theatres which are based on the print that you've been cutting for these many months.

The way this is done is quite simple in theory. The workprint that you have been working with was struck directly from the original negative that ran through the camera on the set (the *camera original* as it is sometimes called). In fact, this workprint is such a faithful copy of the original negative that it even includes the key numbers printed through from the negative. Any further prints from this negative will also be identical to your first prints from it.

When the film is locked someone goes back to the original negative and matches, cut for cut, everything that Wendy did on the workprint. At the end of this *negative cutting* you will end up with one reel of cut negative for every reel of cut workprint, and the two will be identical in every way. When you then make a positive print from this cut negative you will end up with a clean, spliceless print of the reel that will match your cut workprint.

The process by which you turn over your workprint to the negative cutter will be discussed in more detail shortly but the process by which he or she will cut your negative should be mentioned now. You have been splicing film together with pieces of tape during the editing. For negative cutting, however, the splices have to be made with cement.

Actually there are three different ways of printing from cut negative in the lab. The first is with your one long strand of cut-together negative. This is the way that 35mm features are done. The second way is to make one long optical negative from the negative incorporating all of the cuts within this optical and printing with that. This is the way commercials are done. The third way is called the *zero-cut* method or *A and B rolling*. It involves printing the film from two (or, sometimes, three) parallel-running rolls of film. At each cut we would switch printing from one roll to the other. We discussed this method in the chapter on opticals (Chapter 10). This kind of printing is used primarily for 16mm films.

The reason why this last type of printing is used in 16mm films can be explained by describing the manner in which negative must be cut. In order to fasten one piece of negative to another, the pieces must be attached using cement. In order to do this, some of the emulsion is scraped off the top part of one frame and the matching part of the last frame of the outgoing shot is attached to this by means of glue or cement. In actuality, the way this is done is to cut the outgoing shot a little long (by one-half of a frame), scraping the first frame of the incoming shot, and overlapping these two frames. In 35mm the amount of frame needed to overlap in order to attain a firm splice is very small (less than one sprocket in length). But in 16mm, nearly one-half of the frame would have to be overlapped in order to make the splice hold. This would be visible when projected. It is for this reason that the *zero-splice* method is used.

Even in the zero-splice method negative must be spliced together using cement, and one-half of the frame scraped away. It's just that in this method the scraping and splicing takes place *before* the splice comes (see Figure 16.1) so that it will not be seen when the film is printed. The switch onto the reel will come one-half of a frame after the splice from black into the shot.

One of the immediate problems with cutting the negative is that, unlike cutting the workprint, once the negative is cut (and that one-half frame is scraped off) you can never add to the head or the tail of a cut. Once that frame is gone it is gone for good. This is the main reason why commercials never cut the original negative but make an optical negative to print from. They very often have several different versions of the same commercial (ten seconds, twenty seconds, thirty seconds, sixty seconds) using differing lengths of the same shots. Though it is vastly more expensive to make an optical negative than it is to cut your original negative it would be impossible for them to make all of the necessary versions of the commercial without this expense. Features have neither the necessity for multiple versions nor the budget to make an optical negative.

Of course, shots can be (and often are) shortened after the negative has been cut. That is not very difficult since the frame that was lost in the first negative cutting is not needed to shorten a cut. But this restriction on lengthening shots makes for something of a sense of finality when the negative is cut.

Previewing

Directors often have a sense of panic when the negative is about to be cut. One director I worked for almost refused to let the negative be cut until I explained to him that not only did every

FIGURE 16.1 In the zero-splice method, cutting from shot A to B and from B to C is accomplished by *checkerboarding* the negative so that the splices attach the picture to black leader which will not print up in the lab process.

feature work that way but that no one was going to be able to see his film if he did not cut his negative. This panic is certainly understandable. Adam, Wendy, you, Philip, and everyone involved with the creation of *Silent Night, Silent Cowboy* will have been working on this film for three-quarters of a year or more. At this point everyone has certainly lost perspective on the film. What works and does not work is a subjective judgment in any case. It is complicated immensely by the fact that you all know the film so well. Things that are perfectly clear to you may not be at all clear to someone seeing the film for the first time.

For this reason, it is a common practice for the director to want to screen the film for an audience before cutting the negative. Some directors, like Arthur Penn on *Four Friends*, felt that open previews (that is, previews for the public as opposed to friends and advisors) were not useful. We screened *Four Friends* for several groups of friends and received feedback from them. Milos Forman, however, screened *Hair* many times for people who were given tickets on the street corners. After each screening we handed out questionnaires and we reedited the film based on any comments that seemed important.

These screenings were always from the workprint, at screening rooms, with a double-system projection (separate track and picture). Some directors, however, will wait until the film is mixed and then take it out to a neighborhood movie theatre to preview it. These sneak previews (or *sneaks*) are the final acid test of a film's acceptability to a normal audience before its release. These sneaks are generally not held in Hollywood or New York City, so that the reactions of a less movie-hip audience can be ascertained.

But screening in Denver, San Diego, Minneapolis, or such cities can create all kinds of other problems. For one thing, it is rare that you will be able to find a theatre that can screen double-system.

For another thing, the audiences are people who are used to seeing only finished films. Scratch mixes, bad prints, visible splice marks, and the like can upset them and taint their reaction to the film.

For these reasons, sneaks are usually only attempted if there is some sort of real worry about a film. Films are usually sneaked with a mixed track only. If there are any shots in the workprint which are scratched, ripped, or missing frames, they must be replaced by reprints. If there are any shots in the film which have a distracting color balance, they are also reprinted. On *Network* we reprinted virtually the entire film in order to get the freshest, cleanest prints for the one preview that we ran.

The film itself must be treated with special care. If you are going to be screening a cut workprint (and you normally will be) you must have the film cleaned thoroughly before every screening. I like to have the film *sonic cleaned* before taking it out on the road. This cleaning, which is usually done at a lab or at a film treatment house, can remove all kinds of ingrained dirt which Ecco cannot. Sonic cleaning can often lighten your code numbers so it is not a good idea to do it more than once, but it does make the film look better than it could otherwise.

The problem of how to accommodate double-system projection is not an easy one to solve. There are two ways to handle this, neither of which is problem-free. The first is to rent a portable double-system projector (many of the big studios own their own), install it at the theatre, and use it instead of their normal projectors. There are many problems with this. The projectors are rarely as good as standard theatre projectors; they tend to break down more often and to be harder on the film. There are also times when, in the middle of a screening, the picture and the track lose sync. These are not good things to have happen during a sneak preview. Most of these problems can be ironed out if the people setting up the projectors get there early enough to locate all of the problems and repair them. Since this will often require flying in extra parts to the theatre, the first installation should be done several days before the actual sneak date. It is a rare case, however, when you will be given this much time. The screening, then, becomes an exercise in making do.

The second way of projecting double-system is to avoid projecting double-system. At this stage in the editing, however, you will not be able to provide the theatre with a composite optical print (which, as we will find out later, is the format in which you will eventually end up). There is, however, another alternative if the theatre you are going into is properly equipped for it, and that is a composite magnetic track format. In this format (see Figure 16.2) a set of magnetic stripes is glued onto the edges of the film. The sound is then transferred onto one of these stripes. If the theatre has a magnetic head on its projector (and many of them do, since it used to be a common format for "spectacle" films in the sixties), and it is still hooked up, then the film can be run using the theatre's regular projectors.

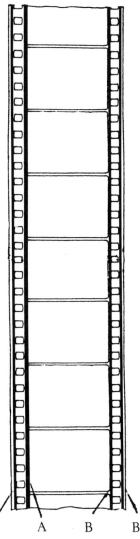

FIGURE 16.2 A composite mag print has magnetic material glued *(striped)* on the edges of the film. This makes the code numbers hard to read. Sound is transferred *(sounded)* onto the stripe marked "A". The stripes marked "B" are put on the film to balance the shape of the film so that it will wind up properly on the takeup reels. If a film is mixed in three- or four-track stereo, these stripes may be used for those extra soundtracks.

B   A   B   B

The advantages of this approach are obvious, the disadvantages less so. Using the theatre's own equipment cuts down on the possibilities of equipment interfacing problems. It also makes for a better working relationship with the theatre owner and theatre projectionist. Many people resent "those Hollywood types" coming in and completely taking over. It often seems to them that nothing that they have to begin with is good enough for "them Hollywood types," and that we want to change everything. In fact, this is usually the case. Most ordinary theatres have equipment which is so primitive and so badly kept up that it horrifies the average filmmaker. While we can do very little about how the released version of the film will be projected in Anytown, USA, we can control how it is projected during sneaks. And so we do. But this inevitably builds up a resentment. There is very little you can do about this except to be very diplomatic and polite while still fighting like the dickens to get what you want.

There are several problems due to the outmoded nature of 35mm magnetic single-system. First of all, since almost no film is released in the format anymore, it is quite likely that the theatre projectors' sound heads are in a state of disrepair. One of the reasons that this method was abandoned in the first place (aside from the added cost of striping and *sounding* the film, as the transfer is called) is that theatre projectionists rarely kept the equipment in good shape. The sound heads got caked with the oxide particles from the soundtrack, making good sound impossible. Years later these particles are still sitting on the sound heads. Be prepared to have to clean the head very thoroughly and, possibly, replace the heads altogether.

Another problem with this form of projection is inherent in the medium itself. You will be striping a skinny little ribbon of oxide onto a spliced workprint. The oxide is placed on as a stream of liquid and allowed to dry on the film. At the splices it can often crack or peel off. This creates a sound dropout at the splice unless the striping, sounding, and projection are handled carefully.

Despite all of these problems, however, I have had good luck with the second method when the theatre is equipped to screen in such a format. As a result I can recommend it, with reservations. The sad truth is that the state of projection in the United States today is so bad that you are fighting a losing battle. No theatre will come near to even a halfway decent screening room.

Taking the film "on the road" is not an easy thing. It is best to carry a mini-editing room with you. A set of rewinds on a board, splicers, tape, reels, cores, a script, all of your editing notes, your logbook, and a host of other things are necessary to be prepared for a problem during the screening or any questions after the screening as to potential recutting.

There is no "normal" procedure for going out on these sneaks. There is only an "ideal" which is never reached. That ideal involves having several days before leaving for the sneak city to clean the film, make all reprints necessary (as well as completing all opticals necessary—including titles if possible), stripe and sound the film if you are going single-system, and to run the film at least once with the materials you will actually be running at the sneak. When you are certain that everything is fine you would then fly out to the sneak city to meet the technician who has been installing your projectors in the theatre (or checking out the projectors already there). He or she will have cleared up any of the problems that have been found. Then, preferably a full day and a half or two days before the scheduled sneak, you will have a full run-through at the theatre with the projectionist who will actually be doing the projection work on the night of your sneak. In this way you can clear up any potential problems in the next day or so before the sneak.

An hour or two before the sneak you will go into the theatre (which hopefully will be closed, rather than on their normal schedule) and run one or two reels of the film. I usually try to pick the reels with the widest range of sound so that I can set a good sound level. Check both projectors. You should then be ready to screen.

As I mentioned, however, this is the rarely attained ideal situation. Most often you will have no more than one day at the sneak site before the screening. If there are several sneaks planned in a row you will be lucky to get even that.

Out-of-town screenings are a nerve-racking experience. Everyone is tense. There is always a lot riding on the sneak, the director's (and the crew's) ego and the company's money, so everyone is incredibly nervous. For that reason you should try to get everything as perfect as you can and, if there are any egregious problems that cannot be resolved, to point them out to the director before the screening. That may not make Adam happy but at least he will know what to expect.

After the sneak there will usually be a hurried reading of the audience cards and all sorts of hotel room meetings that you will not be invited to. This will be rather difficult but you have other work to perform. You should give the film a thorough cleaning on your portable rewinds, either at the theatre or in your hotel room. You should have everything packed up and ready to leave as soon after the screening as possible. If Wendy is going to any of the after-sneak talks you should try and provide her with whatever notes she may need (a reel breakdown, script, etc.). Your primary job at this point is to expedite the movement of the film and the portable cutting room.

Negative Cutting

After all of the paranoia has passed, all of the screenings have been finished, and all of the recutting has been accomplished, you will find yourself at a point in the film that you probably never thought you would reach—the end of the editing.

When the film is finally locked you must begin to prepare for the negative cutting. This involves two things—the first is marking up the film and preparing a negative continuity. Both tasks aim to do the same thing, provide enough information to the negative cutter so that he or she can cut the negative to your film quickly and completely correctly. After all, if there are any mistakes in the negative cutting they can't be corrected easily, if at all.

At this stage of the film you should have all pieces of the film cut into your workprint—including all opticals and titles. Every piece of film will have key numbers on its edges. Make sure that they do. Occasionally the lab will forget to expose the blue edge of the film with the key numbers on it; if this happens have them reprint that piece properly. All marks on the film should be erased so that the only markings there are the ones you will be putting on now.

The idea behind marking up the film is to mark every piece of negative that the negative cutter will be needing in such a way that he or she will be able to easily see just what to do with it. To do this you must mark where every cut in the film should be. You must also tell them where cuts *will not* be if there could be any confusion. You will write on the film any special notes that might help avoid confusion.

To help to understand why this is necessary let me briefly explain how a negative cutter works. The first thing that cutters do is determine exactly which takes they need to cut the negative of the film. Then they will separate out all of these takes and keep them handy. They will then take your cut workprint, put it in a synchronizer, and begin to run down on it. On a second gang in the synchronizer they will be building the matched negative alongside the workprint. In this way they can check key nembers and visual action.

At this point all the cutters will do is cut (with a scissors) the negative on each side of the cut, cutting off one-half of the next frame as well (as discussed earlier in this chapter). They will not actually cement the two takes together. Instead they put them together with a temporary wedge, which is actually a piece of cardboardlike material which holds the two pieces of negative together through their sprocket holes. This keeps the negative and the work print running in sync as well as postponing the messy cement work until later so that the negative cutter is not doing two things at one time. The actual splicing of the negative is done after, often by another person. When the work is divided up like this the first stage is usually called negative matching, and the second negative cutting, though the two terms are often used interchangeably.

As you can probably guess, the process of matching the negative is very exacting. Once the scissors cuts the negative there is no replacing it, so any help that you can give the matcher is that much more safety insurance for you. That is why you must be precise when you mark up your workprint for matching.

Figure 16.3 shows the various notations used in marking up the workprint for the negative cutter. Note that there are two ways to mark cuts.

Often a piece of picture has been ripped so badly that it has been replaced by a white slug. When the matcher gets to that slug he or she will have no idea whether the slug represents the continuation of the outgoing or incoming cut. For that reason you should mark with an arrow just what footage the slug represents (see Figure 16.3).

In addition to marking up the workprint most negative matchers request a negative continuity. This is, simply, a list of every cut in the film. See Figure 16.4 for an example of just how detailed this list must be. When I worked on *Fame* the negative cutter at Metro-

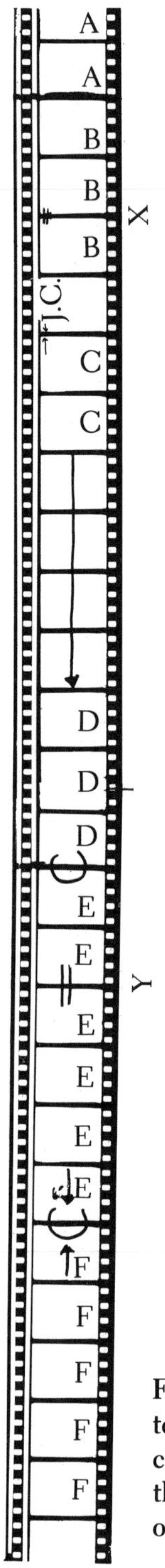

FIGURE 16.3 A piece of film marked for the negative cutter. The markings show where (A) cuts are to be made, (B) cuts were made in the work picture but are not to be made in the negative, and (C) an extension is to be used here instead of the piece shown.

"SILENT NIGHT, SILENT COWBOY"

OCTOBER 17, 1984

NEGATIVE CONTINUITY LIST

Shot #	FTG.	KEY NUMBER
1	12.00	F 32X 63217 $^{+10}$ ———— 228 $^{+5}$
2	22.11	F 32X 54098 $^{+3}$ ———— 108 $^{+2}$
3	32.10	F 32X 54115 $^{+1}$ ———— 129 $^{+6}$
4	45.07	F 32X 54075 $^{+4}$ ———— 088 $^{+1}$
5	66.06	F 32X 63233 $^{+3}$ ———— 254 $^{+2}$
6	74.11	F 32X 63262 $^{+4}$ ———— 270 $^{+9}$
7	81.07	F 48X 21112 $^{+7}$ ———— 119 $^{+1}$
8	93.10	F 48X 21124 $^{+5}$ ———— 136 $^{+8}$
9	99.05	E 23X 26033 $^{+6}$ ———— 039 $^{+1}$
10	107.06	E 23X 26052 $^{+2}$ ———— 060 $^{+3}$
11	115.03	F 32X 63291 $^{+4}$ ———— 299 $^{+1}$
12	124.06	F 32X 63277 $^{+3}$ ———— 286 $^{+6}$
13	131.02	E 17X 14108 $^{+7}$ ———— 115 $^{+3}$
14	139.02	E 17X 14123 $^{+5}$ ———— 131 $^{+6}$
15	149.01	F 9X 32201 $^{+7}$ ———— 211 $^{+6}$
16	161.04	F 9X 32234 $^{+2}$ ———— 246 $^{+5}$
17	168.10	F 13X 18 368 $^{+3}$ ———— 375 $^{+9}$
18	181.06	E 17X 14 136 $^{+7}$ ———— 149 $^{+1}$
19	193.05	F 13X 18 379 $^{+3}$ ———— 391 $^{+2}$

FIGURE 16.4   A sample section of a negative continuity. Some assistants like to include a brief description of the picture for each cut in order to help the negative cutter.

color Labs did not want a negative continuity since they worked by computer and therefore preferred to make their own lists. It was a job that I gave up very gladly.

Answer Printing—At Last

After the negative has been cut, the reels are sent to the lab where a timer will look at them and decide what color balance each should have. The original dailies timing notes are not readily available to the timer so if there is a timing that was difficult to get (i.e., requiring many reprints) you may want to let him or her know just what timing it was that you eventually ended up with. Most often, however, the timer will not want anything of the sort but will prefer to have a chance to do one print completely on his or her own.

Timing involves determining just what percentages of cyan (blue/green), magenta (red-purple), and yellow should be in the image. This is done by varying the amount of red, blue, or green light that passes through the film negative to the print film. Most often the timer will go for what he or she assumes is the best skin tone color and attempt to match the rest of the shots to this.

The timer will determine exactly what balance he or she wants for every piece of negative in the film. When this task is completed this information is put into a machine which senses when each cut is coming up (either by feeling for a metal tab pasted onto the edge of the film or by looking for a notch cut out of the side of the film). At each cut it adjusts the color balance according to the instructions given to it by the timer. For 16mm films items such as fades and other optical effects are also programmed in.

When the first print comes out of the lab the most important thing for you to do is to make sure that the negative cutting was done properly. To do this you would take the first *answer print* (as this print is called) and line it up in the synchronizer with your cut workprint at the start marks. Then roll down, stopping at every cut and making sure that the key numbers match on either side of the cut. Also make sure that no cuts were made when they were not supposed to be made. If there are no miscuts then you can approve the reel for screening.

Occasionally there are some miscuts. This has to be one of the worst kinds of mistakes for a film editor to deal with. At this stage the film is either being mixed or has already been mixed. Depending upon how bad the error in parts of the film may have to be recut and remixed.

The problem here obviously stems from the fact that all of the sound editing and mixing was done to the dupes from the work-print. If a shot of someone talking was cut in one foot later or earlier then the mixed dialogue will be out of sync by one foot. This is by far one of the worst kinds of errors to correct. It may be possible to find another take that can replace the ruined one, though it can never be as good (after all, Wendy originally chose the used take over the other one for a reason—correct?). If there is not a good substitute then some kind of fix in the mix can possibly be made.

The worst case that I've ever heard of regarding major laboratory screw-ups began when the lab storing the negative for a feature film accidentally destroyed a few takes of the film before negative cutting began; when the matchers went looking for the film they found nothing. As bad luck would have it there were no alternate takes that could be used and no possible way to correct the error with existing material. The editor had to make a new negative directly off the cut workprint and use the negative instead of the original. The footage created was, necessarily, of a noticeably different quality than the surrounding material. It was the best solution to an impossible problem.

Horror stories like this are rare. Most problems can be sorted out through the use of alternate takes. The splices in the negative are carefully pulled apart and the new negative is inserted exactly in place of the old one. If the editor is skillful the replacement will not be at all noticeable. On *Fame* there were a few problems with the negative cutting, all of which Gerry Hambling was able to solve with a minimum of fuss.

When the first answer print is complete (or as complete as it can be; often there are a few reels which must be held back awaiting opticals) the director, the editor, the timer, and (most often) the director of photography all get together and watch it. They will usually screen the film at the laboratory, running the workprint reel and its matching answer print reel at the same time. They will look at a bit of one and then ask the projectionist to change over to the other, so they can compare. Then they return to the first, then back again to compare. Changes are requested. The timer then makes new timing notes and the reel is reprinted. Several days later the second answer print comes out of the lab and is screened.

This screening process is repeated until all of the reels are timed to everyone's satisfaction. As the process goes on, reels will be approved. Only the unapproved reels are then retimed and reprinted. It is probable that many reels of your film will be approved after the second answer printing but it is also likely that at least one or two might have to be printed a third time. You will probably want to keep the printing to a minimum since the negative degrades each time it is used.

At this point a *CRI* (or an *IP/IN*) is made of the film. As I've discussed before, the actual prints that get shown in most theatres are not struck from the original cut negative but from a copy of the negative made at the lab. For a long time, to make a negative copy, a copy had to be made on positive stock (called the *interpositive*) and then another copy had to be made from that onto negative stock (called the *internegative*). This internegative was what release prints of the film were made from. However, the extra two generations added on by this process made the print much grainier and more contrasty. Eventually, Kodak developed a one-step process for making this dupe negative. It is called a *color reversal intermediate (CRI)*. The quality of prints made from a CRI was much closer to prints off of the original and so it was vastly preferable. There were still, however, some disadvantages to CRI stock that Kodak could not get around. Recently, they have revamped the technique for making interpositive/internegative prints so that it is now the equal of the CRI process in quality. As a result more films are now going back to making release prints from the IP/IN process.

But whether the IP/IN process or the CRI process is used, the theory is the same. All the color balance instructions are incorporated into the striking of the dupe negative so that when prints are made they can all be made at the same setting and no adjustment of the color controls will be necessary. This brings down the cost of making prints considerably.

The completed mix of your film will be transferred onto a piece of photographic negative for printing along with the picture negative. There are all sorts of individual lab standards that the mixing studio must match when making this *optical track*. (Both film opticals and soundtrack opticals are called "opticals." This occasionally leads to some confusion. Always be careful to let everyone know exactly what you mean when you say "optical.") You should make sure that this information is exchanged properly between the two places.

This optical track is actually a piece of 35mm (or 16mm if that is the gauge of the film you are working in) film with little squiggly

OPTICAL TRACK

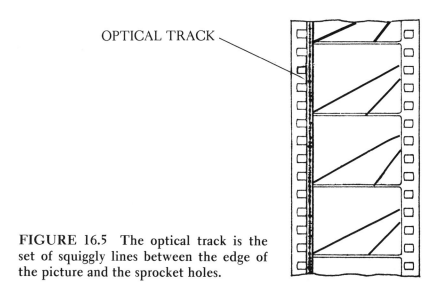

FIGURE 16.5 The optical track is the set of squiggly lines between the edge of the picture and the sprocket holes.

lines on the left-hand side of the frame (see Figure 16.5). When light is pumped through a print of these lines it lands on a photo-electric cell in patterns that can be decoded to form sounds that we recognize. This is how almost all films are projected in theatres. This is why you had problems trying to sneak-preview a film with a magnetic soundtrack. Theatres are not used to anything other than an optical soundtrack (except in certain showcase situations—all 70mm films, for instance, have magnetic soundtracks).

When the laboratory has one or two track negatives and has completely timed the film and struck the IP/IN for release printing (the number of IP/INs or CRIs struck will depend on the number of prints needed; distribution companies try and get about 150 to 200 release prints out of each dupe negative), they can begin striking the release prints. At the same time you will also be able to get a few original negative prints (sometimes called *EK prints*). Since these prints are made directly from the cut negative they will require timing at the lab printing. As a result they will be more expensive. They will, however, be much better prints than the dupe negative prints since they will be at least one generation closer to the original (second generation as opposed to third or fourth). For that reason a few EK prints are usually struck for the two or three big premiere cities. These are the prints that the big critics usually see as well as the ones that open at the classy downtown theatres.

EK prints, since they degrade the negative, are usually struck only for Los Angeles and New York openings, though sometimes they will be made for London, Chicago, or Boston. In such cases, two prints are usually made per theatre. On *Hair* we opened at the Ziegfeld Theatre in New York City and the Cinerama Dome Theatre in Los Angeles. Both theatres received two EK prints—one for projection and one for backup. Other major opening theatres, in Chicago, Washington, D.C., San Francisco, and Boston received two prints, though at least one of them was a dupe neg print.

Once the mix is over, therefore, you will be responsible for organizing the printing of the movie. You will be organizing the lab screenings for answer prints and making sure that the lab personnel have all of the materials they need to make a perfect release print. Once the release printing of the movie has begun then your tasks begin to get much simpler. They revolve around special requests from the distribution company and closing down the cutting room.

Special Requests

In the months before the release of a movie the distribution company is going to be gearing up for the release of *Silent Night, Silent Cowboy*. They are going to want to see the film as soon as possible so that they can begin to plan a marketing strategy and an advertising campaign for the film. Usually, their needs come almost at the same time as you are going through the worst crises in the editing room. You will probably be trying to lock the film as well as turning the picture over to the sound department. You will be involved in optical work and many other complicated items. Then the film company will call and ask if they can see the film.

The temptation at this point is to tell them all to go to hell in a handbasket and call back when you've got the time to talk to them—like in two months. Unfortunately, two months will be too late for them. I have seen directors so protective of their movies that they did not let the film companies have a look at the film until it was much too late. As a result, the advertising campaign was rushed and, usually, terrible.

Supplying the distribution company with its needs is part of your job as well. Though you should never release anything to them without the prior knowledge and consent of Wendy and Adam, you must make it part of your job to do so. It can only help the film.

Early on, after they have already seen the film, the distribution company will want to get a black and while dupe of the entire film so that they can begin cutting a trailer. This is the "coming attraction" short you see in the theatres. The best time to give them this dupe is after the film has been turned over to sound. The reason for this is that you will then have already made an unmixed track (which is what the trailer people should receive) to go with the dupe. It is possible that the company may need the film earlier, but in normal cases the sound editors begin to come on three months or so before the mix and the mix is often six to eight weeks. At the absolute worst, this leaves five or six months between the first black and white dupe for sound and the release of the film, which is normally plenty of time for the trailer to be made, printed, and shown in theatres.

There are some cases where you will not have the luxury of this much time, especially as more and more companies try to shorten the postproduction schedule. On a recent Dino DiLaurentiis film there were only three months between the end of shooting and the completion of the film mix. On many low-budget Hollywood films this schedule might even be considered generous.

But let's say that *Silent Night* is a normally scheduled film. You can then make an extra black and white dupe for the trailer department when you make the dupes for the sound department (we are assuming that the film is in good enough shape at this point to show the trailer people—there is no point, after all, in making a trailer from a dupe which will not resemble the finished film). When you find out who the trailer people are going to be (they are often an outside service that the distribution company contracts to do the job) ship them all of the material that they need. This will often be just the black and white dupe. If you have any music already recorded for the film they should receive that too. At the least, they should be given the name and phone number of your music editor who can supply them with music materials as they become available.

After the trailer people have finished cutting the trailer they will do their own mix on it and make their own release prints of the trailer. In order to do that, however, they are going to need a negative. You of course, cannot give up your own negative since you need it for the film. Trailers, therefore, are made with dupe negatives. When they have finished cutting the trailer you will receive a list of all of the takes used in the film. Either you, or the assistant at the trailer house (from a copy of your logbook), will then order registration IPs struck from the original negative of the relevant scenes. In no case is the negative to leave the lab!

If your film mix has already been done then it would be helpful to give them a copy of the mix in its D-M-E format. In this way they can do their mix from already mixed tracks. This will make for a better and faster mix.

However, it is more than likely that you will not have finished your film mix when the trailer people want their tracks. In that case they may want track reprints of some takes in order to do a reasonable mix. They are not going to be splitting tracks to quite the degree that your sound editors will be. However, they will need to split some of the tracks for overlapping dialogue as well as for some smoothing of backgrounds. You will have to get those reprints for them.

Throughout all of these tasks it is important to make sure that the bills for these orders are not charged directly to your production. This makes the accountants crazy. Even though all of the money will be coming from the same big pot, this pot has a lot of little categories in it. The making of the movie is considered a different thing from the selling of the movie and it is important that the bills for the trailer be separated from your own.

After the answer prints have started to come out the distribution company is going to start asking for prints of the film which they can screen for critics. It is a fact of life that a film which gets no publicity and no reviews is almost never going to make any money. Film companies, therefore, spend huge sums of money publicizing a film; often more than the film cost to make in the first place. Magazine critics must see a film months or more before it is released because their magazines have long lead times. This means that the time between when the writer writes the review and when it is published is often upwards of a month. Often, as with *Life* magazine, it is over two months. The publicity department will be anxious to get as many stories in as many magazines as they can. As soon as a print is available, and often before, they will begin demanding a print to screen for influential critics.

Often these requests can be accommodated quite easily. You will have a print or two at your disposal that can be shown (the first

EK print that was fully approved should stay in the editing room for all of your screenings). As soon as another print of the film is made it should go to the distribution company so they can set up their own screenings without continually bothering you. However, you should always make sure that you check the prints before sending them to the company. In their passion to sell the film the publicity people will often be willing to screen inferior prints simply to get the film seen. Make sure that no unacceptable prints go out for screening or, sure as the sun rises, they will be used.

The only time to break this rule (and only because it is normally impossible not to) comes because of the rash of anti-blind bidding laws passed in many states recently. Previous to these laws, theatre owners who wanted to show a film would bid against each other for it whether or not they had already seen the film.

In an attempt to thwart some of the more unsavory bidding practices, many states have been passing anti-blind bidding laws, which require film companies to make the film available for viewing at least once in their state before offering it for bidding. There is a thirty-day minimum time between screening and opening in many states as well. What that means is that, often, exhibitors in those states must get a chance to see the film before it is really ready to show. On *Fame* we ended up making a quick print with a bad mix just to have something to show. That was the only time that I ever knowingly allowed a bad print to get into the hands of the distribution company. I made sure that it was returned to me after the blind bid states screenings and I kept it under lock and key after that so it could not be shown without my knowledge.

Wrapping Out

Eventually, after all the screenings have been completed and all the prints delivered, it will be time to *wrap out* of the cutting room. That is, it will be time to pack up all of the footage for storage and close out the editing rooms. There are, of course, certain proper ways to do this.

At the time that the producer originally made the money deal for *Silent Night* he signed a contract with the distributor. That contract, called the producer/distributor agreement, specified, among other items, exactly what things the producer had to hand over to

the distributor at the end of the filmmaking process. A wording of
the section of one such contract is shown below:

Delivery: Delivery of the Picture shall consist of making physical delivery, at the sole cost and expense of Producer, to the Distributor of the following items, it being agreed that Producer
shall include in the Final Production Budget for the Picture, and
pay for, as a production cost of the Picture, the cost of each of
the items of delivery required hereunder:

1. One positive print,
2. One picture negative,
3. One set of separations (or an interpositive) and two soundtrack negatives,
4. Three negative copies of the textless main and end titles,
5. One music and effects track,
6. A multitrack tape 15ips of the entire score of the Picture,
7. TV Version of the Picture, as below:
   —One positive print of each TV reel,
   —One 35mm CRI of each TV reel,
   —One 35mm soundtrack negative for each TV reel,
8. 125 copies of the Picture's dialogue continuity,
9. Twenty copies of the music cue sheets,
10. Such materials as Producer may have on hand at time of the
    completion of the Picture and also such material as Dis-
    tributor may require for the making of trailers, TV spots,
    and teasers, and similar advertising and publicity devices
    to be used in connection with the distribution of the Pic-
    ture. In this connection, Producer shall deliver the
    following:
    —35mm black and white copy of cut picture,
    —35mm copy of magnetic work soundtrack,
    —35mm three-stripe magnetic soundtrack of Picture
    —IP of sections of Picture used in trailer,
11. Three copies of the statement of credits,
12. Three copies of proposed main and end titles, and
13. One copy of the conductor's musical score.

We will now cover these delivery requirements in order.

One positive print—Simply, the final EK print which comes
from the lab.

One picture negative—This is the cut negative, with all opticals cut in, including main and end titles.

One set of separations and two soundtrack negatives—The first (the separations) are the IP/INs or CRIs used for release printing the film. This particular contract requires two soundtrack negatives.

Textless main and end titles—When a copy of the picture negative is delivered to the distributor it will, of course, have the main and end title credits in them. For certain forms of release (such as television or foreign releases) a different set of titles may be needed instead of the ones that you've put on. In that case, the distributor must have a copy of the background scenes used in the title sequences so that they can lay new titles on top of it. The easiest way to do this is to have the optical house, at the same time that they make your titles, also strike the required number of copies (in this case, three) of the title sequences *without* the titles. In the case of our main titles, where they begin in black and then fade into picture, that is exactly what we would see in the textless background negative. The length of the textless background should exactly match the length of the titles. The only exception to this delivery requirement is when the entire set of titles is over a non-pictorial background. There is no delivery requirement in this case.

One music and effects track—This is the M&E track discussed in Chapter 15.

15ips tape of the music score—This is the half-inch four-track tape discussed in Chapter 14.

TV version requirements—In the next chapter we will discuss the television version of your film. At this point, it will suffice to say that any reels that contain dialogue or action which needs to be replaced for a television version must have new positive prints, CRIs (or IP/INs), and soundtrack negative delivered.

Cutting continuity—Though this requirement is sometimes handled by the distributor and then charged to the producer it is often handled, or at least expedited, by the editing room staff. For many reasons the distributor would like to have a detailed script of the film as it was actually cut (rather than as it was scripted). This rather tedious job is handled by a number of specialists who run the completed print of the film (often with a separate soundtrack) on a Moviola or flatbed and list every shot in the film and every piece of dialogue or special sound effect. This list is cued by footage so that the location of any shot in the release reels can be exactly pinpointed. There are cases where the editing room staff will hire the person to do this task. However, more often than not, the most involvement that you will have in this job is to supply a separate mixed soundtrack of the film. Please note that even though release reels are double reels (that is, made up of two of your editing reels) I have usually supplied continuity with the reels as they were balanced in the editing room. This is to help the continuity person know where the editing room reels have been joined to form the double release reels. In the cases where I have supplied double reels I have also given the person doing the continuity a list of my LFOAs so that he or she could see where the breaks came anyway. This information should be listed on the cutting continuity because the original cut negative for the film is always maintained on 1000-foot reels not the double reels that the IP/IN is made up of for the release printing. That is also why you will find that all prints off of the original negative come on single reels and all prints off of the IP/IN come on double reels.

Music cue sheet—See Figure 14.5.

Trailer and other materials—This has already been covered in this section except for the "other" item. What the contract means by, "Such material as the Producer may have on hand," is almost all of the material in the editing room. This is explained in more detail below under "Packing Up."

Credits lists—These lists should be supplied by the producer.

Conductor's score—Supplied either by the music editor or the music copyist.

Packing Up

These delivery requirements should be delivered to the address supplied by the distributor. All of the special requirements, like the negative and release printing material, will probably already be in their hands (or at the lab that will be doing the release printing). In addition, certain of the materials may be sent to different addresses. For instance, if there is a music department at the distribution company the scores, cue sheets, and 15ips tape may be sent to the music department. The various bits of paperwork will probably go to some office of the company.

In the end, you will be left with several editing rooms full of material, most of which the distribution companies do not want.

What they will want is all of the original negative not used in the cut negative, all of the original quarter-inch tapes, all of the workprint and work track reels, all of the trims and outs, all of the mixing elements, the wild tracks, the lined script, and the logbooks. The reason for this is quite simple. Often, years after the completion of the editing of the film, changes will need to be made in it. This may be because of a possible rerelease of the movie in a different version (such as was the case with *New York, New York* or *Heaven's Gate*) or a new television version (as was the case with the combined version of the two *Godfather* films on NBC-TV). All of the material needed to recut the movie should be accessible.

It is therefore important that you pack the editing room material in as orderly a manner as possible. Thorough lists should be made of exactly what goes in every packing carton. Packing cartons are large cardboard boxes which are designed to hold a dozen of the two-piece, white trims boxes. The easiest way that I have found of packing is simply to begin at the AA trims and begin putting them into one box after another. On a packing list (such as shown in Figure 16.6) I list exactly what is going into each sequentially numbered packing carton. I also list the information on the outside of every box. I leave the boxes with the paperwork for last and, when everything is ready (and before packing the last box), make a dozen copies of the packing list. One copy goes into the last box, along with the logbooks and lined script. It is sealed and marked very plainly as "PAPERWORK—CONTAINS PACKING LIST." It will also have the highest sequential number (every box is marked with its number and the last number; e.g., "Box 45 of 103"). Copies of the list also go to the distributor and to the producer. I also find it helpful to keep one or two copies for myself.

Every box is then sent to wherever it is supposed to go. Normally these boxes are sent into storage, never to be seen again. It is only the most important paperwork and the release and foreign release printing materials that are saved in a more accessible place.

While the boxes are being packed you should also be returning any equipment that you do not need (I usually hold onto one or two table setups and one Moviola until there is no more film left in the editing room since it is always necessary to check and repair things as you are packing them). Every piece of equipment should be accounted for and returned to the lessor. Any supplies that were bought and not used can often be sold back to the supplier or to

```
                                        Page 1 of 36


          "S I L E N T    N I G H T ,    S I L E N T    C O W B O Y"


                              --Packing List--

                              (Total -- 103 boxes)



     Box # 1        Trims              AA1000 - BB2000

     Box # 2        Trims              BB3000 - CC4000

     Box # 3        Trims              CC5000 - DD5000

     Box # 4        Trims              DD6000 - EE6432

     Box # 5        Trims              EE6433 - GG7000

     Box # 6        Trims              GG8000 - HH9000

     Box # 7        Trims              HH0000 - JJ2000

     Box # 8        Trims              JJ3000 - KK4000

     Box # 9        Trims              KK5000 - LL7645

     Box # 10       Trims              LL7646 - MM8000

     Box # 11       Trims              MM9000 - RR1000
```

FIGURE 16.6   A sample page from a packing list. Note that when trims with the same code prefix are packed in different boxes the last code number in the box (see box 4) is listed. Otherwise the number refers to the entire scene. For instance, box 6 would contain all of the HH9000 trims whether they are coded HH9236 or HH9999. Note also that because we have chosen to omit the code prefix letters II, NN, and OO (since they might be confused with 11, MM, and 00, respectively) they do not appear on our packing list.

another film which needs them. Sometimes the producer will want them if he or she has another film going into production.

After everything has been packed, shipped out, sold, or thrown out the editing rooms should look pretty much as they did when you walked into them on the first day of your job—empty and somewhat depressing. I always feel a tinge of sadness at the end of a job, no matter how much I'm looking forward to a long time off. There is something a little naked about an editing room that has no editing being done it it. I check around the room one last time, close the door behind me, making sure that it locks, march to the front office to turn the keys in, and then leave.

Usually for a long vacation.

17

ODDS AND SODS

Now that you've been through the lengthy process of doing a film the "normal" way I should clue you in to a few of the kinks that you may occasionally meet along the way. These include 70mm films, Dolby films, and video "films." This will only skim the surface of the various oddities that you will be encountering as you work in film editing, but it will be a start.

70mm Films

There are several reasons why a filmmaker might want to shoot and/or release a film in the 70mm format. The first is that saying "in 70mm" on the marquee will bring in a larger audience (or so the prevailing "wisdom" goes). As a result some distributors will insist on a 70mm release for certain kinds of films. A second reason you might want to shoot in 70mm is for better picture quality. The picture area of the 70mm frame is about four times the area of a 35mm frame. This means that the film needs to be magnified less than a 35mm frame to fill a similar-sized screen. In turn, this means that the picture quality of a film shot and released in 70mm will be better than that shot and released in 35mm. Certainly, some of the tricky optical work in the *Star Wars* series of films could not have been done as effectively in 35mm. In fact, whether the original negative was shot in 35mm or 70mm, all of the opticals in the most recent *Star Wars* films were done in the larger format.

There is another plus that you can get with 70mm prints that you cannot get with 35mm, and that is good sound. All 70mm prints have a magnetic soundtrack placed on the film as shown in Figure 17.1. This leaves room for six separately running soundtracks. For this reason any film which wants to release in a six-track soundtrack format must release in 70mm. The sound quality will be better on

FIGURE 17.1   70mm film format. There is room for six magnetic sound tracks, two on each of the wider outside stripes and one on each of the thinner inside stripes. Note that the height of a 70mm frame is five sprockets, not four as in 35mm film.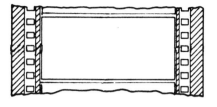

B   A

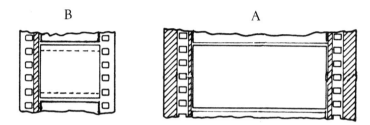

FIGURE 17.2   Differences between 70mm (A) and 35mm (B) film formats. The dotted lines in the 35mm frame show the 1.85 cut-off.

70mm than on 35mm. This is particularly desirable for musical films, which is why musicals are often released in their initial engagements in a 70mm format.

A film need not be shot in 70mm in order to be released in 70mm. An optical blowup can be done to enlarge the 35mm frame to the 70mm size. However, there are two main problems with this. The first is that the quality degrades a little bit as a film goes through the optical process. A blowup (since it will be blowing up a film's deficiencies right along with the image) suffers worse than most opticals. The picture will also become a little grainier. Any film which has a lot of shots right on the edge of sharpness will suffer quite a bit in a blowup.

The second major problem in a blowup is that the frames are of different shapes. As you can see in Figure 17.2 the frame sizes and shapes of 35mm and 70mm film are quite different. In actuality the common screen ratio, as I've mentioned, for 35mm film is 1.85 to 1, which is achieved by chopping off the top and bottom of the frame as shown in the chart.

Since the 70mm frame is far more elongated than the 35mm frame the 35mm image will not fit properly onto the 70mm blowup negative without some adjustment. There are several ways in which this can be accomplished.

The first, and most problematic, way is to blow up each shot in the film in a slightly different manner, attempting to blow up the most important areas of action while losing the least important. In practice this means deciding how much of the top or bottom of the frame you can afford to lose. This way of blowing up is the worst when considered from all sides. It is extremely costly since each shot must be blown up separately. It also destroys whatever composition the cinematographer and camera operator chose for the frame; you are liable to end up with very many ugly-looking frames.

The second way is to do something that we did on *Fame*. *Fame* was shot in 35mm but released in 70mm in its Los Angeles and New York premieres to take full advantage of the magnetic soundtrack for the music. Rather than lose much of the frame we decided to optically place a black matte on either side of the 70mm frame to reduce the screen ratio to more closely approximate 1.85 to 1. This was done as shown in Figure 17.3 and resulted in an image that was smaller than a normal 70mm image. As a result, we ended up with a 70mm print which looked very much like our 35mm prints but with a better soundtrack.

The third way to shoot in 35mm but release in 70mm is to shoot in what is called an *anamorphic* or *squeezed* format. In this format the image that is being shot is squeezed horizontally to fit onto a standard 35mm negative, much as the writing on a balloon appears to squeeze together as the balloon deflates. During projection the image is unsqueezed (or reinflated, if you will) by the exact amount that it was squeezed. This results in an image ratio of 2.2 to 1, the same as the 70mm print ratio. The 70mm prints are then made after unsqueezing the 35mm image. In this way no image is lost in the transfer to 70mm. This is definitely the preferred way to go if it is known that the film is going to be blown up to 70mm. The only problem with this method is that all of the 35mm prints made for the rest of the theatres in the world (and there will be far more 35mm prints made than 70mm prints) will be in this squeezed format. This will require a special lens to unsqueeze the image at the theatre. Most theatres are equipped to show anamorphic prints but since the alignment of the projector and the frame within the projector gate is much more crucial than with regular 35mm film, anamorphic 35mm prints are rarely perfectly shown. The edges of

FIGURE 17.3 On *Fame* we utilized a special 70mm blowup. We took the 1.85 image and placed it as large as we could get onto the 70mm frame. We then blacked out the two edge portions of the 70mm frame that were not utilized. In this way we took advantage of the superior sound of the 70mm format without ruining the picture image (which had been shot for showing in 35mm 1.85 format).

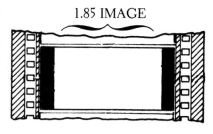

1.85 IMAGE

the frame tend to be out of focus and frame lines at the top and bottom of the screen are often visible. For that reason, the standard 35mm print is usually the best choice for projection unless it is impossible (such as when the 35mm negative is squeezed).

70mm film is never edited in 70mm. 35mm reduction prints are made of the 70mm negative for dailies and cutting purposes. Opticals are, of course, done in the same manner. The negative cutter matches the 70mm negative (actually the negative is 65mm, since no room is left for the soundtrack areas) to the 35mm workprint.

If the film is shot in 35mm squeezed format, however, the workprint will be in squeezed format (so that all cutting can be made with the full frame visible). In that case, a large bulky lens must be mounted on the front of the Moviola to unsqueeze the image. This makes it a little more difficult to work with but otherwise it does not affect the cutting process at all. On a flatbed, the adjustment is much easier—there is a dial that you can turn to switch from a normal lens to a anamorphic. In addition, on KEMs, you can get a special large wide-screen head so that you can see a very large image.

Dolby Films

If you have been living anywhere but in Antarctica for the last five or six years you have been aware of the Dolby phenomenon in motion pictures. The Dolby name seems to pop up on some of the biggest movies—*Star Wars, Raiders of the Lost Ark, E.T.*, and many others. As an assistant film editor you will have to be familiar with what Dolby is and what it can do because you are liable to be working on a Dolby film at some point.

Basically, Dolby does two things for movies. To describe just what they are let me take a short detour, to explain about normal film sound.

As I briefly mentioned in the last chapter, sound is placed on the release print in the form of an optical track. The optical track system has been in use in the industry since the introduction of sound (magnetic soundtracks are a relatively recent development). As a result there are some standards that have been developed that are a bit outdated. The most important one of these standards is something called the *academy roll-off*. This academy, by the way, is the same one that developed the standard for the countdown leaders. This roll-off is, simply, a standard way of degrading the sound so that it will not harm most of the theatre sound systems. More specifically, it gives a standard for the sound mixer (at the film mix) to take out many of the high-frequency sounds in the soundtrack. This standard was much more practical in the old days of theatre sound but remains today and is something of an albatross in terms of cinema sound. It is just not possible to have very good sound when there is no sound above 8000 hertz, and decreasing amounts above 2000 hertz.

The first advantage of using Dolby in films is the Dolby noise-reduction system (similar to that on a home cassette deck), which puts much of that high-frequency range back into the soundtrack. In essence, it sets its own standard, rather than adapting to the academy standard. Using this you can get sound up to 12,000 hertz. Though this hardly touches the upper range of human hearing (the upper range of an organ scale is almost 20,000 hertz, for instance), it does add much to the fullness of the sound that we hear from a movie soundtrack. Dolby is, therefore, ideally suited to the soundtrack of a musically oriented film.

The second use of the Dolby film system is the practical achievement of stereo sound in the theatres. Previous to Dolby the only way to get stereo sound for a film was to print separate tracks on magnetic stripes directly onto the film. In this way you could get four tracks onto a piece of 35mm film. The drawbacks of a magnetic soundtrack on 35mm were discussed in the last chapter, however, and it was never a very effective or cheap way of attaining stereo. The Dolby system takes advantage of the fact that there are *two* squiggly lines on an optical track. It uses a special matrix to encode four channels of sound into two. These two are then put onto the film via an optical track. At the theatre, during projection, these two are then decoded back into the original four tracks. This method is often referred to as the 4-2-4 method, for obvious reasons.

Since the Dolby four-track process is an optical process it costs no more to print (once the optical negative is made) than a normal optical soundtrack print. For this reason, stereo is now easier to accomplish than it used to be.

For the assistant editor, there is more work involved in the preparation of a Dolby release than for a monaural one. This comes primarily because the tolerances for a Dolby release are far stricter than for a normal film (you didn't expect there *not* to be a tradeoff, did you?). One of the most frustrating things about making a Dolby film is that the tremendous increase in sound quality that you hear in the mixing studio is rarely matched in the theatres. In order to make sure that the best possible sound does reach the theatres it is necessary to do more policing of the prints and theatres.

On *Hair* three assistant editors sat screening release prints of the film almost around the clock in the weeks before the film's mass release. They were checking not only the quality of the picture print but whether the soundtrack was good. Because of the tighter tolerances of the Dolby soundtrack it is essential that better quality control exist at the lab. Many labs offer high-speed printing of release prints at a reduced cost. Most distributors take advantage of this savings. However, this increased speed usually results in reduced sound quality, especially if the lab allows their print bath to get dirty. It is important to check on these prints, as much as your budget will allow (obviously, you can't check every print of a mass release; but you can try and check every print that is going to a major city or to an important theatre in a major city).

Another important check comes at the theatre showing the print. One of the biggest deficiencies of the Dolby process is that it is incumbent upon the theatres to upgrade and service their equipment so that they can play the improved soundtrack. Most theatres, being financially marginal operations, rarely invest the money needed to make sure that this better sound is played back properly. And, even if they do invest in new amplifiers, preamplifiers, and speakers, they rarely know how to keep them in top-notch operating condition. Dolby has set up no policing policy for this and, as a result, many theatres which have the Dolby playback units still cannot play back proper Dolby sound. There is no point, after all, in having increased high frequencies if you are playing back your sound through a 30-watt amplifier that can't reproduce that better high end.

On the two Dolby films I've worked on—*Hair* and *Fame*—I actually went into the theatres where we were going to open the film and tested the sound. We then equalized the theatre (that is, made sure that the playback of the sound fit the Dolby standard) and then ran a few reels of the film and adjusted the sound again, until I was hearing a sound as close to what I had heard in the mixing studio as I could. I should say here that *no* theatre sound is going to equal the mixing studio sound. In fact, no two theatres are going to sound alike. Room acoustics are too different for that. I have even been in theatres where no two parts of the theatre sounded alike (this is especially true with domed theatres). It is most important to go for the best sound that the individual theatre can reproduce, even if it is not exactly what you mixed.

Dolby stereo prints on 35mm are actually four-channel prints. There are three channels fed behind the screen—one each on the left, the center, and the right—and one channel is fed to the *surround speakers* which can be anywhere that the theatre chooses to put them. Common locations for surround speakers are on the rear wall or down the two side walls. I have been in theatres where they are placed in the ceiling, behind the screen, or all over the theatre.

You can also get Dolby stereo on 70mm prints but it is of a slightly different type. First of all, it is a magnetic track, not an optical one. Second, there are six tracks of sound, not four. Dolby uses these two additional channels in a special way. They lead to speakers behind the screen in between the center speaker and the outside ones (for this reason the two additional channels are referred to as left-center and right-center). These channels, called *baby boom channels*, will only reproduce very low frequency information— rumbling or low notes of a score. *Close Encounters of the Third Kind* used these channels extremely effectively during the landing of the spaceship. The low-frequency sound practically rattled the theatre seats.

By and large, Dolby films are mixed in the same way as mono films. The effects and music need to be recorded on the tracks slightly differently. Effects will have to be planned to go either in the left or right channels (the surround channels are good for certain very specific effects—crowd sounds and the like—which come from all around rather than from a specific place).

The major difference between Dolby and mono film mixing comes after the mixing is over. First of all, the film is not mixed onto a single D-M-E full-coat. It must be mixed onto a four-track full-coat (or a six-track if it is a 70mm six-track Dolby stereo release). This four-track will not be split in the normal way, since it will reflect exactly what is intended to appear in each of the four channels in the theatre. Therefore, music will always be mixed with effects and often dialogue (which almost always goes into the center channel) will be mixed with effects. You will have nothing comparable to the D-M-E. You will therefore have to do a completely separate foreign mix.

At M-G-M studios (and one studio in England) they have a very expensive but very handy system where, in addition to recording onto a four-coat Dolby mixed mag, you also will be recording three other Dolby four-coats, one each for dialogue, effects, and music. You thus end up with the equivalent of a D-M-E, spread between three full-coats. This makes creating a foreign Dolby version much easier. These separate full-coats are called *stems*.

The second way in which mixing a Dolby film is different is that, obviously, you will have to mix a second version of the film—in mono. It won't take as much time to mix it as a normal film would since most of the film is already mixed. But a good mono mix cannot be gotten just by collapsing all of the four channels into one. Some finessing must be done.

The third way in which the Dolby process is different from the monaural is in the creation of the optical track. Because the Dolby stereo format works by collapsing the four tracks into two in a special way, it must be treated differently. First a Dolby two-track master must be made from the four-track mix. Then this two-track goes to a special transfer house (usually the Phil Boole Recording Service in Burbank, California) where a Dolby optical track negative is made. *This* is what then goes to the lab. Care should be taken to listen to the first print from this optical track since Dolby sound is more sensitive than monaural sound to dirt and printing errors and may not be correct on the first try.

There is much else to be learned about Dolby sound, enough to fill a small book of its own, but armed with these facts, and a knowledgeable helper, you can control the quality of the picture and sound of your film.

Video in the Editing Room

Over the last few years there has been an increasing awareness of video technology among film directors. This awareness first began on the set, where a simultaneous video recording of the scene being shot could give everyone an instantaneous playback (almost like an immediate dailies session) so that decisions as to whether to do another take could be made more easily. Many directors liked this ability.

Then, on *Apocalypse Now*, Francis Ford Coppola began doing some of the editing of the film on a small videotape editing system. Using this system he was able to experiment with opticals in a way that would have been extremely costly and time-consuming to do on film. Though all of the optical and editing work was ultimately done on film, the time saved in the video editing obviously intrigued Coppola enough to try and edit his next film, *One from the Heart*, all on video. Woody Allen has begun editing his films on videotape as well. Video editing is plainly the wave of the future. As more and more filmmakers begin to turn to video in the editing process the technology will have to improve. And as the technology improves more and more films will be edited in that way. Already, film editing at the television networks is fast disappearing in their news departments. Many independent filmmakers are turning to video to help speed up their schedules and to save them money. Can feature filmmaking hold out forever?

Obviously, no one really knows the answer to that question. But my instinctive feeling is that the editor of the future who knows nothing about videotape will be in an anachronistic minority.

Until videotape technology settles into some kind of pattern it will be difficult to know exactly what position the assistant editor will have in a videotape editing situation. Some people feel that there will be no need for an assistant. Others feel that it is the apprentice's job, rather than the assistant's, that will undergo the most change for there will be no trims to put away. Every edit will be saved on tape (or on videodisc, if the project that the people at Lucasfilm is working on succeeds) through the use of a small computer. It seems to me that everyone's jobs—editors', assistants', and apprentices'—will have to be redefined.

The basics of the video editing process rest on something called the *SMPTE code*. This is a sync signal (much like the 60 hertz tone used to synchronize recording tape and film) which rides on the videotape. It is actually a number that looks something like this: 12:34:56:29 (which is a readout of sequential hours, minutes, seconds, and video frames—thirty frames per second). It can be printed out on the bottom of the screen (a *visual time code*) or just as numbers on a track of the tape (an *audio time code*). In this manner every part of the tape has its own unique time code number, just as you gave every foot of film a unique edge code number on *Silent Night*. A computer reads these numbers and remembers where you want to make a cut and where you want to cut to. It then adjusts the tape electronically so that the images will line up perfectly and then, on another piece of tape, makes the edit for you. On many systems you can preview the edit before transferring it onto the other tape. If it doesn't work, you can adjust it. Then, when you are satisfied, you can make the edit and watch the cut sequence.

The biggest drawback that videotape editing has had up until now has been its method of saving the stored cut picture and track. If a change was to be made in the cut, even of only a frame or two, the entire cut from that change on had to be retransferred onto videotape. There was no way to splice in those additional frames (or, for that matter, to take them out). Videodisc editing systems get around that problem by remembering the cuts on a computer and recreating them each time it is played back. But making videodiscs is a tremendously expensive and lengthy process. When a fast and cheap method of making videodiscs is perfected (it is already in development) so that dailies can be seen on videodisc the day after a shoot, we will truly see the beginning of video and the computer in the editing room.

Television Versions

It is no secret to the millions of viewers of television that movies that have played in the theatres and are later broadcast on television are "edited for television." This is usually because of excessive sex or offensive language in the original version which the television censors will not allow on network television. Six or seven years ago it was not uncommon for the network to reedit the film for their needs and, in the process, completely butcher the film. Recently, however, distributors have taken to insisting that directors shoot alternate versions of potentially objectionable scenes. In *Fame*, for instance, there was a scene where some boys in the boys' bathroom were looking through a hole in the wall into the girls' room where a number of girls were walking around bare-breasted. The director, Alan Parker, shot an alternate version of the boys' point of view in which none of the girls was uncovered. This type of *television coverage*, as it is called, is now more the rule than the exception in shooting films. No one is particularly proud of knowingly creating a bowdlerized version of their own film but the prevailing wisdom is that it is better to do it yourself than let the networks do it.

After the completion of the feature version of the movie it is the responsibility of the editor to create a television version of the potentially objectionable dialogue and action in the film. On *Fame* one of the M-G-M vice-presidential types came down to the editing room and, for a few days, went through the entire film compiling a list of everything that *he* thought would have to go. The list was actually quite amusing, being topped with a tally sheet counting the number of occurrences of each "dirty" word.

Someone, either the editor or a vice-presidential type, must make up such a list. After it is made up, the director and the editor should decide just how to deal with each occurrence. Some of the objectionable words will be easily replaced simply in the sound editing—words like "shit" can be replaced by "shoot." It is the responsibility of the looping editor to get these replacement lines when he or she is doing the original looping sessions. If some were missed then the actors or actresses must be called back to do these lines.

Other objectionable items (either dialogue or action) must be replaced by recutting. In some cases a shot of someone saying an objectionable word can be replaced with a shot of another person. The offending word/sentence is either removed or looped. Always remember when making these reedits that any time a picture cut is made one frame is lost in the already existing material for the negative cutter's splicing.

After all of the reediting is done you will have a black and white dupe of the film with the color print changes cut into it, and a soundtrack with additions and deletions made in it.

For all of the reels that have had changes made in them, then, a mix and a new cut negative must be made. Obviously, you won't want to recut the negative made for the proper version of the film. You will, instead, want to make an alternate cut negative. There is, of course, no way to do this with the original negative. However, this version can be made with a dupe negative. This is done by making a dupe negative of the reels that need to be changed. The negative cutter receives your television recut of those reels (if you've been a good assistant, these TV recuts should be plainly leadered as such) and will match to this new cut. It is also very helpful if you submit a television conformation list—that is, a list of all of the conformations made for the television version (the sound department will get a copy of this conformation list as well so they can create a television soundtrack). The negative cutter can then match the new negative to this print, cutting the new negative into the reel's dupe negative.

In actuality, however, if the negative cutter were to cut the new negative into the dupe negative, any resultant print would look very odd since the difference in quality between a print from the duped portion of the reel and a print from the original negative portion of the reel would be quite extreme. This happens because of the difference in generations; when prints from different generations are cut together it is usually noticeable.

The way to solve this problem is to make a dupe negative of the new material and cut it into the reel, not the original negative. When a print is made from this new cut there will be no difference in generation between the two verisons of material—the IP/IN of the original film and the IP/IN of the new footage.

You will also have to have a new mix made for the reels where sound changes occurred. You will often find that many more sound changes will be necessary than picture changes. It is your responsibility to make sure that all such changes are communicated to the sound department. When they have had a chance to make the adjustments in all of their reels then they will remix those reels and end up with new optical track negative for the television reels.

There is one potential source of confusion here. Since the television version is often the version of the film that is sold almost immediately to the airlines for in-flight showing it is usually necessary to have both versions of the movie printed simultaneously (or almost simultaneously). It is possible that the two versions of the film might get confused. I have found it helpful in such cases to make a complete set of television dupe negatives and optical track negatives, even if some of the reels have not been changed. These new picture negatives and track negatives should be plainly marked "SOFT VERSION" or "TELEVISION VERSION." In this way, it is much harder for someone at the lab to mix up one with the other.

18

THE HARDEST JOB OF ALL—FINDING A JOB

Anyone who has ever tried to find a job in the film industry—or any other industry in the known world—has heard of something called the catch-22 of job seeking. Put simply it goes like this—you can't get a job without experience though you can't get experience without a job. It is a revolving door of missed opportunities. You can't get a job without first having a job.

Somehow, people still get that first job. It is not impossible, merely absurdly difficult. This chapter will try to give you some hints to help you get that first job.

The Resume

When people come to me looking for work I always ask them for a resume. I don't really do this so that I can see all of the experience that a job applicant has; but for two reasons. First, it gives me an association between a name and a face (often I can use one of the jobs listed on the resume for a mnemonic key). Second, it gives me an address and phone number in case I do decide to hire that person.

This illustrates something about how people look for work. There are so many people who would like to work in film editing that it is all to easy to forget just who everyone is. Anything that can differentiate you from the next job applicant is helpful.

This is advice that I give everyone who asks me for work. Find out what makes you more valuable than the next person—if you speak a foreign language, if you used to work in social services, if you can read music, etc., etc. List *that* on your resume. Your differences will be what gets you, as opposed to the next person, hired.

Your resume need not be an elaborate one. Most people get by with a simple typed list of their jobs, including short descriptions of the tasks they performed on each. The resume should, however, be neat and well organized. Editing situations require both characteristics and if a person's resume is lacking in either category I would think twice about hiring them. There are so many people looking for work that anything that gives an indication that you would be unsuitable for the job should be avoided on your resume.

A sample resume is given in Figure 18.1. Betty has worked in features for the last several jobs. Since she is looking for feature work, that is what she is listing on her resume. She mentions who she has already worked with and that she is in the New York editors' union. This is the type of resume that she can give to almost any editor in New York and be guaranteed consideration for a job.

Most jobs at the level that Betty is at are given to people with whom editors have already worked. A look at Betty's rise in the editing room would will show you this. She began as an apprentice sound editor on a film that Charles Simpson cut. She apparently impressed him enough that when it came time to hire an apprentice editor on his next film he asked her. On the basis of this experience she was asked to be Nate High's assistant music editor on a film; she continued in that function on *Silent Night, Silent Cowboy*. Though Betty's rise is a bit more meteoric than most (many sound apprentices work three or four jobs before being able to move up— either to apprentice picture editor for four or five jobs or to assistant sound editor) it is illustrative of the way in which most people move up in the field—through impressing the people with whom they've worked enough to be asked onto other jobs with them.

Unless your father happens to own a film studio this kind of proximity to those who do the hiring will probably not be available to you. In this case, the only kind of proximity that you can get is to constantly go out on job interviews. A sample of the kind of resume a newcomer might take around is given in Figure 18.2. Edward Zee, being someone with no contacts in the film industry, has had to stretch his credits a bit. The truth of his career, as opposed to his resume, is as follows. The trailer company that he worked for in 1983 was a small trailer company run by a friend of his. They had one job in the entire week that he was there and Ed

---

BETTY BOUND
123 Alphabet Street
New York, NY 10000
212/123-4567

Member Local 771, IATSE

May–July 1983
SILENT NIGHT, SILENT COWBOY — Assistant Music Editor. Feature film
directed by Adam Free. Edited by Wendy Libre. Music Editor —
Nate High.

January–March 1983
BOOTLEG, BOOTLEG — Assistant Music Editor. Feature film directed by
Cecil B. DeMille. Edited by Beeg Editor. Music Editor — Nate High.

January–December 1982
*THE ESCAPE OF THE MONSTERS FROM OUTER SPACE WITH FLASHY
CARS* — Apprentice Picture Editor. Feature film directed by Eric von
Stroheim. Edited by Charles Simpson.

August–November 1981
DADDY WEIRDEST — Apprentice Sound Editor. Feature film directed by
Eric von Stroheim. Edited by Charles Simpson. Supervising Sound
Editor — Wallace Foley.

References Available On Request

FIGURE 18.1   Resume for an experienced person.

really didn't do much except order IPs from the lab. But he did learn
how to do that. The film *The Apple of Your Eye* was a low-budget
short that a friend of his directed after he graduated from UCLA.
The short, paid for through family money, never went anywhere
but Ed's friend does have a print lying around his house somewhere.
Ed, though he did not get paid a cent for working on the film, did
learn a lot about editing from the woman who cut the film (who was
working as an assistant editor on a low-budget feature during the
day while cutting this film at night with Ed).

E D W A R D   Z E E
987 Sixth Street
Santa Monica, CA 90000
213/555-1212

Objective — To work as an Apprentice Editor or anything that will lead
to a job in an editing room.

Experience
1983 — *Sample Trailer Company* — Worked in this trailer editing house
in all facets of the editing process. Ordered IPs from labs, assisted
trailer editors in the editing, prepared tracks for dub, etc.
1982 — *The Apple of Your Eye* — Worked as an assistant editor helping
with dailies and trims on this low-budget short. Sunk dailies, filed
trims, helped preparing for the dub.
1982 — Edited the following films at UCLA Film School:
"Cheaper By The Baker's Dozen"
"Smoked Out"
"Enough Is Too Much"
1978-1982 — UCLA Film School, graduated BFA
Have edited several films of my own.

References
B. I. Hertz — Editor, Sample Trailer — 213/936-1212
Phyllis Murphy — Editor — 213/312-6427

FIGURE 18.2   Resume for a newcomer.

You can see how to subtly stretch the truth in a resume. The
idea is never to misrepresent what you know but to give your experience in the best possible light.

What the editor who needs an apprentice is really looking for
is someone who seems enthusiastic about working hard and long
hours, someone who knows enough about filmmaking and film editing that it won't be necessary to explain what a frame line is, and
someone who gives the impression that they will be easy to work
and live with for a long duration of time in a confined area.

Hitting the Pavement

Instead of working with other people, most beginners have only their own personalities to sell themselves. The only way that they can be seen is to go out and knock on doors. They should try and visit every editing company or editing room that they can find so that they may introduce themselves, drop off a resume, and make their needs known.

How does one find these editing rooms? Sometimes you can call the phone numbers of production companies listed for movies being shot in *Daily Variety* or *The Hollywood Reporter* and ask them where the movies are being edited. Sometimes they might even tell you. There are several books which are published which list, among other things, editorial services. Motion Picture Enterprises Publications, Inc. (Tarrytown, New York 10591) publishes a book called *Motion Picture, TV, and Theatre Directory* which is a yellow-covered book listing services for film and television. Called the "yellow book," it is a good place to begin looking for locations of editing rooms either under the "Editing Services," "Cutting Rooms," or "Editing Equipment—Rental" categories. This book is primarily useful for the East Coast, however. On the West Coast there is another guide published, called the *Pacific Coast Studio Directory*.

The best way to reach these people is to go to their cutting rooms. This is a minor annoyance to the editors but it is impossible to effectively sell yourself otherwise. And, make no mistake about it, you *will* be selling yourself. You will be in competition with at least twenty or twenty-five other people for each job that is available. On an average six-month job in New York an editor will accumulate about a hundred resumes.

Once again, the best things to try and sell are your differences. There will be plenty of people looking for work who will have worked more than you. They can sell themselves on the basis of their experience; you cannot. You must sell yourself on the basis of your energy, and your willingness to work hard and learn.

Often it is necessary to work for free while you are looking for a toehold in the industry. Everyone I know has worked for nothing or next to nothing at the beginning of their careers. It is one way of getting experience; it is also one way of getting to meet people. In the introduction to this book I talked of my first week on the movie *Lenny*, my first paying editorial job. Let me briefly describe what went before that for you.

I went to a public university in New York State, a school which is much better known for its science students than for its theatre students. There were about forty students altogether in the Theatre Arts department (the department I eventually ended up in). There were, at the time, four film courses, all taught by one professor. One day in my junior year Karl, a Columbia University graduate film student who was doing a project near the college, called and asked if there was anybody who would be interested in working on the set of his film for two weeks for no money. My film professor announced it in his class and several people expressed interest. I, however, was the first one to the phone after the class (I remember dashing into the department office so fast that I lost several papers I had been writing; but that is another story).

I got the job and ended up working fourteen hours a day for two straight weeks on a rather charming fiction film about a boy who was an outcast at his school. I ended up working in a crew composed of the director, a cameraman, an assistant camerawoman (who later edited the film), and a soundman. I was the "assistant everything." I learned more in those two weeks than I could have learned in two years in my film classes.

The next year, when Karl was shooting another film, he called me directly and asked if I would like to work on the new film. I did.

The summer after I graduated Karl had begun to get work that paid. He was directing public service announcements for a small production company. He had been given enough of a budget to hire someone to help out on the set as a production assistant (also known as a "gofer" since they "gofer coffee" and "gofer sandwiches," etc., etc.). Karl hired me. But after having made a few of my own films at college (in lieu of term papers) I had discovered that I liked editing more than any other part of the filmmaking process. I asked to be able to assist him in the editing room. I would do it for free. Karl agreed.

These little jobs did not occur very often. In order to support myself I worked as a temporary secretary, typing at accounting firms and law offices. Finally, a job came where Karl had enough money to hire an editor—a woman named Kathy. We worked together and liked each other a lot. While we were working together she was hired to be the supervising sound editor on *Lenny*. She asked me if I would work on it. I thought about it for about two nanoseconds and said "yes."

I tell this story not to bore you but to show you the difference between being lucky and making your own luck. It was luck that Karl called my college to ask for help but it was my doing that I raced to the phone as soon as I found out about the job. It was Karl's doing that he got paying work but it was my work on the earlier films that got him to call me for that offer. And while it may have been luck that Kathy was hired to work on the little public service announcement at about the same time that she was hired onto *Lenny* it was I who volunteered to work for nothing in the editing room on these films and it was my work that Kathy liked enough to prompt her to ask me to work on *Lenny*.

There is no such thing as pure, unadulterated "luck." There is only the need to put yourself in the position where luck can work, and that requires the proper aggressive attitude and *need* to work in the field. Sometimes, that aggressiveness will mean you work for free. I don't think that it is a bad idea to accept those kinds of jobs, if you can afford it. People get paid in many ways besides money— experience is more valuable in the long run than money in this field.

When you go around looking for jobs the best thing that you have to sell is yourself, your desire to give the person who will hire you a lot of effort and energy. Everyone starts with no experience. Most editors remember that when it comes time for them to hire someone.

Unions

One of the first stops in looking for work should be the editors' unions in whatever city you are looking for work. In New York, that is Local 771 IATSE. In Hollywood and San Francisco it is Local 776 IATSE. There are other editors' unions in Canada and Chicago. There are also other unions, most notably NABET. Though their editors rarely do feature films they are fairly active in commercials and other low-budget ventures.

The main job of a union is to serve its membership and, for many, that means to keep the number of people looking for work low so that their own members will have more of a chance at the available work. This makes it very difficult to get into the union. There is a federal law which states that any person working on a job for more than thirty days must not be denied the right to continue working. This law, the Taft-Hartley Law, means that, after working in a union job for thirty days you must be allowed to join the union. What this law does, however, is to introduce another catch-22 into the work equation—you cannot work on a union job without being in the union, and you cannot get into the union without working on a union job. Like all catch-22s, it is not an easy catch to get through. Like all catch-22s, however, it is constantly broken by people who have the right combination of luck and the ability to generate opportunities for luck.

The Los Angeles working situation is also complicated by something called the *producers' experience roster*. Basically, this is a roster of people who have worked on union films. It is divided into three categories, called Groups One, Two, and Three. When you first get on the roster (if you can get on the roster) you are placed in Group Three. Two years later you rise to Group Two and three years after that you move up to Group One. Producers and editors are supposed to fill open positions first from any available Group One people before looking in the Group Two list. And, only if all available Group One *and* Two members are working or not available for work, are they allowed to hire from Group Three. Needless to say, the number of times when all of the members of all three groups are working are few and far between. This leaves virtually no chance for the unknown job seeker to break into a union film.

Yet people do it all the time. How? Some people do it because their parents or their friends are already on the roster and are willing to hire them despite the rules. Thirty days later they can join both the union and the roster. What these people have going for them is their connection into the industry. *That* is what makes them different from other job seekers, however unfair it may seem to those who cannot get into the union.

So how does a person break into film and the union? The easiest way is to acknowledge to yourself that this is really two separate tasks, not just one. Your first step should be to try and get into film. *Then* you can try to break into the unions and the roster. Once you have worked enough in nonunion film work (and there is a lot of it around, both in New York and Hollywood, though New York nonunion filmmaking is rarely in features) then you can begin to accumulate the contacts and knowledge to make a break into union work.

I have always found that good work does not go unrewarded. If you work hard enough and learn well enough you will be able to move in whatever direction you want. First you must hit the pavements and meet a lot of people; you will get work (if you are persistent enough without being obnoxious). Then you must be good enough at that work to impress people. Once that happens, you will be able to move toward whatever kind of filmmaking you want to do—whether it be features, television, documentaries, or anything else. There are too many people in this industry for it to be easy. But it is never impossible.

APPENDIX I

To convert the length of your film, in feet, into time, you could use a calculator; but there's an easier way.

Find your film's length, in feet, in the column marked "feet" in the first chart (forget about the number of frames for now). The time will be directly across from it, in the proper column for your film gauge (each film format runs at a different number of feet per minute). Then use the second chart to find the number of seconds corresponding to the number of frames. Add this to the time obtained from the first chart and you've got it!

For instance, *Silent Night, Silent Cowboy*, the film in this book, runs 9432'12 (9432 feet 12 frames).

9000	feet is	1:40:00.0	(1 hour 40 minutes)
400	feet is	0:04:27.0	
32	feet is	0:00:21.0	
12	frames is	0:00:00.5	
	Total	1:44:48.5	

Footage-to-Time Conversions			
FEET	16mm	35mm	65/70mm
	Sec	Sec	Sec
1	2	1	1
2	3	1	1
3	5	2	2
4	7	3	2
5	8	3	3
6	10	4	3
7	12	5	4
8	13	5	4
9	15	6	5
10	17	7	5
11	18	7	6
12	20	8	6
13	22	9	7

FEET	16mm Min/Sec		35mm Sec	65/70mm Sec
14		23	9	7
15		25	10	8
16		27	11	9
17		28	11	9
18		30	12	10
19		32	13	10
20		33	13	11
21		35	14	11
22		37	15	12
23		38	15	12
24		40	16	13
25		42	17	13
26		43	17	14
27		45	18	14
28		47	19	15
29		48	19	16
30		50	20	16
31		52	21	17
32		53	21	17
33		55	22	18
34		57	23	18
35		58	23	19
36	1	0	24	19
37	1	2	25	20
38	1	3	25	20
39	1	5	26	21
40	1	7	27	21
41	1	8	27	22
42	1	10	28	22
43	1	12	29	23
44	1	13	29	24
45	1	15	30	24
46	1	17	31	25
47	1	18	31	25
48	1	20	32	26
49	1	22	33	26
50	1	23	33	27
51	1	25	34	27
52	1	27	35	28
53	1	28	35	28

FEET	16mm Min/Sec		35mm Min/Sec		65/70mm Sec
54	1	30		36	29
55	1	32		37	29
56	1	33		37	30
57	1	35		38	30
58	1	37		39	31
59	1	38		39	32
60	1	40		40	32
61	1	42		41	33
62	1	43		41	33
63	1	45		42	34
64	1	47		43	34
65	1	48		43	35
66	1	50		44	35
67	1	52		45	36
68	1	53		45	36
69	1	55		46	37
70	1	57		47	37
71	1	58		47	38
72	2	0		48	39
73	2	2		49	39
74	2	3		49	40
75	2	5		50	40
76	2	7		51	41
77	2	8		51	41
78	2	10		52	42
79	2	12		53	42
80	2	13		53	43
81	2	15		54	43
82	2	17		55	44
83	2	18		55	44
84	2	20		56	45
85	2	22		57	45
86	2	23		57	46
87	2	25		58	47
88	2	27		59	47
89	2	28		59	48
90	2	30	1	0	48
91	2	32	1	1	49
92	2	33	1	1	49
93	2	35	1	2	50

FEET	16mm Hr/Min/Sec		35mm Hr/Min/Sec		65/70mm Hr/Min/Sec	
94		2 37	1	3		50
95		2 38	1	3		51
96		2 40	1	4		51
97		2 42	1	5		52
98		2 43	1	5		52
99		2 45	1	6		53
100		2 47	1	7		53
200		5 33	2	13	1	47
300		8 20	3	20	2	40
400		11 7	4	27	3	33
500		13 53	5	33	4	27
600		16 40	6	40	5	20
700		19 27	7	47	6	13
800		22 13	8	53	7	7
900		25 0	10	0	8	0
1,000		27 47	11	7	8	53
2,000		55 33	22	13	17	47
3,000	1	23 20	33	20	26	40
4,000	1	51 7	44	27	35	33
5,000	2	18 53	55	33	44	27
6,000	2	46 40	1 06	40	53	20
7,000	3	14 27	1 17	47	1 02	13
8,000	3	42 13	1 28	53	1 11	7
9,000	4	10 0	1 40	0	1 20	0
10,000	4	37 47	1 51	7	1 28	53

APPENDIX II

To find the length, in feet and frames, for a piece of film of a given length of time, locate the amount of time you want to convert in the "seconds" or "minutes" column. The length, in feet and frames, will be directly across from it in the proper column for your film gauge.

For example, a 16mm film that lasts 21 minutes 11 seconds is 762'24.

Frames-to-seconds conversions			
Fr	Sec	Fr	Sec
1	0.0	21	0.9
2	0.1	22	0.9
3	0.1	23	1.0
4	0.2	24	1.0
5	0.2	25	1.0
6	0.3	26	1.1
7	0.3	27	1.1
8	0.3	28	1.2
9	0.4	29	1.2
10	0.4	30	1.3
11	0.5	31	1.3
12	0.5	32	1.3
13	0.5	33	1.4
14	0.6	34	1.4
15	0.6	35	1.5
16	0.7	36	1.5
17	0.7	37	1.5
18	0.8	38	1.6
19	0.8	39	1.6
20	0.8	40	1.7

Sec	16mm		35mm		65/70mm	
	Ft	Fr	Ft	Fr	Ft	Fr
1	0	24	1	8	1	11.2
2	1	8	3		3	9.6
3	1	32	4	8	5	8
4	2	16	6		7	6.4
5	3	0	7	8	9	4.8
6	3	24	9		11	3.2
7	4	8	10	8	13	1.6
8	4	32	12		15	
9	5	16	13	8	16	11.2
10	6	0	15		18	9.6
11	6	24	16	8	20	8
12	7	8	18		22	6.4
13	7	32	19	8	24	4.8
14	8	16	21		26	3.2
15	9	0	22	8	28	1.6
16	9	24	24		30	
17	10	8	25	8	31	11.2
18	10	32	27		33	9.6
19	11	16	28	8	35	8
20	12	0	30		37	6.4
21	12	24	31	8	39	4.8
22	13	8	33		41	3.2
23	13	32	34	8	43	1.6
24	14	16	36		45	
25	15	0	37	8	46	11.2
26	15	24	39		48	9.6
27	16	8	40	8	50	8
28	16	32	42		52	6.4
29	17	16	43	8	54	4.8
30	18	0	45		56	3.2
31	18	24	46	8	58	1.6
32	19	8	48		60	
33	19	32	49	8	61	11.2
34	20	16	51		63	9.6
35	21	0	52	8	65	8
36	21	24	54		67	6.4
37	22	8	55	8	69	4.8
38	22	32	57		71	3.2

Sec	16mm Ft	16mm Fr	35mm Ft	35mm Fr	65/70mm Ft	65/70mm Fr
39	23	16	58	8	73	1.6
40	24	0	60		75	
41	24	24	61	8	76	11.2
42	25	8	63		78	9.6
43	25	32	64	8	80	8
44	26	16	66		82	6.4
45	27	0	67	8	84	4.8
46	27	24	69		86	3.2
47	28	8	70	8	88	1.6
48	28	32	72		90	
49	29	16	73	8	91	11.2
50	30	0	75		93	9.6
51	30	24	76	8	95	8
52	31	8	78		97	6.4
53	31	32	79	8	99	4.8
54	32	16	81		101	3.2
55	33	0	82	8	103	1.6
56	33	24	84		105	
57	34	8	85	8	106	11.2
58	34	32	87		108	9.6
59	35	16	88	8	110	8

Min	16mm Ft	35mm Ft	65/70mm Ft	65/70mm Fr
1	36	90	112	6.4
2	72	180	225	
3	108	270	337	6.4
4	144	360	450	
5	180	450	562	6.4
6	216	540	675	
7	252	630	787	6.4
8	288	720	900	
9	324	810	1012	6.4
10	360	900	1125	
11	396	990	1237	6.4
12	432	1080	1350	
13	468	1170	1462	6.4
14	504	1260	1575	

Min	16mm	35mm	65/70mm	
	Ft	Ft	Ft	Fr
15	540	1350	1687	6.4
16	576	1440	1800	
17	612	1530	1912	6.4
18	648	1620	2025	
19	684	1710	2137	6.4
20	720	1800	2250	
21	756	1890	2362	6.4
22	792	1980	2475	
23	828	2070	2587	6.4
24	864	2160	2700	
25	900	2250	2812	6.4
26	936	2340	2925	
27	972	2430	3037	6.4
28	1008	2520	3150	
29	1044	2610	3262	6.4
30	1080	2700	3375	
31	1116	2790	3487	6.4
32	1152	2880	3600	
33	1188	2970	3712	6.4
34	1224	3060	3825	
35	1260	3150	3937	6.4
36	1296	3240	4050	
37	1332	3330	4162	6.4
38	1368	3420	4275	
39	1404	3510	4387	6.4
40	1440	3600	4500	
41	1476	3690	4612	6.4
42	1512	3780	4725	
43	1548	3870	4837	6.4
44	1584	3960	4950	
45	1620	4050	5062	6.4
46	1656	4140	5175	
47	1692	4230	5287	6.4
48	1728	4320	5400	
49	1764	4410	5512	6.4
50	1800	4500	5625	
51	1836	4590	5737	6.4
52	1872	4680	5850	
53	1908	4770	5962	6.4

Min	16mm	35mm	65/70mm	
	Ft	Ft	Ft	Fr
54	1944	4860	6075	
55	1980	4950	6187	6.4
56	2016	5040	6300	
57	2052	5130	6412	6.4
58	2088	5220	6525	
59	2124	5310	6637	6.4
60	2160	5400	6750	

GLOSSARY

Academy Leader   Leader which conforms to the standards set up by the Academy of Motion Picture Arts and Sciences. From the projection start mark on this leader, it is exactly eight seconds (12 feet in 35 mm, four feet and 32 frames in 16 mm) until the beginning of the picture.

Academy Roll-Off   A standard, established by the Academy of Motion Picture Arts and Sciences, for movie theatre sound. It involves decreasing quite a bit of the high-frequency sound. This roll-off is what Dolby® film sound tries to avoid.

Add-A-Plate   See *Console*.

ADR   Automatic Dialogue Replacement. See *Looping*.

Anamorphic   A method of getting wide-screen images from normal 35 mm film. In the shooting, a special lens is used which squeezes the image. A matching lens reverses the process for projection. If you were to look at a frame of anamorphic film without "unsqueezing" it (such images would be called "squeezed") it would look like the image on a balloon after the air has been let out of it.

Answer Print   A timed (color-corrected) print of the film. It may or may not have a soundtrack married to it.

Assembly   A rough piecing-together of the cut, sometimes called a "rough cut." The assembly consists of all of the scenes shot, and usually runs quite a bit longer than the finished film.

B-negative   Takes which were shot and developed but not printed.

Balance Stripe   See *Stripe*.

Balancing   See *Reel Balancing*.

Base   The bottom side of the film. It is shiny, as opposed to the top part of the film—the emulsion—which is dull. Actually, the base is a plastic material onto which the three layers of color film stock (or the one layer of black and white) are glued. See also *Emulsion*.

Beep Tone   A short tone which can be used to mark a specific location on a soundtrack. It is commonly used at the beginning of reels, two seconds before the beginning of the picture (nine feet after the start mark in 35 mm, three feet and 24 frames in 16 mm).

Bump   When two sounds are cut together it is possible that the background sounds will not match exactly. The effect of the different sounds cut together is called a bump. The tasks of "dialogue splitting" and "mixing" are designed to smooth out these bumps and end up with one seamless soundtrack.

Camera Original   The actual film that went through the camera on location.

Card   A particular kind of credit optical in which the names remain stationary, fading in and out.

Changeover Cue   The second changeover cue. When the projectionist sees it, he or she is supposed to switch the projection from one projector to the other.

Changeovers   The marks which are placed in the upper right hand corner of the frame to cue the projectionist to change from one reel to another.

Character Reel   A reel set up for an ADR session which contains one character's lines only.

Cheated Track   A piece of track which is cut into the work track purposely out of sync with the picture.

Cinetabs   Small tabs which are used for identification of individual rolls of film or sound. Also called "trim tabs."

Clapper   See *Slate*.

Click Track   A musical rhythm. Each click represent one musical beat. A click of 12/0 denotes that one beat of music comes every 12 frames.

Code Number   A number which is physically printed onto the edge of the film, in ink. It is used to identify pieces of film and track in the editing room and to keep the picture and track in sync. These numbers usually run one every foot. Also called an "edge number."

Color Cards   Standardized cards which contain a scale of colors. When these are shot, it is easy to tell just how far the filmed colors deviate from the actual colors. Such cards facilitate the color correcting of a film.

Color Correction   See *Timing*.

Conformation   A change made to a reel after it has been locked.

Console   A moviola with one picture head and two sound heads. Often a second sound head is attached onto a regular moviola. This attachment is called an "add-a-plate."

Core   A two- or three-inch diameter plastic disc which is exactly the width of the film. The film or mag is wound onto the cores for editing or projection. See also "split reel."

Coverage   The various angles that a director shoots for a scene.

Crawl   A particular kind of credit optical in which the names move up or down the screen.

CRI   Color Reversal Intermediate. A particular kind of reversal (original) film which can be struck directly off of another negative, without going through an intermediate positive stage, such as with an I.P.

CRI Print   A release print off of a CRI, as opposed to an EK print.

Cut   The cut-together work picture and work track, either together or singly.

Cut Picture   See *Work Picture*.

Cutter Moviola   A type of upright moviola which has no arms on it, is easier to take film on and off of, and is gentler on the film than a regular moviola, all of which facilitates its use as a cutting machine.

Cutting Copy   The "work picture."

D-M-E Track   An M & E full coat track which also includes, usually on channel one, the mixed dialogue to be used as a reference for foreign dubbing.

Dailies   Every day during the shooting of a film, the director and some members of the cast and crew view the footage shot the preceding day to verify that everything is satisfactory. If it is not, some of the footage may have to be reshot. These screenings are called "dailies screenings" or "rushes."

Degaussing   The process of erasing all sound from a piece of magnetic stock or tape.

Dialogue Splitting   The process of separating work track pieces which bump together onto separate elements so that each may be treated separately at the mix.

Dissolve   An optical in which one image slowly changes into another.

Domestic Version   The major release of a film, in the United States and English speaking countries.

Double Reel   When the film is ready to be distributed, the 1000 foot editing reels are combined into 2000 foot reels for theatres. This is accomplished by combining reels one and two into Double Reel One, editing reels three and four into Double Reel Two, and so on.

Drop Shadow   A design for titles in which a small, darker, extra copy of the words is superimposed onto the title, slightly askew of it. This gives the words more readability.

Dubb   See *Mix*.

Dubbing   1) Mixing the film. 2) Looping.

Dupe   A copy. Picture is often duped onto a piece of black-and-white film. Such dupes are called "slop dupes" or "slop prints." When tracks are duped it is normal to ask for a one-to-one copy, to preserve the same volume level and equalization as the original track.

Edge Number   See *Code Number*.

Editing Bench   A wide table on which most of the editorial equipment sits. As a result, most of the physical cutting of the film is done on it. Both the rewinds and the synchronizer are on this table, as well as the splicers and a host of other equipment. Editors who edit their films on flatbeds do not use editing benches as much as editors who cut on an upright since the flatbed itself functions as the bench for most of their editing work. Sometimes referred to as the *Editing Table*.

Effect   1) In picture, an optical or special photographic manipulation of the film. 2) In sound, a specific sound, such as of a tire squeal or water dripping. 3) Also used to mean a special manipulation of elements during the shooting of the film, such as the creation of rain or snow.

EK Print   A release print-off of the camera original, as opposed to an IP Print, or a CRI print.

Element   An individual sound track at a mix. Also called a "unit."

Emulsion   The top side of the film. It is dull, as opposed to the bottom part of the film—the base—which is shiny. Your lips will leave a mark on the emulsion side of film.

EPS   Electronic Post-Sync. See *Looping*.

Extension   In sound or in picture editing, a trim which is added to a piece already used in the film.

Eye Sync   The process of synccing up picture and track without slates. It involves finding points in the sound which can easily be located on the picture as well, such as door slams. Certain letters of the alphabet also provide good sync points, such as the letters *b, d, k, p,* or *t.*

Fades   Opticals in which an image gradually goes to black (fade-out) or emerges from black (fade-in). It is also possible to have images fade in from or out of other colors besides black, such as white.

Fill   Waste film. It is used to space out soundtracks within a reel to preserve synchronization with the picture. It is also called "slug" or "spacing."

Flash Frames   As the camera is slowing down at the end of a take it lets more light in. This shows up as a frame or two on the film where the image is very bright. Flash frames are handy for identifying the ends of takes.

Flatbed   A kind of editing machine. The separate film and soundtrack are run horizontally across this table-like device in sync with each other.

Flipped Track   Track which has been turned upside down, so that it will not read. Track is flipped so that it will be in sync and ready to be used in case it is desired by simply unflipping the track.

Flop   An optical effect in which the frame is turned around so that what was the left side of the frame becomes the right and vice versa.

Foleys   Effects, usually body movement of some sort, such as footsteps or clothes rustle, which is recorded in sync with picture.

4-2-4   The method of recording and playing back Dolby Stereo sound for film. The tracks are mixed down from their four-track format to a two-track form. It is this two-track version that is transferred to optical track and married with the picture. At the theatres, Dolby equipment expands the two tracks back into four.

Four-Stripe   See *Full Coat.*

Four-Track   See *Full Coat.*

Frame   An individual picture on the film. Each frame is exposed for ⅟₄₈th second. The camera shutter is then closed for

⅟₄₈th of a second while the film is pulled down to the next film frame, which is then exposed for ⅟₄₈ of a second. It is the rapid projection of succeeding frames, in which the postion of the elements in the picture changes slightly from frame to frame, which gives the audience the illusion of motion.

Frame Line   The space between two succeeding frames.

Full Coat   35 mm track which is completely covered with oxide. As many as six tracks of sound can be recorded onto it. Other configurations are four and three tracks. For that reason, full coat is also known as "three-track," "three-stripe," "four-track," or "four-stripe."

Grading   An English term for "timing."

Gray Scale   A standardized card which works exactly like a color card except that it shows gradated black-to-white rather than colors.

Handle   An extra few frames attached to the head and tail of an optical, beyond what is needed.

Head Trim   See *Trim.*

Hi-Con   A black and white optical stock often used for credits or special effects.

Hole   A portion of a soundtrack which has no sound in it.

IP/IN   The process of making a new negative of a film by striking an interpositive and then, from that, a new negative—the internegative. In recent years, this two-step process was replaced by the CRI process. But advances in the IP/IN stocks now make this a preferable method for release printing.

I.P. Print   A release print off of an I.P., as opposed to an EK print.

Interpositive   A positive film stock, used for optical negatives. Sometimes called an "I.P." Technically, a color fine-grain positive print used for making color dupe negatives.

KEM   A brand name for a common flatbed editing machine.

Key Number   A number which is imprinted into the edge of the film negative. This number is then exposed on to the print film, giving a permanent record of every piece of film used in the movie. Also called a "latent edge number."

Latent Edge Number   See *Key Number.*

Leader   White-coated film which is used at the heads and tails of film and soundtrack. It serves several purposes. It protects the film itself since *it* is wound on the outside of the reels rather than the valuable picture. It also provides the thread-up necessary for projection. Since it can be easily written on, it is also used as identification.

LFOA   Last Frame of Action. The last frame on a reel of film or track before the leader begins.

Lift   A piece of cut picture or track which is removed from the film and stored intact, rather than being broken apart and stored as trims.

Lock   That point in the editing of the film when the picture editing is over. The cut is then "locked."

Loop   A piece of track which has been joined at its ends to form a continuous band. When played, it will go around in a circle until stopped providing a nice continuous sound.

Looping   Dialogue replacement. Sometimes called dubbing. Also called "ADR" or "EPS."

M & E Track   A mixed full-coat which has the music on one channel (usually channel two), the mixed effects on another (usually channel three) and no dialogue. This track is sent to foreign countries for foreign versions of the film. There, they lay their own dialogue on top of the already completed M & E mix, saving them the job of remixing the entire film.

Mag   Soundtrack stock.

Married Print   At no time during the shooting or editing of a film are the sound and picture on the same piece of film. It is not until the film is ready to go into the theatres that the two are combined, or "married," together. See also *Optical Track*.

Matte Shot   An optical in which part of one shot is combined with part of another to create another shot which did not exist to begin with. An example would be taking a shot of an astronaut shot in a studio, combining it with a shot of a lunar landscape to give a final frame in which the astronaut appears to be on the moon.

Mix   The combination of many sound elements—dialogue, music, and sound effects into one cohesive and balanced soundtrack. Also called a "dubb."

Mixed Mag   A single mono stripe of the final mix of a film.

MOS   Literally "mit-out-sound." Used to denote a picture take for which no sound was shot.

Motor Cue   The first changeover cue. When the projectionist sees it he or she is supposed to start up the motor on the other projector.

Moviola   A brand name for a common editing machine. The separate film and soundtrack are run vertically from the feeding reels onto the take-up reels in sync with each other. Also called an "upright moviola" to differentiate it from a Moviola Flatbed.

Moviola Flatbed   A brand name for a common flatbed editing machine.

Negative   Original film exposed in the camera.

Numbering Machine   A machine which inks code numbers onto the edge of the film and track.

One-to-One Copy   A sound transfer which is at exactly the same level and equalization as the original sound.

Optical   A piece of film which has been manipulated in some special way, after it has already been shot, to create some special effect.

Optical Track   The soundtrack on a married print. It appears as a set of squiggly lines at the left side of the picture. When light is projected through the optical track it is read by a photocell behind the film. This photocell decodes the patterns of the light into sounds—providing us with the dialogue, music, and effects that we hear on a film's soundtrack.

Out   A take, no part of which has been used in the cut work picture.

Phasing   The hollow sound that occurs when two identical tracks are run in near-perfect sync.

Pick-Up Shot   After a shot has been made on the set, the director sometimes wishes to re-do only part of the take. This re-do is called a pick-up shot since only part of the shot is picked up. It is slated with the same set-up letter, and the letters "p.u." are added at the end. For instance, a pick-up to shot 11A would be 11Apu.

Pre-Mix   When many units are involved in a mix it is difficult, if not impossible, to play them all at one time. In this case, several of them are mixed together and this new mix (called the pre-mix) will replace those many elements at the mix. Also called pre-dubb.

Protection I.P.   See *Registration I.P.*

Reel Balancing   The act of apportioning the footage between all of the reels so that no reel has too little or too much film, and so that changeovers can be made without the audience noticing.

Registration I.P.   A certain type of interpositive which is printed in so particular a manner that the I.P. can be used as a replacement negative. For this reason, a registration I.P. is made whenever the original negative is being removed from the lab, so as to have a protection in case something were to happen to the original negative. A registration I.P. is, therefore, sometimes called a "protection I.P."

Release Print   The married print which is sent to theatres for showing. Normally it is not made directly from the original camera negative, but is made from a dupe negative, either a CRI or an IP/IN copy.

Reversal   An original film which results in a positive image rather than a negative one. Camera original comes in two forms— negative, which has a negative image on it, and reversal, which has a positive image.

Rewinds   Two high posts which stand up on the edge of the editing table. Shafts, which stick out of the rewinds, are used to hold the reels of film. These reels are fed off the left rewind, onto the right one.

Rough Cut   The first assemblage of the cut footage.

Rough Mix   See *Scratch Mix*.

Run-Out   The extra thirty feet or so placed at the end of any reel or unit going into the mix. This will prevent the mixer from running past the end of a reel when it is not desired.

Rushes   see *Dailies*.

Scratch Mix   A temporary mix used primarily to combine dialogue and music or an important sound effect. No attempt is made to correct sound problems. Also called a "slop mix" or "rough mix" or "dubb."

Set   The location where the film is being shot.

Set-Up   1) An individual camera position. A given scene will usually be covered with several different camera angles and lens sizes. Each of these is a different set-up. In American notation, each set-up for a given scene (say, scene 11) will be given a different set-up letter (11, for the master, and 11A, 11B, 11C, etc., for other angles). In English notation, each succeeding set-up, from the first day of shooting until the last, regardless of what scene it is meant for, is given a sequential set-up number, beginning with Scene 1, Take 1 on the first day. 2) Can also refer to the editing room table equipment—synchronizer, rewinds, splicing block, et al.

Single-Card   A credit in which only one name appears on a card.

Slate   The black-and-white board which is struck together at the beginning of every take. It is used to provide a visible and audible sync point as well as providing a visual record of the set-up and take numbers of the take. Also called a "clapper."

Slop Dupe   See *Dupe*.

Slop Mix   See *Scratch Mix*.

Slop Print   See *Dupe*.

Slug   See *Fill*.

SMPTE Code   A method of sync which is used for tape media, such as music recording tape or videotape.

Sound Reader   An amplifier. Sound from the track is picked up from the sound heads on the synchronizer and fed into this reader, where it is translated into sounds that we can understand and amplified so we may hear it. It is also called a "squawk box."

Sounding   The process of transferring sound from onto a striped magnetic 35 mm picture print.

Spacing   See *Fill*.

Split Reel   A take-up reel which can be unscrewed into two sides. A core is placed inside and, after the sides have been screwed back together again, it can be used as a regular take-up reel. Since flatbed editing machines use film wound on cores, rather than on reels, this permits easy manipulation and projection of film cut on a flatbed without having to wind it all off the cores and onto take-up reels.

Spotting Session   A meeting in which the director, composer, editor, and music editor determine exactly where the scoring for the film shall fall.

Sprockets   The teeth on the film driving mechanism. These teeth link up with the sprocket holes on the film, those tiny perforations at the edge of the film, and transport the film forward at a designated rate. 35 mm film has four sprocket holes for each frame, 16 mm film has only one, 70 mm has five.

Squawk Box   See *Sound Reader*.

Squeezed Image   See *Anamorphic.*

Steenbeck   A brand name for a common flatbed editing machine.

Streamer   A long line, usually three feet in length, drawn on the film to cue someone—either for an actor or actress to let them know that a line to be looped is coming up, or a conductor to let him or her know that a musical cue is upcoming.

Stripe   35 mm track that contains one location for sound. Oxide has been glued onto part of a piece of clear 35 mm film. In order for the track to take up correctly on reels, another, thinner, stripe is also glued onto the top of the film. It is called the "balance stripe" and is usually not recorded onto.

Striping   The act of gluing a thin layer of oxide onto the 35 mm picture. Later on, sound will be transferred onto it in a process called "sounding."

Superimposition   Also called a "super." An optical in which one image is seen at the same time as another.

Sync   The condition when the sound and the picture that was taken on the set line up in the manner in which the events actually occurred during the shooting.

Synchronizer   A machine which has several rotating wheels with sprockets on them. By placing pieces of film or soundtrack on these wheels these pieces can be run in perfect sync with each other.

Sync Point   Any visual or aural place in the film which can be used to find the sync between the two. The normal sync point is the slate.

Tail Trim   See *Trim.*

Take   The single recording of a set-up. If take one is not satisfactory to the director he will do take two, then take three, until he is satisfied. The next set-up will start with take one again.

Take-Up Reel   A metal or plastic reel on which film is stored.

Three-Stripe   See *Full Coat.*

Three-Track   See *Full Coat.*

Timing   The act of correcting the color balance of the individual takes in the cut negative. Each shot must be balanced individually so that the slight differences between them can be evened out. Also called "color-correcting" or "balancing."

Transfer   A sound copy. After a day's shooting, the sound is on ¼ inch tape. It is then transferred onto mag stock for use in editing.

Trim   A piece of a take which is left over after a portion of that take has been cut out and used in the cut of the film. A piece which comes *before* the section used in the film is called a "head trim," a portion *after* the section used is called a "tail trim."

Trim Bin   A large barrel into which takes of film are hung. They are usually rectangular and lined with a felt-like material to prevent the film from scratching as it hangs down into the pin from a rack of pins above it. Also called a "trim barrel."

Trim Tabs   See *Cinetabs*.

Unit   See *Element*.

Virgin Stock   Soundtrack stock onto which no sound has yet been recorded.

Walla   A background sound effect of a crowd murmuring.

Wild Sound   See *Wild Track*.

Wild Track   Sound recorded on the set with no accompanying picture. Also called "wild sound."

Work Picture   The cut-together film. Also called the "cut" or "cut picture."

Work Track   The cut-together sound track.

Zeroing Out   Setting the synchronizer, moviola, or flatbed footage counter to zero.

BIBLIOGRAPHY

Arijon, Daniel. *Grammar of the Film Language*. New York: Hastings House, 1976. A discussion of the most basic of editing concepts—the shot, especially in regard to how one shot will cut with another. Extremely thorough though undeniably dull. Useful for directors, editors, and script supervisors who want to have an encyclopedia (in the smallest detail) of how scenes should be staged so they will cut together.

Baker, Fred, and Ross Firestone. *Movie People*. New York: Douglas Book Corporation, 1972. Has a wonderful interview with editor Aram Avakian in it, in which he discusses some of the thought processes behind cutting.

Bazin, Andre. *What Is Cinema, Vols. I and II*. Berkeley and Los Angeles: University of California Press, 1971. Not really a book on editing though parts of it discuss the theoretical aspects of montage.

Chase, Donald. *Filmmaking: The Collaborative Art*. Boston: Little, Brown, 1975. The very short section on editing has fragmented interviews with several established editors, a few of which occasionally go beyond the anecdotal into the practical.

Eisenstein, Sergei. *Film Forum* and *Film Sense*. New York: Harcourt, Brace, 1949. Both of these works show the initial stages of an editing philosophy. Eisenstein, perhaps justifiably, is considered the titular father of montage. These works are a careful combination of theory, experiment, and inspired conjecture on the nature of editing.

Lipton, Lenny. *Independent Film Making*. San Francisco: Random House, 1972. This is one of the many how-to books for the independent or college filmmaker who knows very little to start with. It is also one of the best of the lot. It caters largely to the 8mm and 16mm filmmaker but discusses much terminology and procedure that all filmmakers must go through.

Lustig, Milton. *Music Editing for Motion Pictures.* New York: Hastings House, 1972. A little reference work on the details of preparing a motion picture for scoring and dealing with other musical problems in films. Though not particularly thorough or detailed it does compile many facts for the first time, all in one place.

Nizhny, Vladimir. *Lessons with Eisenstein.* New York: Da Capo, 1979. Notes from Eisenstein's teachings. Largely concerned with the purposeful choice of camera angles and blocking. There is much to be learned from all of this as it applies to editing.

Pudovkin, V. I. *Film Technique and Film Acting.* London: Vision Press Ltd. Possibly the seminal work on film editing. Though a bit dated by developments in other branches of film (notably writing, sound, and acting) his theories stand up today as among the most basic and important.

Reisz, Karel, and Gavin Millar. *The Technique of Film Editing.* New York: Hastings House, 1968. A down-to-earth discussion of editing principles which never gets too theoretical and nearly always has a valid point to make with pertinent examples.

Rosenblum, Ralph, and Robert Karen. *When the Shooting Stops.* New York: Viking, 1979. Basically an anecdotal look at the editing process. Some amusing incidents are recounted.

Sarris, Andrew. *Interviews With Film Directors.* New York: Bobbs-Merrill, 1967. Some of these directors mention their editing theories. Some of them even make sense.

Spottiswoode, Raymond. *A Grammar of the Film.* Berkeley and Los Angeles: University of California Press, 1950. Though the book is rather turgid and pretentious, for some unknown reason friends of mine have found some wisdom in the theoretical discussion of editing.

Walter, Ernest. *The Technique of the Film Cutting Room.* New York: Hastings House, 1973. An excellent and thorough work on the editing process from the technical point of view. It primarily covers the English system and is, at present, a bit dated. But it remains a readable and reliable guide to the editing room.

INDEX